Doc Holliday
in Film and
Literature

Doc Holliday in Film and Literature

SHIRLEY AYN LINDER

Foreword by Paul A. Hutton

McFarland & Company, Inc., Publishers
Jefferson, North Carolina

LIBRARY OF CONGRESS CATALOGUING-IN-PUBLICATION DATA

Linder, Shirley Ayn.
    Doc Holliday in film and literature / Shirley Ayn Linder ; foreword by Paul A. Hutton.
      p.   cm.
    Includes bibliographical references and index.

    ISBN 978-0-7864-7335-9 (softcover : acid free paper) ∞
    ISBN 978-1-4766-0330-8 (ebook)

    1. Holliday, John Henry, 1851–1887—In motion pictures.
2. Holliday, John Henry, 1851–1887—In literature.   I. Title.
PN1995.9.H525L56 2014
791.43'651—dc23   2013045555

BRITISH LIBRARY CATALOGUING DATA ARE AVAILABLE

© 2014 Shirley Ayn Linder. All rights reserved

No part of this book may be reproduced or transmitted in any form or by any means, electronic or mechanical, including photocopying or recording, or by any information storage and retrieval system, without permission in writing from the publisher.

On the cover: Val Kilmer as Doc Holliday in *Tombstone*, 1993 (Buena Vista Pictures/Photofest)

Manufactured in the United States of America

McFarland & Company, Inc., Publishers
  Box 611, Jefferson, North Carolina 28640
    www.mcfarlandpub.com

If your actions inspire others
to dream more, learn more, do more
and become more, you are a leader
—JOHN ADAMS

With great appreciation and thanks
to Paul A. Hutton

Table of Contents

Acknowledgments	ix
Foreword by Paul A. Hutton	1
Preface	3
Introduction	5
ONE—Facts and Early Fantasies	7
TWO—The Legend Begins	38
THREE—The Great Depression	52
FOUR—The War Years	66
FIVE—The Glory Days	77
SIX—The Tragic Sixties	97
SEVEN—The Sinking Seventies	108
EIGHT—The Ignoble Eighties	116
NINE—The Legendary West at the Turn of the Century	123
TEN—Doc Holliday in the New Millennium	140
Chapter Notes	157
Filmography	171
Bibliography	174
Index	183

Acknowledgments

It's quite difficult to thank all the people who have encouraged, supported, and helped me bring this book to fruition since it began in 2000. I fear that I may omit someone.

First on the list is Paul A. Hutton, As my teacher, mentor and chair, he guided me through five years of study—providing much research and material from his own files. Through the years, he has continued to acquire and send pictures, magazines, articles, and other newly discovered information to which I otherwise would not have access. It is to his 18 years of ongoing interest and encouragement that I owe a great part of this book.

Kathleen Chamberlain of necessity is next—for her endless hours at the Red Robin trying to explain the "myth of the west" to me. Her continued friendship and advice is priceless. Richard W. Etulain's tireless editing of my first article in 1998 taught me so much—many thanks. John L. Kessell and Robert Himmerich y Valencia often kept dismay from the door. I would also like to thank Peter C. Rollins of Oklahoma State University, who early on officially recognized my efforts and never relented from his determination I would someday publish. All the co-workers at the New Mexico Historical Review laughed at the non-academic nature of my topic, but embraced me as a fellow student and friend. Thanks to Byron Price and Paul Fees, who supplied my first History of the U.S. West job at the Buffalo Bill Historical Center. I apologize to all the above for my rather extended trip up Fool's Hill before returning to their carefully tended fold—to Doc Holliday and the history of the U.S. West.

Despite my exile in West Texas, family and friends continued to prevent me from despairing. Sharon Cunningham, a Tennessee friend made in New Mexico, did a wondrous job of editing. She has continued as my aide de camp in finding lost articles and putting me in touch with the right people. Thom Nicholson came all the way from Chicago to offer his expertise and set me back on the path. Jeff Morey and Gary Roberts, true Doc Holliday aficionados, have never failed to answer my email queries and lift me over many a bump. A very special note of appreciation to Michael F. Blake for all his knowledge and contributions. To Johnny Boggs (despite my living in Texas) for helping find me an editor. I took a side flight into Scotland, which proved a land as interested in western lore as I am in their wars of independence. Robert Carmichael has assisted me in so many ways there, ultimately bringing one of their favorite subjects, History of the U.S. West, to Scotland, via Doc Holliday and me.

Love and thanks to my children Mitchell, Dariush, Erin, and Linder (who did ask once that I come home for Christmas but "not bring Doc Holliday"). They took the time, while presenting me with eight grandchildren, to keep my spirits up. Matt, it is a joy having you with us. Thanks to Frey for providing a safe haven in which I could work. I cannot leave out companions of the dog park who, having no comprehension of what I am doing, still greet me with a smile and send me home to work in a better frame of mind. Border collie, Siabhra, a special hug for your constant companionship.

To the truest and best friends who have so blessed me — in order of their appearance in my life — Paul Rutter, Trudy Karr, Kristin Jensen, and Amber McNeely Smith.

And to all, if unnamed above, who have borne with, encouraged, taught, and continue to teach me. Despite my independent spirit — I would have never completed this without each and every one of you: You know who you are.

Lastly, this story is for my Daddy, Forrest Egbert Linder, who taught me laughter and survival. It is for my children, who tested and honed those skills. It is for my grandchildren, whom I hope to teach; and it is for all my friends who have kept it alive during the dark times, and who never let me forget.

It is also the story of an ultimate survivor with a wicked sense of humor — John Henry (Doc) Holliday, who brings it all full circle.

Foreword
by Paul A. Hutton

Few figures in the history of the American West have captured the world's imagination as has the Georgia dentist turned gambler and gunfighter John Henry "Doc" Holliday. His story is replete with romance and tragedy — the doomed, fatalistic Southern aristocrat roaming the frontier in search of an end to a tortured life–and is one perfect for history, fiction, and film. His friendship with Wyatt Earp and his participation in the most famous gunfight in American history has added to this fabulous reputation.

The Holliday-Earp relationship is often central to these stories, especially as they concern the gunfight at the O.K. Corral. The Holliday role is so full of romantic possibilities that good actors have used it to full effect, often overshadowing the Wyatt Earp actor in films. Actors from Harry Carey to Kirk Douglas to Val Kilmer have had star turns as the deadly dentist (often promoted to surgeon in the movies). Often these tales play off the tension of the ironic friendship between the paladin of law and order and the notorious gunman. "The strangest alliance this side of heaven or hell, between the most famous lawman of them all and the most feared of all gambler-badmen" ran the breathless poster headline for Paramount's 1957 feature *Gunfight at the O.K. Corral*. In reality, of course, there was nothing at all strange about their friendship, for the real Holliday and Earp both made a living off the underside of frontier boomtown life. Far from being an attraction of opposites, their friendship was based on mutual interests. Earp was much closer to Holliday in terms of how they each made a living, although they remained worlds apart when it came to temperament. It is an irresistible story.

Shirley Linder has long been fascinated by Doc Holliday, both the real man and the larger-than-life legendary frontier character. She turned her interest into a well-crafted master's thesis in history at the University of New Mexico, which is the genesis of this book. Her years of careful research into the real Doc pay rich dividends in her ability to thus interpret the legendary character so celebrated in fiction, film, and television. The Janus-faced Holliday of history and popular culture are but two sides of the dark American fascination with violence. Each Holliday reflects how we, like moths to a flame, are endlessly attracted to those who live out our violent fantasies. The cultured, tortured, and ultimately doomed Holliday may indeed be the most fascinating of all those who inhabit that Wild West fantasy world of quick violence — a sort of frontier James Bond.

Join author Shirley Linder on a delightful and informative journey into the frontier world of that dapper, deadly dentist Doc Holliday, both the man of our history and the man of our dreams. You could not find a better guide to take you on a quest to discover the difference between the actual life and the imagined legend of this enigmatic, larger-than-life character.

Paul A. Hutton, a University of New Mexico professor, is an expert on the history of the West, its film, literature, and popular culture. He has served several terms as executive director of the Western History Association and president of Western Writers of America.

Preface

Doc Holliday in Film and Literature began in a West Texas Dollar Picture Show. Or — it may have actually begun in Jackson, Tennessee, one day long ago. When I was very young my family said, "Shirley Ayn won't watch anything where they don't ride horses, shoot guns, and it happened at least a hundred years ago."

Tombstone (1993) and Val Kilmer (as Doc Holliday) were really the catalyst. It was seconded by Paul Hutton, my graduate chair at UNM who actually smiled (not laughed) when I mentioned Doc as a topic for my thesis. I was then over fifty, had likely seen 95 percent of any western filmed to that date, then gone back to school when my youngest went off to college herself, which made me a "non-traditional" student. Truthfully, I've always rather liked being non-traditional.

My original intention was only to finish a BA in journalism. Having wandered through the ivy-covered halls of eleven different colleges and universities as I followed the oil patch, however, there were a lot of credits that fell through the cracks. The great documentaries on television around that time, often narrated by Paul A. Hutton, made it easy enough to become totally intrigued by the Myth of the West. It was those same documentaries that led me to the University of New Mexico with a curriculum in History of the U.S. West. I was already a historian (of the Civil War, genealogy, and numerous other battles and wars throughout time), so stepping back into the western frontier of America was a logical one.

I thrived on the university background and was easily convinced to continue in an MA program. Likely I was still not looking at a book, just at writing the best thesis possible. That took four full years with my taking about 90 percent of all frontier classes and studies offered and no way left to advance any further. During that time I had the privilege of working with Dr. Richard Etulain, who gave me the privilege of contributing my first article to *Journal of the West*. I enjoyed four years of working with *The New Mexico Historical Review*, was published in *True West Magazine* and *The Cavalry Journal*, and learned to like single malt Scotch whisky.

An opportunity to work at the Buffalo Bill Historical Center engulfed me an even deeper and wider aspect of the U.S. West. Doc Holliday, of course, was always at the forefront of my interest and somewhere in there I decided to convert my thesis into a book. Anyone who has done that fully understands the folly of thinking it would be easy.

Essentially, I have been writing this book for 17 years. But for continued encouragement from academic and personal friends, I might still be revising it.

I have come a long way from the twelve-year-old who won breakfast with Gene Autry, who drove three hundred miles to see Dale Robertson when my first child was less than a week old, and interviewed Harry Carey, Jr., in Cody, Wyoming.

And just so you know, my all-time favorite gunfight is in *The Wild Bunch*.

Introduction

Doc Holliday spent most of his life dying.

Born nine years before the Civil War that split the nation, uprooted to escape General William T. Sherman's burning march across Georgia, and a survivor of the brutal Reconstruction of the South, John H. Holliday lived to graduate from the Pennsylvania College of Dental Surgery before his twenty-first birthday and be accepted into one of Atlanta, Georgia's, more prestigious practices.

Family tradition and countless legends state that Holliday was diagnosed with tuberculosis late in 1872 and given a year or less to live. John evidently decided to make the most of the time left him. He surprised everyone, perhaps himself most, by surviving past his thirty-sixth birthday, living a riotous and dangerous frontier life that would have proven deadly to even a hardy young man, a life of late night gambling, heavy drinking, cigar smoke, and wild women.

Through the years, many have wondered at his motives in making such a dramatic change of lifestyle. Did Doc Holliday really have such a strong desire to live, or was he making the most concerted of efforts to die with his boots on? Possible this failure at self-destruction accounts for his last words: "This is funny."

It is not surprising that Doc Holliday captured the imagination of his own generation, and has enraptured those of succeeding readers, viewers, well-intended novelists, biographers, quasi-historians, and screenwriters. As the minds of the curious have ever turned to seek out the mysterious and different, the American public has also noted Doc's story and wondered at it.

The result is a Doc Holliday still alive and going strong in the imagination of the world now in its twenty-first century. His popularity has not faded and, if anything, has enjoyed regeneration. No biography can explain the heroic Doc Holliday that the imaginations of journalists, literature, Hollywood, television and, above all, the minds of the American public, have conceived. Never a myth and always a reality — today Doc Holliday is a legend.

How then, you may ask, do myth and legend differ? B. Wyatt Brown noted: "History, shorn of all myth is ... impossible."[1] This is perhaps as good a starting place as any.

For the answer does not lie in history, or in fact versus fiction. Stories once considered mythic have been proven based in reality by archaeology, anthropology and research. Certainly greatly embroidered, frequently taking on parable-like proportions, but based on actual people and events.

Dictionaries have great difficulty finding distinction between myth and legend. Words such as *fictional, half-truths, imaginary, popular story*, and *romanticized* appear in definitions of both, thus leaving the seeker in further confusion.

Added to the dilemma is that our United States history is of such short duration that the majority of our myths can easily be researched and nailed down. Although some are purely imaginary (Paul Bunyon, Pecos Pete, etc.), the basis for most of our stories are of such recent origin as to be traceable to actual people, places, and events.

Leaving us still with the question of who merely existed and who is truly legendary? The answer lies in the charismatic, individual character set apart from the commonplace person. Every major event throughout history has contained a cast of hundreds, often thousands. What element separated the hero from the mundane, the colorful from the drab, the exciting from the dreary? Who merely took on grandiose proportions as opposed to the absolutely unforgettable?

Perhaps most simply put, myth is a tale everyone knows. Legend is what time and public imagination have made of that story.

Yet a special kind of person is required to gain such respect and admiration as is consummated in legendary proportions. It is a gift granted to few, and only to the deserving. Although that person may be contrary to popular moral or legal ethics, he emits a spark, a fire, an energy that overshadows those around him and causes him to stand out like a bolt of lightning against a black desert sky.

Whether that attribute is born or developed, I cannot answer. What I can tell you is that by 1887 John Henry Holliday had that unique gift. That is why he remains today the legendary Doc Holliday.

ONE

Facts and Early Fantasies

Certainly the facts as they first emerged concerning the life of John Henry Holliday came much closer to being a fantasy than anything approaching a true story. Only two sources, one late in the twentieth century, and another early in the twenty-first, established the actual facts of his life.[1] You may know nothing of John Henry Holliday and have been completely confused by film portrayals, magazine stories, and fictional books. You may know nothing except the two versions given in the epic movies *Tombstone* and *Wyatt Earp*.[2] This, a quick overview of his real life, may give you some better perception of how his image has evolved from fantasy to fact to legend over some 161 years.

John Henry Holliday's date of birth is recorded in the family Bible as August 14, 1851, in Griffin, Georgia, a small hamlet some thirty miles due south of Atlanta. An older sister had died in infancy, so he grew up the only child of Alice Jane McKey and Henry Burroughs Holliday. Both families were of Scots Irish descent and had moved to Georgia from South Carolina. John Henry appears to have been frail, and was not christened in Griffin's First Presbyterian Church until the following March. Home-schooled, while his cousins received public education, he may have been termed a sissy, and it can be conjectured that perhaps some of his anger and violence stemmed from having been called a "mama's boy" in his adolescence. According to Susan McKey Thomas, a descendant on his mother's side, John spent his first nine years much as any young man in the antebellum South.[3]

Without a shadow of a doubt, however, his life dramatically changed forever when Georgia seceded from the Union in late December 1860, and his father, Henry B. Holliday, marched off to fight for the Confederacy, the last of his family to join the cause.[4] Twelve-year-old John Henry experienced further upheaval when his father resigned his commission less than two years later for reasons of chronic diarrhea. Fortunately for General Robert E. Lee and the Confederacy, all such sufferers did not desert their obligations so readily.

With the Union victory at Gettysburg on July 4, 1863, combined with the fall of gallant Vicksburg, Mississippi, the next day, it became apparent that northern Georgia was not a safe place to be. Henry Holliday chose to sell his north Georgia property and move to Valdosta, located in Lowndes County on the Georgia-Florida line. The exact date of their move is unclear, but it was before General William Tecumseh Sherman's departure from Atlanta on November 15, 1864. Southern Georgia escaped Sherman's march south from Atlanta when he turned east-southeast at Macon and continued on to Savannah. His "bummers" would have surely raped Griffin. Sherman's infamous "March to the Sea" was 800 miles long and 8 miles wide. Total destruction was placed at eight billion dollars in 1865 currency. The cost today is unfathomable. An intriguing note is that the Confederate Cabinet, in its 1865 flight from Richmond to the Florida Keys, spent two nights about 40 miles on either side of John Henry's new Valdosta, Georgia, home.

Both during and after the war, several of John's McKey and Holliday relatives were exiled in or near their household. One such cousin, three years older, was Martha Jane (Mattie) Holliday. Her friendship with the young John Henry would be the cause of speculation throughout much of his adult life, and continues until the present day. However, for the five years remaining of his adolescence, young John attended the Valdosta Institute, where he studied the classics and probably continued the music lessons begun with his mother.

Any study of a Southern boy's upbringing leaves no doubt that his education also included card playing and the consumption of alcoholic beverages, as well as horsemanship, hunting, fishing, and courting. The fact that woman whose menfolk were away at war structured him, or that his mother had taken to her bed with tuberculosis, still leaves little question but that John Henry Holliday was raised to be a man in every sense of the word. An astounding story has surfaced about John Holliday concerning this time immediately following the end of the war. Its origin is a letter from family relative Susan McKey Thomas, and bears repeating.[5]

What remained of the Confederate Army straggled home, not knowing what faced them on their return. Sparsely clothed, wounded, sick, and near starvation, many were a dangerous lot, worried and embittered by defeat and humiliation. John's family knew he had an uncle among that ragged band and contrived a scheme to aid him. They would send help in the form of a frail, 14-year-old boy. Only a mother could know the true mettle of her only son, but how she must have feared for him.

As the story goes, young John Henry set off on horseback, leading a second steed for his uncle. Oddly enough, the family apparently had little doubt of his success. Other than the clothes on his back, he carried food tied up in a tablecloth and was armed with his father's revolver. Some say the weapon had been brought back from the Mexican War. Other accounts label it a Colt Dragoon, which is possible, but not as a Mexican War relic, for the Dragoon was not patented until 1849. All firearms were allegedly confiscated from Confederate soldiers at war's end. It is impossible, however, to envision any Southerner either graciously or voluntarily handing in a weapon.

This story attests primarily to John Henry Holliday's courage and sense of survival, traits that followed him the rest of his life. An imaginative writer declares he shot at least one would-be thief. Knowing those times in the South, it can be suspected he may have dispatched more than one to defend his food, gun, and extra horse. How far he rode through those starving, desperate men is not recorded, but the family maintains he returned safely, and with his uncle.

Tragedy, however, continued to haunt young John Henry. Seventeen months after Appomattox, and barely a month past his fifteenth birthday, his mother died of tuberculosis. His grief was rudely interrupted just three short months later when his father married a young woman very near his son's own age. John was shocked and outraged at such disrespect and lack of mourning propriety; any semblance of stability in the boy's life was totally destroyed, and the strained relationship with his father led to several refuted stories of his getting into trouble. In all fairness, however, trouble was a handy item for any young Southern boy during Reconstruction Georgia. Admittedly, it is for a teenager of any era.

Two intriguing tales haunt the last few years John was living at home. In truth, not a single official record of either event exists, but they remain entrenched in all Holliday folklore. Both are easily accepted, given the climate of Reconstruction Georgia and John Henry's rebellion against a father who had proved a traitor to both his mother and his beloved South. The stories are even more acceptable when you consider the character reflected in the remainder of John Henry Holliday's life.

One such story was reported by W.A. Griffith, a Holliday-worshipping young Valdostan with unproven claims of visiting Doc in the West and later corresponding with him. Griffith related Holliday's involvement in the placement of powder kegs beneath the County Courthouse, location of the Freedman's Bureau.[6] Hated arm of Reconstruction, the Freedman's Bureau employed Henry B. Holliday and attended to the rights of the newly freed slaves. However, there are neither newspaper stories nor court records of an explosion. Such an event would surely have been highlighted. It would not, of course, if it happened as some say, and the kegs were never detonated. Anti-federal activities occupied most young Rebel boys' time in the late 1860s and make this story plausible.

Who made the career choice is unclear, nor how rumored incidents played into it, but tuition was paid in September 1870 and John began his professional training at the Pennsylvania College of Dental Surgery in Philadelphia. He studied chemistry, mechanical dentistry, metallurgy, dental pathology, histology, operative dentistry, physiology, anatomy and surgery. Returning to Valdosta, young Holliday was apprenticed with Dr. Lucian Frederick Frink.[7] *The Dental Times* of April 1872, together with a commencement announcement, confirm that John Holliday graduated after writing his thesis on diseases of the teeth. He was, however, five months shy of the age required for state certification.[8] Research by Holliday biographer Gary L. Roberts disclosed that John spent the time with a classmate in St. Louis, gaining experience in a great many things.[9] Roberts confirms it was at this early date that Doc became involved with Mary Katherine Harony, the woman with whom his name is forever linked.

The second legend takes place during this same time frame between his graduation from dental school and his reaching the age of certification to practice in Georgia. It originated with William Barclay (Bat) Masterson, who hated Doc, and was intensely jealous of his friendship with Wyatt Earp.[10] This casts even more doubt on the story, which has been soundly refuted by the family.

Masterson's story follows several commentaries that also added fuel to the early infamy that surround Doc's myth. This fable, titled "Shot a Crowd of Negroes," places in Doc's hands, for the first time, that well-known double-barreled shotgun. According to Masterson, John, not yet 21, ordered a group of young blacks from what was considered the family swimming hole. He "waited until he got a bunch of them together ... then turned loose with both barrels, killing two outright, and wounding several others." The family admits to an incident, but states adamantly there was no murder. They swear that John fired his revolver (not a shotgun) into the air. Once again, no court or newspaper account exists to verify or deny anything and, considering the times, any such event remotely would have met with serious reprisals. Alas, the story haunted Doc until his dying day.

Once licensed and settled into a practice, John moved up quickly, and on Friday, July 26, 1872, Dr. Arthur C. Ford published the following announcement in *The Atlanta Constitution:*

I HEREBY inform my patients that I leave to attend the Sessions of the Southern Dental Association in Richmond, Virginia, this evening, and will be absent until about the middle of August, during which time Dr. Jno. [sic] H. Holliday will fill my place in my practice.[11]

Despite this prestigious professional position, in November of 1872, and again in January of 1873, John sold properties inherited from his mother and placed other real estate in his father's trust.[12] His abrupt departure would indicate that during this interim he had, indeed, received the dreaded diagnosis of tuberculosis. Family tradition declares he was given less than a year to live.[13] Tuberculosis is but one of several theories for Doc's sudden departure. His alleged love for his cousin, Martha Ann (Mattie) Holliday, is yet another. While cousins often married in the Antebellum South, Mattie was Catholic and canon law denied marriage between first cousins.[14] There is also mention that young John Henry was sowing too many wild oats, at which account it should be noted he was of Scottish descent and Celts are known for their wanderlust. William Wallace, the great freedom fighter of Scotland, had a nephew, also his second in command, by the name of Tom Halladay.[15] Doc's name was often misspelled that way in both literature and film, and it is really not a far stretch to make the connection.

Whether John Holliday availed himself of the various patent remedies for "consumption" on the market at the time is unknown. Many of these "cure-alls" contained large amounts of purgatives. Most were comprised of at least 32 percent alcohol and many contained opium.[16] Addiction, not cure, was often the result. Experimental treatments of placing glass balls in the pleural space and lung collapse were also popular at the time, but not utilized by young Holliday. He seems to have chosen the route most commonly recommended, a higher and dryer climate.

It is fortunate that John H. Holliday was not included in the sixty percent of tubercular patients who died during their first year in "The Well Country," which is what parts of the West were sometimes called. The death rate in Los Angeles rose so high the area became known as "a mortician's paradise." Other popular cures of the day included "the ranch cure," such as Theodore Roosevelt had utilized, and "the tent cure," which consisted of very rough outdoor living. The strong sulfuric air of highly advertised spas like Las Vegas, New Mexico, and Glenwood Springs, Colorado, literally ate up what little lung tissue remained to the patient. Needless to say, the railroads continued to hail these health spots on their routes, ever anxious for another buck.

In New Mexico, the combination of altitude and bright sun additionally caused a twenty-two percent increase in skin cancer, and the widely advertised wonders of high altitude rarefied air could actually prove lethal to pulmonary function. The migration caused further economic problems in uprooted families with few ways to earn a living. Dallas, Texas, filled none of the recommended attributes, but that would be John Holliday's destination.[17]

Moving West is obviously the only admonition John Holliday followed. He certainly thereafter assiduously avoided fresh air, a healthy diet, and rest.

GTT

In the aftermath of the Civil War, many Southerners, driven off their land by an inability to pay taxes, often carved "GTT" into the door, indicating they had "Gone to Texas." Returning fathers and sons given no more chartered course than that often never saw their families again. Doc Holliday did not likely carve the initials in a wooden edifice, but the words must have been forever etched in his heart.

Modern-day travelers might conceive a trip from Valdosta as a short hop to Atlanta or Jacksonville, then non-stop to Dallas–Fort Worth or Love Field. Bob Boze Bell, noted western illustrator, believes that John Holliday's trip was much more arduous.[18] Although some parts could have been made on horseback, the time of year and his health likely dictated the first leg constituted an all-night train ride in cramped sleeping cars from South Georgia to Chattanooga, Tennessee. A famous writer of the times commented that the three rows of berths made sleeping conditions akin to undressing under a sofa. Now, 345 miles north of his home, he would board yet another train, this one bound for Memphis, Tennessee, 310 miles and 29 hours to the southwest. His interim journey to New Orleans was 395 miles by riverboat, although the Civil War had ended the glory days of the mighty paddle wheeler, despite advertisements of exotic drinks and gaming. Another ninety-mile train ride jolted him along the Gulf of Mexico to Galveston, Texas, for his final smoke-filled, bone-jarring 288 miles into Dallas on the Houston and Texas Central Railroad. In all probability, any "adventure" encountered on this journey was clouded by homesickness and a heavy heart. His destination was, after all, death.

John Henry Holliday arrived in Dallas with sufficient time to be included in the 1873 City Directory.[19] He is listed as a partner with Dr. John Seegar, officing in the Elm Building, located on the corner of Market and Austin. Evidently the partnership got off to a grand start as the pair won three prizes at a local dental contest. The awards were for the best set of teeth in gold, the best in vulcanized rubber, and the best set of artificial teeth and dental ware.[20] By the following March, however, the partnership was dissolved, with Holliday assuming his portion of the indebtedness.[21] His patients would not have welcomed the hacking cough associated with his disease.

Nine years later Holliday would tell a Gunnison, Colorado, reporter that while in Dallas he had belonged to a Methodist-Episcopal congregation and, according to his own statement, was "a prominent member of a temperance organization" until he "deviated from the path of rectitude."[22] A far deviation, indeed, as the following May, John Holliday was included in a roundup of local gamblers who were fined.[23] Perhaps in an attempt to stay out of trouble, Holliday moved to Dennison, Texas, some seventy-five miles away on the Red River. He had returned to his old haunts by the first of the year, when the *Dallas Weekly Herald* reported on January 2, 1875[24]:

> Dr. Holliday and Mr. Austin, a saloon keeper, relleved [sic] the Monotony of the noise of firecrackers by taking a couple of shots at each other yesterday afternoon. The cheerful note of the peace-full six-shooter is heard once more among us. Both shooters were arrested.[25]

The State of Texas indicted J.H. Holliday for the crime of assault to murder, but a grand jury returned a verdict of not guilty.[26] Holliday appeared again before a Dallas County Court in April on another gambling charge. This time he was found guilty and fined ten dollars.[27]

Here arises a great deal of what has led to much of the Doc Holliday myth. He was probably in Fort Griffin, Throckmorton County, Texas, shortly after the Dallas gambling charge in April. Subsequent writers would weave all sorts of tales around his time along the Texas Fort Trail.[28] This Trail had its origin during the mid–19th century's westward movement, necessitating armed troops and forts to protect the settlers from Indians. Connected to other outposts by the Butterfield Overland Stage, Fort Griffin was one of the toughest places on the Texas frontier, and the largest town between Fort Worth and El Paso. A major source of troops and supplies for the Indian campaigns, and a marketing depot for professional buffalo hunters, it was situated on a plateau eight hundred yards south of the Clear Fork of the Brazos, sixty feet above the valley. Most of Fort Griffin's seedier activities took place on The Flat, down by the river. Things were pretty wide open in those days, with Sheriff Henry Jacobs only cracking down when matters got too far out of hand. Local righteousness had dictated such an effort shortly after the dentist's arrival.

Factually, John Holliday was in Shackelford County, Texas, on June 12, 1875, when he first appears as "Dock."[29] He and Mike Lynch were charged and found guilty of playing cards "in a house in which spirituous liquors were sold." It would be thought the one always accompanied the other, but seemingly not. It is fairly established that Kate Elder and other names were in town. Doc was dealing at Johnny Shaunessy's tavern where he later made a historic friendship. The two were seemingly reluctant to pay the fine, for an *alias capias* was forwarded to the sheriff of San Angelo, in Tom Greene County, Texas, on the 30th of that month.[30]

John H. (Doc) Holliday appearances between June of 1875 and July of 1877 are vague, as he is alleged to have assumed the alias of an uncle, Tom McKey. Doc himself later recalled to a Denver newspaper reporter that he had dealt Faro at "Babbit's House" in the Mile High City.[31] Roberts' book confirms he was in all probability in both Deadwood and Cheyenne, the rich mining towns, during those years. The Earp brothers were clearly documented as having been in them all, although evidence indicates they were not associated with Doc, who managed to stay out of trouble. No court or newspaper records pinpoint his whereabouts under either the Holliday or McKey name.

In any case, well before his twenty-fourth birthday, any intentions John might have entertained of becoming a legitimate and professional businessman had succumbed to the lure of whiskey, smoke-filled bars, and gambling. He had, by this time, already outlived the short life predicted for him in Georgia and would, surprisingly, defy death for yet another twelve years. Several stories from this period, whether fact or fiction, bear telling, as there are no primary records.[32]

Mary Katherine Harony Cummings, better known to Holliday fans as "Big Nose Kate," stated in her memoirs that they were at Sweetwater "when Bat Masterson shot Sgt. King."[33] Now here is a story worth the telling, whether Doc observed the drama or not. The Cantonment on the Sweetwater lies some forty-two miles west of Abilene, Texas, and was originally established as a sub-post of Fort Sill, Indian Territory (Oklahoma), during the Red River Indian War.[34] Its purpose was to protect the interests of cattle traders who, compelled to find eastern markets for their great herds, were forced to drive them through Kiowa and Comanche country to the Kansas railhead of the Union Pacific Railroad. Its name was changed to Fort Elliott, Texas, in February 1876. Several accounts regarding the Masterson-King shootout over a young lady who was allegedly a bit too free with her affections are related in three books on the life of Bat Masterson.

Despite its adobe and sod construction, Bill Thompson and his partner ran the elaborate "Lady Gay" saloon-dancehall-gambling house at

Sweetwater. It sported the only wood floor in the neighborhood. Bat Masterson was in that winter, fresh from buffalo-hunting on the prairie, and either was (or was not, depending on the rendition) involved with a girl named Mollie, who may have (or may not have, again according to the story) followed Ben Thompson to his brother's place on the cantonment. Corporal Melvin A. King, Company H, Fourth U.S. Cavalry, was a Civil War veteran wont to "take up with Texas cowboys and cause trouble" (according to Wyatt Earp).

The upshot of the January 24, 1876, incident was that Sgt. King's bullet intended for Bat passed through Mollie and killed her, lodging in Masterson's groin. Before hitting the floor, Bat shot King dead. Those are the facts, and it is a good story any way you read it. Doc Holliday was very likely not at Sweetwater. Subsequent findings indicate Kate may well have been, in a professional capacity.[35]

Kate's account of the pair being at Eagle Pass makes sense. A Mexican consulate had recently been opened there to stimulate commerce along the border. The resultant influx of money would have doubtless attracted any gambler, thus giving credence, although not necessarily truth, to her story. Directly across the border lay Piedras Negras, Mexico, nowhere near the Texas Fort Trails or Doc's usual haunts. From the southeast corner of the Trail's route, then to San Antonio, down to Uvalde, and across would have been wild and woolly, and not an easy trip for anyone. But Mexican gold was Mexican gold.

Bat Masterson interjects another theory at this point. He claims that Doc killed yet another Negro, this time a soldier at Jacksboro, Fort Richardson, in Jack County, Texas. Fort Richardson lay less than a hundred miles from the new home of the Comanche, Kiowa and Plains Apache, who did not want to live like white people. The post of Jacksboro was established in July 1866, with troops so severely deprived of clothing and food that morale was low and desertions high. When the Sixth U.S. Cavalry retook command eighteen months later, conditions were so poor that the post was relocated to Fort Richardson, Texas, about half a mile southwest, on a tributary of the Trinity River.[36]

On the night of March 3, 1876, Private Jacob Smith was shot and killed by "persons unknown." Roberts' note from the *Dallas Weekly Herald* says he was a member of the Tenth Cavalry and a "dusky warrior."[37] No arrests were made and no record of either John Holliday or Tom McKey can be found from January 1876 until Doc's reappearance in Texas some eighteen months later. This opens the door for any imagination to run totally amok. Wherever he was, Doc was keeping a mighty low profile, quite an accomplishment for one who managed so many court appearances in prior years. Did he believe himself wanted for murder? The fact is, nobody knows exactly where Doc was. Conjecture is, not in the Lone Star State. In any event, you can bet he was where the pickings were good.[38]

Wherever and however low he lay in the weeds, by July 4, 1877, Doc was soon back in Texas, and back in trouble. The account of his having taken a cane to Henry Kahn following a disputed card game and subsequently being shot and killed was, obviously, greatly exaggerated. It was, however, reported as fact by the *Dallas Weekly Herald*.[39] Of interest is that he was probably already walking with a cane, more likely from the tuberculosis in his bones than any attempt at being debonair.

Doc was, by now, evidently incorrigible. Neither the arrival of a cousin, George Holliday, to assist the wounded dentist in Fort Worth, nor alleged family pressure, persuaded the now-seasoned gambler to return to the bosom of home and family. When cousin George went back to Valdosta, Doc paid another visit to Fort Griffin.[40]

Unfortunately, his return coincided with a new vigilance regime in Shackelford County. John Selman and his "Tin Hat Brigade" carried out lynch law and increased their herds by other than ordinary multiplication. Local cattlemen objecting to their system were silenced by six-gun. Doc Holliday's reputation as a gunfighter and troublemaker was well established by now and, had he availed himself of the opportunity, history may well have linked his name with Selman and other period killers such as John Wesley Hardin and Jesse James. Then a chance encounter led him to a fame all his own.

Wyatt Earp

Wyatt Earp, in interviews with Stuart N. Lake between 1924 and 1929, claimed his and Doc's meeting had occurred in the fall of 1877.[41] Wyatt, possibly acting on behalf of the Santa Fe Railroad, but more likely as a freelance bounty hunter, had followed train robbers Mike Roarke and Dave Rudabaugh out of Dodge City, Kansas, as far as Fort Griffin.[42] There the trail grew cold. Inquiring of local saloonkeeper John Shaunssey, an old acquaintance from Cheyenne, Wyoming, Wyatt was directed to a tall, thin man seated at a nearby card table. He had probably not met Doc anywhere in "the northern" gambling country, despite claims from many South Dakotans that he was in Deadwood. If so, he did not recognize him. The possibility exists, of course, he recognized but was not acquainted with him, which puts us back to Square One on the 1875–77 question. Seemingly they were not friends at the time.

Whether Holliday did not know the thieves' whereabouts, or refused to tell, is unknown. One account states he sent Earp on a wild goose chase to West Texas. The fact is, Earp returned to Dodge City without his prey. The two, however, seem to have struck up a conversation of sorts, with Doc inquiring about the pickings in Dodge City. This is Wyatt's account and nobody questions Wyatt Earp. Or do they?

The next episode in the life of Doc Holliday is recorded by almost every one of his so-called biographers. It originated with Wyatt Earp, who admittedly did not witness the event, stating he heard it from Bat Masterson. Where Bat got his information is a complete mystery. No newspapers graced Fort Griffin and no records remain in Shackelford County, Texas. "All references to Doc Holliday disappeared in 1988." This is easily believed as entire pages have disappeared from many official records all over the West. The larcenous extent of some historical collectors knows no bounds.

According to Masterson's story, the setting was the obvious poker table with two of the players being Holliday and a local by the name of Ed Bailey. An unwise gentleman, Bailey had a bad habit of "monkeying with the deadwood," trying to look at the discards. Doc warned him repeatedly to "play poker," ultimately resorting to what etiquette of the game dictated: He pulled down a pot without showing his hand. As would be expected, Bailey began to draw his gun, possibly expecting a fair shoot-out. Instead, the gambling dentist jerked his knife and caught Bailey "just below the brisket." The variations on this story are numerous to the point we can believe that something of the sort happened, although not necessarily in Fort Griffin. Anywhere along the Texas Fort Trail that Doc frequented is possible.

From this incident arises another colorful but somewhat unbelievable tale. Wyatt Earp, again, is the storyteller. With Holliday held for murder and under guard at a local hotel, rumors of a planned lynching began to circulate. According to Wyatt, and picked up by others, Kate acquired two pistols and two horses, and proceeded to set fire to a shed as a distraction. She then disarmed the deputy and rescued Doc, and the two headed for Dodge, four hundred miles straight through the heart of Indian Territory, where nobody in their right mind would go. The fact of the story's continued retelling indicates that Kate was no shrinking violet, and had a reputation of being loyal. Even Kate herself, ever ready to be a heroine, disclaimed this odyssey, pointing to the many impossibilities and inconsistencies. What cultivated such a captivating fabrication is puzzling, possibly an effort to cover the truth, which remains unknown. Historically, however, it accounts for the first of three deaths inflicted by Doc Holliday upon humankind. At least, "the only three" confirmed by Wyatt Earp which were Ed Bailey in Texas, Mike Gordon in Las Vegas, New Mexico, and Tom McLaury in Tombstone.

Much conjecture surrounds Doc's involvement with the notorious lady gambler Lottie Deno. There is little to substantiate such a relationship at the time, other than proximity of place and time, the Old Texas Fort Trails. We can accept as fact, however, that Mary Katherine Harony Cummings (Kate Elder, Kate Earp, Kate Holliday, Big Nose Kate, *ad infinitum*) was undoubtedly Doc's consort from Fort Griffin until at least midway of his Tombstone, Arizona, stay (from 1880 to 1882).

The simplest explanation for this assortment of names can best be explained by the fact that "ladies of the evening" usually adopted the name of the person who ran the establishment. As they were constantly being fined for prostitution, they would appear in court records from town to town, by the name of their employer at the time. Harony was Kate's maiden name. The first marshal of Wichita was Ike S. Elder; most of the Earps were involved in gambling and prostitution, and Kate did marry a man named Cummings after she left Doc and Tombstone. Interestingly, Kate did not have a big nose. She got the name from her habit of sticking it in other people's business.

Their relationship was a volatile one, with Kate wandering about in somewhat of a nether world between Doc Holliday's woman and prostitution.[43] This was neither unusual nor unremarkable for a woman in her trade. About this time, Doc wrote home that he had "enjoyed about as much of this Texas as he could stand."[44] He and Kate pulled up stakes and headed for the cowtowns of Kansas.

Cowtowns and Railroading

Kansas in the 1870s and '80s was best defined in a local newspaper headline of the times: "As of this edition, hell is still in session at Ellsworth." Wyatt Earp's legend as a lawman had begun there when the railroad left Abilene, then wove its way across and into 1872 Wichita.[45] Astride the Arkansas River, Delano, the entertainment section of town, stood on the west bank and was described by the *St. Louis Republican* as a "brevet hell."[46] Earp's career in Wichita ended in a political fistfight the summer of 1876. He then moved on to Dodge City. He was affiliated with his brothers Virgil and Morgan, Bat Masterson and other fellow lawmen. Until this time, Wyatt had never taken another man's life.

The summer of 1878 was one of the rowdiest in Kansas cow town history. An unexpected shooting with more Texans, which resulted in the death of one young cowboy, earned Wyatt his first mention of fame.

Although he, Jim Masterson, or any one of several involved in the altercation could have fired the shot, Wyatt received credit in *The National Police Gazette*.[47] The three Earp boys, the Masterson brothers, Bill Tilghman, and Charlie Bassett kept things pretty much in line. Enter the good dentist.

Doc evidently intended to "go straight" in Kansas after the somewhat fictionalized and often over-dramatized flight through Indian Territory. The couple registered at the Dodge House as "Mr. and Mrs. John H. Holliday" and shortly thereafter an ad appeared in the local newspaper:

DENTISTRY
J.H. Holliday, Dentist, very respectfully offers his professional services to the citizens of Dodge City and surrounding country during the summer. Office room No. 24, Dodge House. Where satisfaction is not given money will be refunded.[48]

One can visualize a "dissatisfied" patient requesting his money back from Doc Holliday.

Wyatt Earp had returned to Dodge City, Kansas, the month before and the friendship was firmly grounded in September when Doc allegedly saved Wyatt's life.[49] Assistant Marshal Wyatt Earp and another officer were pistol-whipping a bunch of drunken Texas cowboys in the Comique Theater. The official title for this activity is "buffaloing." As he was laying about with a ready hand, one of the Texans took direct aim at Earp's back. Holliday, more than likely drinking and gambling out of action's way, hollered, "Look out, Wyatt," and discharged his revolver. As in so many cases involving Doc Holliday's gun firing, no one was injured. Evidently either his reputation or the gunshot scared the rowdies off and Wyatt forever claimed that Doc "saved his life." It forged a friendship that would stand the test of time as Doc's one redeeming character trait, fidelity. Not a single author, historian, or screenwriter has ever denied him that: his loyalty to Wyatt Earp.

An old Ashland, Kansas, man left an interesting letter that lies pretty much unnoticed in the Glenwood Springs' Frontier Historical Society's files.[50] Written by a Jim Talley, and undated, the story allegedly came from Talley's uncle who claimed to be a conspirator with Doc during his gambling days in Dodge. Then only a boy, Ely Vanmetter would wander around the table aimlessly. When Doc had a coughing fit, Ely would run over, pound him on the back, and whisper the other players' hands in his ear. Jim Talley claimed to have other stories, but this is the only written account to be found. Probably an occasionally used joke to amuse the boy, it sounds like Doc humor, but not his character. Just how funny the losers thought it, is certainly questionable, as is the truth of it all.

New Mexico and Colorado

Cowtown winters were intensely boring. A few days before Christmas 1878, Doc and Kate arrived in Las Vegas, New Mexico, a mining boomtown ripe for the picking. Another attraction may have been the hot springs although, as has been noted, they were almost instant death to a lunger. Holliday did again establish a dental practice, in the same building with a jeweler named William Leonard, an association that would cause Doc serious problems a few years down the road. Still, he just could not stay out of trouble, and in March 1879 was indicted for "keeping [a] gambling table."[51]

Following an extremely cold winter and slow economy, Doc and Kate returned to Dodge. Jeff Morey, noted Doc Holliday researcher, is of the opinion that Doc's problems in New Mexico stemmed primarily from the fact that his large winnings came not from the more common soldiers, as they had in Texas, but from notable people in authority. Or, Doc simply may have found, as former New Mexico Governor Lew Wallace wrote, "every calculation based on experience elsewhere, fails in New Mexico." It is for sure Doc never had any (good) luck there.

Even back in Dodge City, however, Doc just could not settle down. He soon joined with a group led by Bat Masterson, then a deputy U.S. marshal, to assist the Santa Fe Railroad in its battle with the Denver & Rio Grande over the Raton Pass right-of-way. The group hung out in Pueblo, Colorado, until about June, when peaceable terms were negotiated. Doc pocketed what might have been his share of the $10,000 paid Masterson by the Santa Fe, and traveled to Trinidad, Colorado.[52] By this point, Doc had shown a decidedly greater skill with the carving knife than the six-gun, perhaps attributed to his medical training. It could very possibly have been attributed to poor eyesight, a concept sometimes advocated.

A small notice in the *Otero Optic* on Thursday, June 5, 1879, shows where Doc placed a five-dollar bet on a "splendid violin" raffled at Henry & Robinson's place.[53] He lost the toss of the dice and we can but hazard a guess as to what was on his mind. Oh well, it was Saturday night, and Doc would gamble on anything.

In July 1879, Doc claimed his second victim. A newspaper article at the time reported a Coroner's Inquest found persons unknown had inflicted the wound.[54]

> On July 19, 1879, a number of places of amusement were opened in East Las Vegas. Among those attending the festivities was Michel Gordon, a former member of the Fifth Cavalry, who had been under the influence of liquor for several days. His mistress was at a hall on Center St. Gordon tried to

persuade her to accompany him to another hall on Railroad St. When she refused to go, he flew into a drunken rage and swore that he would kill someone or be killed himself before morning.

Gordon was found shot through the breast later that night and died the following morning. The *Las Vegas Gazette* and the *Santa Fe New Mexican* observed the next day that no one would talk about the matter for fear of being called to testify in court. The case was dismissed as excusable homicide.[55] Two years later the *Las Vegas Optic* publicly identified Doc as Gordon's killer.[56] Wyatt Earp and others later attested to the fact that Doc had done the deed. This establishes that the deadly dentist was evidently back in Las Vegas and had upped the level of his sins.

On July 20, 1879, Doc Holliday's Saloon opened its doors. A nearby competitor was advertising a schooner of beer for ten cents. Although Doc purchased various real estate properties in Las Vegas, the town seemed to be a jinx for him, as he was indicted twice within the next two months for "keeping a gaming table."[57] Pages have been cleanly cut from the San Miguel County, New Mexico, Deed Book that would have pinpointed out exactly where his saloon did, and may still, stand.

Although much has been made of Doc's preference for poker, it is a fairly established fact he would have been an excellent Faro dealer. The game demands total concentration and is an involved form of dealings in high finance.[58] It utilizes a rectangular table with players on three sides and the dealer always with his back to the wall. A deck of cards is slipped into the dealing box, open on the top and at one side. The top card, called "soda," is visible to everyone and counts nothing. The game begins with the soda being removed and put to one side; the first counting card can then be viewed. A card in the box is a winning card, one on the side is a losing card, and either can be bet on, to win or to lose. A strip of green felt contains the thirteen Spades and some of the old decks showed a Tiger as the Ace. Thus evolved the term, "bucking the tiger." To play, you put your money on a card, by itself if you were betting to win, or with a penny or copper token if you expected it to lose. Twenty-four turns made up the game, with three cards comprising the last, or cat-hop, and paid double. A case keeper operated an abacus-like affair comprised of colored beads representing each card in the various suits that had been played, just not whether it had won or lost. Yes, it was complicated, made more so by whisky, noise, busty women, and smoke.

Keeping the case was known as "riding the hearse," as many a gambler too drunk and/or dim-witted soon discovered the reasoning behind. The dealer was faced with the same challenge as each player, remembering what had been played, which card had won and which had lost. The fact that Doc Holliday was considered a top-notch Faro dealer is evidence of his quick and intelligent mind. Also perhaps to Wyatt Earp's attestation that no matter how much Doc drank, he rarely seemed affected.

Gone Again

About this time, Wyatt once again intervened in Doc's life. Most stories say Earp arrived in Las Vegas in October 1879, accompanied by his own "wife" at the time, Mattie (Celia Ann Blaylock) and three members of his brother James' family.[59] Understand that Mattie, like many women referred to as "wife" during those times, never legally held that title. Kate would later recall that she and Doc just pulled up stakes and headed for the reported glories of the Arizona silver strikes with the Earps. Wyatt never mentions Kate in his account. He simply states that Doc caught up with him at "Trail's End," tied his horse on the back of the buckboard and climbed in.[60] Wyatt also told Stuart Lake that "Mike Finnerty" was with him.

Now "Mike" has never been further identified nor mentioned, but considering Wyatt's penchant for naming his animals after people, and considering he was a somewhat educated man, leads to at least one supposition. *The Life and Times of Col. Daniel Boone* had been published when Wyatt was a boy and Mike Finerty was Daniel Boone's nemesis in many of the tales.[61] It is not stretching it too far to give Wyatt the imagination to name his dog after a childhood story character.

The strange entourage was probably comprised of Doc, Kate, Wyatt, Mattie, and the James Earp family. This included Jim's "wife" Bessie, and "stepdaughter" Sallie Earp (possibly *nee* Haspel who also was likely one of Wyatt's consorts from Peoria, Illinois, a few years earlier).[62] Kate wrote a good bit about the trip in her memoirs many years later. So much conjecture surrounds these few months in the life of John H. Holliday, it is difficult to separate truth from fiction from hearsay. The facts simply do not exist to sort it out. Apparently Doc returned to Dodge City, missed Wyatt (who had spent about a month in Las Vegas), and left before Doc could get back to New Mexico and take off after him. The facts are fairly certain the entire group made what would prove a three- to four-week overland trip to Prescott over the only likely route afforded.[63]

The fifty-year-old wagon trail out of Las Vegas crossed the Pecos River at San Miguel del Vado three miles south, then swung north and west through Glorieta Pass into Santa Fe. "Trails End" is the terminus of the Santa Fe Trail where a monument has marked the spot for centuries.

"Trail's End" in Santa Fe, New Mexico: the site where Doc met Wyatt en route to Tombstone (courtesy John P. McWilliams, reprinted from *New Mexico: A Glimpse Into an Enchanted Land*).

San Miguel County, notoriously slack in its care of courthouse records as previously mentioned, does show that J.H. Holliday sold property to A. M. Johnson *et al.* on September 30, 1879. Wyatt was in town the same month and his party did not arrive in Tombstone until late in the year, with a wagon Wyatt intended to convert into a stagecoach.[64] This fact, together with the length of time involved, indicates they did not avail themselves of railroad comforts, with tracks between Santa Fe and Flagstaff. The Santa Fe Railroad did not go through Albuquerque until April of the following year.

The military road, built by the Army with convict labor, was the only other choice out of Santa Fe, New Mexico. It wound down the escarpment through La Bajada, malingering along Aderavedero, the main east-west street of Pena Blanca, then the seat of Santa Ana (now Sandoval) County. Shortly thereafter it crossed the Rio Grande at Abrevadera ("Watering Place"), followed the military road briefly, then turned back east on Camino Real into Cuervo and San Felipe. There the Rio Grande was crossed again at Angostura ("The Narrows") with a short trip end run into Bernalillo, about fifteen miles north of Albuquerque. Whether directly out of Bernalillo, or through Albuquerque for supplies, there was still but one option for travel west, the military road.

The Army provided supply stations about every thirty miles where supplemental rations could be purchased. That part of New Mexico is not overabundant with either water or grass, so they likely had to pay for them regularly. It is 328 miles today, on Interstate 40, from Albuquerque to Flagstaff, Arizona, just northeast of Prescott. Their route was very similar, whereby they would have traveled past the monolith at Torreon and stopped at Fort Defiance, near Window Rock, on the Arizona–New Mexico border.

Pushing your horses, you can make thirty to forty miles a day from sunup to dusk, ten hours in the saddle or on a splintery plank seat. In places the buckboard and belongings would have to be portaged up or down the sides of a mountain pass. At Window Rock, things got higher and even rougher. One of the first places to be crossed was the Wide Ruins. There was no water at Winslow, until the railroad later dug wells, and after crossing the 8500-foot Hutch Mountain, Camp Verde was finally reached. There was no road from there into Prescott; we can only imagine what paths they may have struggled to find.

But make it they did, Wyatt hooked up with Virgil and Allie, and the three Earp families moved on to Tombstone. Wyatt reported that "Doc was on a roll" and stayed behind.[65]

The June 1880 census for Yavapai County, Arizona, shows "Holladay [*sic*] J.H.: W.M. (White, Male) 29; Single; Dentist; born Georgia; Father and Mother born South Carolina."[66] No mention is made of Kate (although who knows what name she may have been using). Shortly thereafter, new anti-gambling and liquor laws were enacted in Prescott, leaving little of interest to the good dentist. Things were riding high until the end of the year.

Roberts offers further evidence that Doc returned to Las Vegas for yet another go at the land of his (dis)enchantment, again meeting with misfortune.[67] On the third trip to his nemesis city of Las Vegas, he sold his businesses.[68] Prior to pushing on to Tombstone, however, he met up with Charlie White (Wright), a man he had earlier run out of town.

> The two commenced blazing away at each other in the Old Town Plaza Saloon and when White fell to the floor, Doc thought he had killed him. Only grazed, White recovered and left shortly thereafter for Boston. All charges were dropped against Doc who gave up for the third and final time on New Mexico and headed further west.[69]

This is neither the first nor the last account of blazing shootouts, virtually dozens of cartridges (from two six-shooters?), signifying nothing. Despite Wyatt Earp's words to the contrary, Doc Holliday may not have been "the deadliest man with a six-shooter." Perhaps the reason these stories are not repeated is they blemish the bloodthirsty image most want to paint of Doc.

Some credence must be given to this shootout story, however, as it is recounted in the memoirs of Miguel Antonio Otero, governor of the New Mexico Territory from 1897 to 1906.[70] Otero lived in Las Vegas at the time and was quite an admirer of Doc's, referring to him as "a very likable fellow." Few others of his day agreed with this appraisal, but Doc could probably be quite the charming Southern gentleman if you were not sitting across the card table from him.

Wyatt told Stuart Lake that Doc did not arrive in Tombstone until the spring of 1880, and that the gambler brought $60,000 in winnings. Certainly some "roll," although some of it could have been from property sales in Las Vegas.

Kate declares she was with Doc during some of this time but that when he insisted on meeting up with the Earps in Tombstone, they split. It is not surprising; when you consider the amount of trouble they seem to be constantly getting into, that neither Kate, nor any of the Earp women, cared for their menfolks' friendship.

Tombstone and Beyond

The Great Register for Pima County (Arizona) listed "Holliday, J.H., age 24" in September of 1880.[71] Yes, the age is wrong, he was 29, having just had a birthday. By that time Virgil was a U.S. marshal and Wyatt was riding shotgun for Wells Fargo. He was also serving as a deputy county sheriff. Brother James was bartending directly across the street, and Morgan had arrived the previous spring from Butte, Montana.[72] Doc allegedly partnered with his friends in several business ventures and held a quarter ownership with them in the Crystal Palace.[73] Gambling and drinking the night away were, however, more the general routine, sprinkled with disputes and disorderly conduct.

October 1880 found Doc confronting Johnny Tyler, a former dealer at the Oriental Saloon, and the two drew their pistols. Milt Joyce, the bartender, tried to interfere and was shot in the hand by Doc for his efforts. A bystander was shot in the foot. One of Stuart Lake's notes indicates a part of Holliday's altercation with Tyler may have included an interest in the same woman. Which one is unmentioned. Doc pled guilty to misdemeanor and assault charges, and paid a $20 fine.[74] The incident accelerated the hard feelings between Holliday and Joyce, who hated both Doc and the Earps. Johnny Tyler would prove a problem for Doc several years later in Colorado; he was building quite an entourage of enemies.

The following spring, an old friendship almost got Doc in serious trouble. Nearly every written or filmed account of Holliday's life mentions this incident, yet it is impossible to denounce or vilify Doc. The facts remain unknown.

William (Billy) Leonard, formerly of Las Vegas, New Mexico, had turned from the jewelry business to stagecoach robbery. He resided with Bill (Luther) King in a shack about two miles north of Tombstone. According to Wyatt Earp's interviews with Stuart Lake, Doc visited them often.[75] On March 15, 1881, Holliday rented a horse at Dunbar's Livery Stable and rode out to "The Wells." He returned about 4:00 P.M., riding on the water hauler's wagon. Wyatt testified that Doc "went to playing Faro," after he returned and ate supper, and was still playing when word arrived from Bob Paul, shotgun messenger for Wells Fargo, that the Benson Stage had been attacked and driver Bud Philpot killed. Paul testified a masked man had stepped into the stage's path a few miles from Contention, shouting "Hold!"

"By God, I hold for nobody!" the guard retorted, standing and aiming his shotgun at the gang of men now grouped in the road. Shots ensued, hitting Philpot, who fell among the traces, setting the horses off at a wild gallop. The stage was a mile down the road before it was brought under control. The robbers had been unsuccessful in getting an estimated $80,000 in gold bullion on board.

A posse was quickly formed, comprised of the three Earp brothers, Bob Paul, and Bat Masterson (in town for a few days). Wyatt and Masterson were fellow lawmen and friends from Kansas cowtown days, while Paul had been the shotgun messenger on the stage. It should be noted here that this story was recorded in several early tellings as the Bisbee Stage. Most recent and well-documented historians have agreed, however, that it was indeed the Benson Stage. It is also not to be confused with the Sandy

Bob Stage robbery of September 8 of that same year, which was definitely laid at the feet of Johnny Behan's deputy, Frank Stilwell. A second posse, led by Sheriff John Behan was comprised of William M. Breckenridge and "Buckskin" Frank Leslie. Billy Breckenridge was never a friend of Doc or the Earps, and would continue his animosity long after their deaths.[76] Tennessee-born Leslie, appointed deputy by the city council to keep peace in the Oriental, was known for his bad temper and quick trigger finger. He was, however, an excellent tracker.[77] The posses met up and were together when Deputy Morgan Earp arrested Luther King, who admitted he had held the horses during the holdup attempt. William Leonard was allegedly one of the robbers. Doc was incriminated primarily because of his friendship with Leonard, his absence from town on the day of the robbery, and the fact that he had ridden with neither posse. Nevertheless, editor John Clum of *The Epitaph*, always a staunch supporter of Wyatt Earp, his family and friends, wrote a few days later that he would personally "make a sieve out of the next low-down blankety-blank who repeated [this] gossip."[78]

In a letter written years later, Wyatt would state adamantly, "Doc was not in the Benson stage holdup and he never did such a thing as holdups in his life. He was his own worst enemy."[79] Stuart Lake, however, substantiates the charge based on a July 6, 1881, issue of *The Tombstone Nugget* (anti–Earp and Holliday), stating a warrant was issued for Doc "upon the affidavit of Kate Elder with whom Holliday has been living for some time past." The story behind this is that Kate got drunk, briefly took up with Johnny Ringo, swore out a deposition that Doc was guilty, then recanted when she sobered up. Wyatt demanded that Doc send her out of town. Kate went.

Fred Dodge, in his recollections, records six men guilty, adding Luther King, Jim Crane, and Johnny Barnes.[80] Dodge writes that one of the robbers told him, "Billy Leonard and Doc Holliday were the men who planned it." If Doc were involved, it would have been in the planning. He had a very keen mind for detail. Passengers on the stage were emphatic: There were eight holdup men, which has extended to possibly include "Curly Bill" Brocious, Ike (or any one of the Clantons), Frank C. Stilwell, and/or Peter Spence. William Graham ("Curley Bill") Brocius was possibly from Indiana and may have known Doc from Fort Griffin days.[81] Stilwell, according to Tombstone researcher Roy B. Young, was a legitimate businessman with mining, livery, saloon, and liquor interests, who claimed to have been born in Texas.[82] Spence, born Eliot Larkin Ferguson, a former Texas Ranger, ran afoul of the law and wound up in Tombstone.[83] The resultant popularity of these men in the Tombstone saga has generally tended to indict them by association. There is also the "glint off a rifle in the distance" story related by one of the stage occupants. This added further to the confusion of not only who, but just how many holdup men there really were.

We must wonder what Doc was doing at his friends' house all day when they were not at home, but obviously off attempting to rob the Benson Stage. He said he was in Charleston playing cards, which poses the question, with whom? What happened to the horse he rented? What on earth was he doing up so early in the morning? Doc's routine was to gamble until three or four, sleep until noon or later, eat breakfast, then return to the bar for another 12 hours of drinking and cards. Although his innocence or guilt is by now a moot point, it has furnished much material for the creative minds that have served up his story. Doc's statement "If I had pulled that job, I would have shot a horse and got the eighty thousand" makes a valid defense.[84]

As a sidebar, William Leonard was unable to testify in either the affirmative or negative. The Haslett brothers gunned him and Harry ("The Kid") Head down in the Animas Valley of New Mexico before they could be brought to justice.

The truth, not the myth, is that John H. "Doc" Holliday was a major participant at the now famous Gunfight at the OK Corral. Much of the *myth* lies in where the fight really took place, in its duration, in who was to blame, and in the outcome. However, the part it played in vaulting Doc Holliday to fame among western good men/bad men cannot be overstated. The "street fight," as Wyatt Earp called it, may have been the greatest factor in Doc's future legend. Indeed, it may have been the only factor. As the bulk of this book deals with the evolution of not only the legend of Doc Holliday, but of information concerning details of the famous gunfight, it is outlined only briefly at this juncture. Wyatt reported the following month that Doc whistled quietly and nodded as they walked down the street.[85]

Wyatt was adamant in how many shots were fired and by whom.[86] It is his and Virgil's story which research deems most accurate.[87] Wyatt admitted that he and Billy Clanton fired first, whereupon "the fight commenced." Doc seems to have blasted Tom McLaury with the shotgun handed him earlier by Virgil, then thrown down the weapon in disgust and subsequently emptied his pistol. Earp's statement that Doc was slightly wounded when his gun belt was shot off is rarely mentioned in most variations of the tale. He may have been grazed, but whether he wore a gun belt is questioned.

Doc has been accused of firing the first shot. The most likely scenario, however, is that either Wyatt and Billy Clanton did. Ike Clanton's wild and cowardly escape before the shooting began probably shoved Wyatt out of Billy's line of fire and possibly saved his life. When Ike ran, he also changed the odds, leaving only three cowboys to face the four lawmen. Legend says thirty shots were fired in thirty seconds. Gary Roberts states the number of shots was "twenty-five to thirty."[88] Seven men with six-guns could have expelled forty-two, although allegedly Tom McLaury may have had no revolver but was going for the rifle in his saddle when Doc shotgunned him, leaving six shells unaccounted for. We know Billy Clanton emptied his revolver; he died asking for more bullets. Young Billy allegedly died with seven holes in him, one in his right wrist. He fired his last few shots using his left hand. The following chapters of this book will outline the pros and cons of this fateful day's events to its ultimate explanation by California historians Jeff Morey and Casey Tefertiller well into the twenty-first century.[89]

A coroner's jury, after listening to testimony from Billy Claiborne and Ike Clanton, refused to place any blame. Subsequent warrants for the arrest of Doc and the three Earp brothers were issued with charges filed by Ike Clanton and issued by Justice Wells Spicer. Friends raised amounts well above their bail, with Wyatt himself contributing $7000 for Doc's bond. The grand jury never permitted Doc to personally testify.[90] It can only be presumed his attorneys refused him that privilege. The stories rarely varied, however. "The Law and Order Faction," comprised of the Republican Earps and Holliday, stuck with their story of a prompted and unavoidable gunfight. Their opponents, all Southern Democrats categorized as "The Cowboys," perceived of themselves as victimized. For all practical purposes, the end result was the same, a place in western history for all participants.

Doc Holliday fell into neither of the social or political categories. He was a Southern Democrat with no logic for his actions other than his loyalty to Wyatt Earp. His reasons and moral fiber must be left to the mind of the beholder and, indeed, have been more times than can be numbered.

Although Doc and Wyatt languished in Sheriff John Behan's jail, denied bail for over two weeks, probably no one was more surprised than the attorneys when Judge Wells Spicer, after hearing the testimony, refused to turn in an indictment. Everybody walked. There was not even a trial. Public opinion, it cannot be denied, was harsh on Doc Holliday, whose reputation allegedly tainted that of the Earps to at least some degree. It can only be concluded that their having been lawmen greatly altered the status of their past careers, as did Doc's reputation of a hot temper.

Still unswerving in his friendship, Doc was on the so-called "vendetta ride" following a crippling ambush on Virgil Earp three days after Christmas the same year and the murder of Morgan Earp on March 17, 1882.

Three of the "Cowboy" faction were killed, although not a one could be credited to the dentist from Georgia. However, it was Wyatt, and Wyatt alone, who shot Florentino "Indian Charlie" Cruz and Curly Bill Brocious. Australian historian Peter Brand, together with new Tombstone historian Roger Jay, early in the 21st Century, identified the actual members of this famous brigade and brought knowledge of their lives before and after to the fore.[91]

Just who comprised the group with Wyatt and Doc that departed Arizona has undergone wide and varied conjecture over the years. Its resolution is yet another wrought by the new millennium. They did so via Lordsburg and Silver City, stopping in Albuquerque for about two weeks while Wyatt rounded up some money.[92] According to Stuart Lake, Sheriff Bob Paul received a telegram from Earp on May 10, 1882, stating he and Doc were in Gunnison, Colorado.[93] It is fairly certain that Doc and Wyatt quarreled en route to Gunnison, where Doc left him and younger brother Warren and proceeded to Denver. Gary L. Roberts, together with Australian researcher Peter Brand, would later prove Doc rode to Denver with Daniel G. Tipton, only recently identified by Roberts and Brand.[94] A picture of Tipton is available courtesy of the Ohio State Penitentiary.[95] The reason for the quarrel is yet another part of the myth to undergo change during the years, meeting with a "probable" conclusion during the twenty-first century.

Thank Goodness for Denver

Denver proved an unwise decision. Holliday was arrested soon after his arrival in the Mile High City, on May 15, 1882, and a great many newspaper reports relate events during his jail time there. To the reader it may seem that if Doc Holliday ever had any luck at all, it was bad. However, things definitely began a downhill slant following his days in Tombstone. It was a stroke of genius for his historians in the twentieth century. Although the Denver papers split in their opinion on Doc's guilt or innocence, it was there his individual story hit national headlines for the first time. The day following his arrest, *The Denver Tribune* referred to him as a "desperate, blood-thirsty and notorious murderer, stage robber and villain."[96]

The man who caused Doc's arrest was reported to have been one Perry Mallen, who "claimed to be a Deputy Sheriff from Los Angeles."[97] As it turned out, Mallen's story was more mythical than anything concerning Doc to date. Despite being a total fraud, Mallen certainly had the dentist sweating for several weeks. One story Mallen gave out claimed he came directly from the "cowboys in the South" and accused Doc of "every conceivable crime," including being an accessory in the murder of Frank Stilwell. This is perhaps not too fanciful, considering that Wyatt himself later stated that Holliday was with him when Stilwell was gunned down at the Tucson train station. Stilwell's body, however, was riddled with both buckshot and rifle holes, and a verdict has never been reached on that story.

Newspaper accounts from far and wide exaggerated Doc's crimes, with some publications eventually taking his side. During May and June of 1882, public attention was first truly focused on John Henry Holliday. The May 16 *Denver Daily Times* reported, "No fewer than twenty-five men have fallen by his hand, most of them murdered without provocation.... [H]is record [is] stained with blood."[98] The same day's edition of *The Denver Republican* referred to Holliday as "the Jesse James of the West" and "one of the most noted desperadoes of the West," declaring that, "Billy the Kid faded into insignificance by comparison."[99]

The very next day, in an item entitled "Capers of Cowboys," *The Denver Tribune* published Doc's side of the story. It pointed out the fact that Holliday had not been in hiding or using an alias. Again, there is no proof he ever did. *The Tribune* declared him "a defenseless and unarmed man" when Mallen accosted him. Unarmed? The paper further notes that Doc was a friend of both Bat Masterson and Constable Pat Desmond in Pueblo. This is certainly blatant myth; Bat and Doc were never friends. At this time in his life, however, even alleged friendship with a well-thought-of lawman was a boon.

On May 18 the *Denver Daily Times* reported receipt by local officials of a warrant from Pueblo charging Doc as operator in a confidence game whereby his victim had lost $150.[100] According to most reports, this was a ruse to get Doc out of Denver and further confuse the issue of his custody. Another way to avoid extradition to Arizona.

By Friday, May 19, *The Republican* had switched over to Doc and the Earps' side. A lengthy account was printed, including some "Romantic Stories" about Doc. This account states that Bat Masterson told their reporter, "Holliday had killed twenty-seven men," but the account makes haste to note, "[I]t is a very pleasant story, and a fiction." Bat told the reporter he knew Doc well, that he was a good dentist, and had acted in Tombstone out of loyalty to the Earps. Bat hated Doc, but he never once denounced Holliday's loyalty to Wyatt Earp.

The Saturday, May 20, edition of the *Denver Daily Times* announced Sheriff Bob Paul's arrival in Denver and made a "confirmation of Holliday's story." Evidently, Bob Paul admitted that Doc had been his deputy at one time.[101] A *Tribune* account that same date made the rather obvious suggestion, "[Paul] is evidently in favor of Holliday."[102]

But for his arrest there, and the eventual siding of *The Denver Republican* with John Henry Holliday, history would be woefully lacking in actual interviews with the hero of our story.

On May 20 and 22, the paper related how Masterson "asserted positively" that Doc had never been in Utah. Mallen had charged Doc with a killing there. "Awful Arizona," a long piece on the 22nd, printed a "quiet little chat" between Holliday and one of the *Republican*'s reporters[103]:

> Holladay [sic] is a slender man, not more than five feet six inches tall and would weigh perhaps 150 pounds. His face is thin and his hair sprinkled heavily with gray. His features are well formed and there is nothing remarkable in them save a well-defined look of determination from his eyes.... His hands are small and soft like a woman's, but the work they have done is anything but womanly and ... the slender wrist has proved its muscles of steel.
> ... The first thing noticeable about him ... was his soft voice and modest manners.

The article seems careful to tell the story as it was heard from Doc and it is here he mentions having dealt at "Babbit's house" at the time of the alleged Utah killing. This would have been during that 1875–77 time frame.

The *Republican* goes on to recite telegrams, other newspapers, and various individuals, all in seeming support of the Earps and Doc Holliday. The writer appeared to believe that Colorado's Governor Frederick A. Tritle "was conniving with Sheriff Paul" to obtain release of the prisoner. Doc and other sources evidently convinced the writer of this article that the dentist would be murdered if he returned to Arizona. On May 24, the *Republican* announced, "Holladay [sic] *habeas corpus* case had come up and "as was expected ... he was released." This decision pertained to Mallen's charges.

The *Republican,* apparently still in Doc's corner on May 26, reported his arrest on charges in Arizona and remarked, "The general impression is that Holladay [sic] will be acquitted," and "It is rumored that Bob [sic] Masterson is organizing a party to guard the train upon which Holladay [sic] will be taken back."

The following day the same paper reported Doc's arraignment on murder charges in Arizona. On May 30, bold headlines bleated "HOLLIDAY DISCHARGED." It explained how Colorado Governor Frederick Pitkin adjudged the Arizona extradition papers issued against Doc as being "defective."

Interestingly, *The Valdosta* (Georgia) *Times* published an article about their hometown boy on August 19. It was taken from *The New York Sun* and had been sent to them from Silverton, Colorado.[104] The header shrieks "STARTED MANY GRAVEYARDS," with the subtitle of "Pulling His Shooting Iron Often in Behalf of Law and Order." It is doubtful that John Henry's family was intrigued to hear the account of his having "killed thirty men" ... or of his "robbing and killing all along the Southwestern border." This same article threw Doc in "with cattle thieves at Fort Yuma," but allowed him to clear himself by a declaration of, "I have had credit for more killings than I ever dreamt of." In spite of this, the article continued quoting Holliday as declaring that although he had to "fix one or two drunken greasers" [*sic*] he had been charged with murders and robberies he was five hundred miles away from at the time.

This identical article appeared in the *Daily Denver Times* that same day. A *Denver Tribune Republican* account on August 4 reported Holliday arrested for vagrancy. At that time on the western frontier, vagrancy was used to get any undesirable out of town and Denver had strong reasons to suspect Doc of being a troublemaker.

After the Glory

Doc went free and reunited briefly with Wyatt in Pueblo, Colorado, was then bound over on trumped-up swindling charges, but soon freed.[105] That had been Wyatt and Masterson's plan all along, just to keep Doc in Colorado and out of Arizona. Court records substantiate this incident.

The Leadville, Colorado, City Directory indicates that John Henry Holliday was receiving his mail at the Western Union telegraph office there in June 1882.[106] *Doc Holliday, A Family Portrait* has him dealing Faro at Mannie Hyman's Monarch Saloon and frequently playing poker at the Board of Trade Saloon across the street.[107] That author further claims to have learned recently from Mary Billings-McVicar of Leadville that Doc gamed at the Texas House. It is in Leadville that several "prescriptions" may have surfaced, written on Doc's behalf, for laudanum. None are extant, and we can only hope that more than alcohol was somehow relieving the pain that beset him.

Gary Roberts' "The Leadville Years" (December 2001) tells us that Leadville itself warned people with bad lungs or weak hearts to keep away.[108] But it was a gambling town and Doc had friends there, so he stayed. The strength he had regained in Arizona was soon lost to recurrent bouts of pneumonia. It was also here, in 1883, that Doc learned that his cousin Mattie, lifelong friend and correspondent, had entered a convent. Although the true nature of their relationship may never be known, the effect of the news must have been a final blow to any yearning he may have had for an ordinary life.

Not everybody in Leadville were friends, according to Roberts, and soon former rival Johnny Tyler and other toughs from Tombstone began to cause him trouble. The animosity grew more heated in 1884 and drew in William J. (Billy) Allen, with absolutely no ties to Tombstone other than what was whispered in his ear. Doc was repeatedly embarrassed because any troublemaking on his part could have sent him straight back to Arizona and by now he lacked the strength to even protect himself. He so feared being extradited to Arizona that he stopped carrying a gun, and was so broke he borrowed five dollars from Allen. It can surely be said he had fallen on desperate times when Doc sent for the police and asked the help of several friends.

By now Doc was either too sick, too clever, or just did not care enough to keep his name out of the news. Fortunately for historians, however, much of his Leadville activity was political and even public-spirited; he was in trouble only once. So, while most of Doc's life in Leadville had been shrouded in mystery for nearly 120 years, twenty-first century research would reveal most of it. *The Leadville Herald Democrat* reports Doc shot Billy Allen, a crony of Holliday's old nemesis Johnny Tyler, in August of 1884.[109] The gambling dentist was charged and tried for assault with intent to kill. The majority of testimony declared it was over a five-dollar debt owned to Allen and admitted Doc shot in self-defense.

According to Henry Kellerman, the bartender at Hyman's, Doc shot Allen twice, quite deliberately, but almost missed both times. Holliday's friends got together the $8,000 bond posted, while witnesses for the defense attested that Allen called him a son of a bitch and threatened to "knock [Doc] down and kick his damn brains out." The report also noted, "Allen is a stout, active man; Holliday is a small man and delicate besides." Doc testified that he weighed 122 pounds, Allen 170, and that he was unable to protect himself without a gun. The case was heard on March 27, 1885, and Doc was acquitted.[110]

Despite his poor health, Doc stayed out of trouble for two years and built quite a reputation as a good citizen.[111] Roger Jay reports in his 2003 *WOLA* (Western Outlaw and Lawmen History Association) *Journal* account that when a disastrous fire struck the Texas House on December 6, 1881, and raged out of control for several hours, Doc was one of five civilians cited for commendation in helping put it out. Jay proved his serious attention to detail in that December's *WOLA Journal*, again bringing new material to the forefront. Doc Holliday is the focus of his article on the Lake

County Independent Club that contains much Leadville data heretofore unpublished.[112] Jay wound up 2003 with another article in *Wild West,* "Doc Holliday: Last Stand in Leadville."[113]

The most poignant story from Doc's last days is one his advocates sincerely hope is true. In what is known as "The Recollections of Josephine Earp," the woman who spent over forty years with Wyatt, Doc's last reunion with his good friend is reported.[114] It occurred the summer or fall of 1885 at the Windsor Hotel in Denver, where Josephine observed "a thin, more delicate" Doc who sat with Wyatt and talked for some time. She noted his continuous coughing, and related his having told Wyatt he could often not leave his bed. Josephine declared Wyatt was touched, and how he remembered Doc's saving his life. Interestingly, there is no mention of Tombstone or its events, just two old friends whose parting would soon be permanent. It is comforting to know they saw each other one last time.

Doc Holliday reportedly returned to Leadville for a short visit. According to an item in the Western Frontier Museum in Glenwood Springs, Colorado, and confirmed by his *Ute-Chief* obituary the following November 10th, Doc arrived there in May 1887. It was already too late for John Henry Holliday, although there is no doubt the sulfur fumes at the nearby Penny Hot Springs spa accelerated the decomposition of what little lung tissue he had left. Despite many written and filmed accounts that romanticize Doc Holliday as having died at a sanitarium; it is certain his last days were spent at the Hotel Glenwood in a solitary room. But lest we pity him, it was proclaimed the finest hotel in the state outside of Denver.

Virginia Crowne's "Reminiscing: An Account of Early Days in Glenwood Springs, CO," claims Holliday was delirious the last two weeks of his life.[115] She attests that he had been a quiet, docile man who made many friends the short time he had been in town. None of this is substantiated, but fans would like to believe it. Although it is difficult to think of Doc as "docile," he was too sick by this time to be anything else.

Regarding his religious affiliation, a history of the First Presbyterian Church of Glenwood Springs[116] had this to say:

> [T]he murderer, Doc Holliday, felt free to call upon him (the Presbyterian minister) for spiritual assistance in his final days. Although Holliday had been baptized in the local Catholic Church, at the time of his death, their pioneer priest, Father Downey, was away with the troops on the Ute uprising, so Rev. Rudolph conducted Holliday's burial service.

Kate's claim of arriving in Glenwood Springs and nursing Doc until the end is unsubstantiated. Later claims by others are also unproven. Art Kendrick, hotel bellman, remembered buying whiskey for the bedridden Doc, whom he said always greeted him with a brace of pistols. He does not mention Kate or Wyatt Earp, who never made any claim of visiting Doc after Denver. Doc died alone.

Dr. W.W. Crook attested in a letter that Doc was tending bar when he was taken with pneumonia and died.[117] Dr. Crook did not remember the exact date, but it was November 8, 1887. Doc was barely thirty-six years old.

The Aspen Daily Times of November 9 stated that Holliday died of military (galloping) consumption, the usual end for any "lunger." Dr. Crook's letter states Doc was buried, "on the hill at what is known as the old cemetery."[118] He verifies that the grave was not marked and it is possible the body was moved. In November in Glenwood Springs, the ground is frozen solid. Those with the misfortune to die during a Colorado winter were "stored" at various spots and brought out the following spring for burial.

Doc's November 10 Denver *Republican* epitaph noted that he represented a class of men who were fast disappearing in the New West. It continued to call Holliday a bunco man, desperado, and bad man generally. It did compliment him on being a strong friend and a cool, determined enemy.

That same newspaper, on Christmas Day, published "Holliday's Trail of Blood" in which he is touted as the murderer of sixteen men, and as having homicidal tendencies.[119] The closing words of this Yuletide commentary undoubtedly sum up what every student of John Holliday will eventually determine: "Histories of him are very indefinite and unsatisfactory." Indeed they are. Three separate gravestones have marked the spot of his burial. The first two were stolen but pictures of all three are available.

In the Frontier Historical Society archives of Glenwood Springs appears a brief picture and note dated 1956. Around the picture are the words "SIX-GUN GAMBLER John Henry Holliday, DDS, has long been a legend in Glenwood Springs, Colo." This 1956 article declares that his grave was recently located and positively identified by residents in the town's oldest cemetery. A tombstone was promptly erected. In the upper left hand of the headstone appeared an ace-high flush. On the stone was engraved:

> John Henry Holliday D.D.S.
> Born Valdosta, Georgia, in 1852
> Graduate of Baltimore Dental
> School in 1877, at the age of 20
> One of the great gamblers & the speediest
> Man with a six gun in the west.

The present-day headstone of John H. Holliday in Linwood Cemetery, Glenwood Springs, Colorado. Note the year of birth, which conflicts with the data recorded in the family bible: August 14, 1851.

> He lost his biggest bet when he died
> Nov. 8, 1887 in a Glenwood Springs, Colorado,
> Sanitarium with tuberculosis, instead of
> Being cut down by a bullet.

With so much erroneously engraved, possibly its theft is fortuitous. The headstone existing today is surrounded by a wrought-iron picket fence with a footstone declaring "Doc Holliday is buried some place in this cemetery." Even that may be untrue as a large portion of the early graveyard was washed away in a landslide, very possibly taking John Holliday's remains with it.

November 1887.

John Henry Holliday in the flesh was gone.

His myth was well established.

His legend was just beginning.

TWO

The Legend Begins

The Myth Refuted

Contrary to some opinions, Doc Holliday never did a solitary thing to enhance his own reputation. Had he chosen to do so, Texas newspapers would gladly have accommodated in establishing yet another wild character for their rogues' gallery. He quietly made the required court appearances, paid his fines, and just as innocuously returned to his somewhat boisterous lifestyle. The majority of his legal problems involved gambling and selling liquor. What fights he had were when he had "tarried too long at the wine," as some righteous folk might quote.

On the occasion of his first murder he left the country, may have even assumed an alias, and was not heard of for eighteen months. These were hardly the actions of a man seeking notoriety. He left town for a few months after Mike Gordon was shot in Las Vegas, New Mexico. He returned later, paid off a debt, got some gambling charges dismissed, became embroiled in the Charlie Wright affair, briefly co-owned a bar in Albuquerque, and was in Arizona before the *Las Vegas Optic*, two years later, denounced him as the killer.[1] At no time did he seek out newspaper coverage nor was his voice recorded as ever having made any claims to fame, violent or otherwise.

In Prescott, Holliday was residing with two rather prominent gentlemen, Richard E. Elliott, owner of the Occidental Mine, and John J. Gosper, acting territorial governor of Arizona. His friends were not shabby, and neither would have associated with a man of noted ill fame.

His arrival in Tombstone found him in league with Wyatt and Virgil Earp, both respected as lawmen and gentlemen. It was not until he became embroiled with Ike Clanton, the matter of the Benson Stage and, ultimately, the street fight, that he became widely known anywhere in the West. Certainly he was not in the nation.

He uttered not one word at his trial for first-degree murder, possibly at the advice of his attorney. When arrested several months later in Colorado, Doc was much too busy being the soul of discretion and attempting to save himself from extradition to Arizona, to be noted for anything other than his "soft voice and modest manners."[2]

None other than Wyatt Earp himself backs this opinion on the matter. While testifying at the Lotta Crabtree Estate Hearing in 1925, the attorney specifically queried Wyatt if he knew Doc Holliday, and if he was "somewhat of a notorious character in those days."[3] Wyatt replied that Doc was not, "outside of this other faction trying to make him notorious."

Despite headlines during the Denver period declaring him a mass murderer worse than Jesse James and Billy the Kid, he kept the lowest possible profile, which he maintained after his release and mandated remainder of his life in Colorado. He defended himself with a revolver in Leadville, but again said little at his trial where most of his defense was by others. During his last days in Glenwood Springs, he was declared quiet and unassuming. At no time in his life, other than during brief outbursts, did John Henry Holliday depart from his Southern upbringing.

The years following John Holliday's death tended to be confused as to how he would be portrayed. People who had known him did not cherish smearing his name. Inevitably, however, as newspapers in Denver and other parts of Colorado, Valdosta and Macon, Georgia, spread stories about him, a darker image appeared.[4]

He would not be allowed to rest in peace.

The Legend Begins

Doc's one friend had mostly good to say of him.

Wyatt Earp, ten years after Holliday's Glenwood Springs death, agreed to an interview with *The San Francisco Examiner*, believing it would be a tribute to his friend.[5] The paper, of course, was only attempting to get at Earp, but it gives us probably the first and only recorded facts about Doc from someone who truly knew and liked him. Wyatt minced no words:

> He was a dentist whom necessity had made a gambler. A gentleman whom disease had made a frontier vagabond. A philosopher whom life had made a caustic wit.

> A long, lean ash-blond fellow nearly dead with consumption and, at the same time, the most skillful gambler and the nerviest, speediest, deadliest man with a six-gun I ever knew.
>
> Perhaps Doc's strong, outstanding peculiarity was the enormous amount of whiskey he could punish. Two to three quarts of liquor a day was not unusual for him, yet I never saw him stagger with intoxication. Sometimes it would take a pint of whiskey to get him going in the morning.

Wyatt Earp concluded his *Examiner* interview with the explicit statement that Doc Holliday had never killed but three men: Ed Bailey, somewhere on the Texas Fort Trail, Mike Gordon, in Las Vegas, New Mexico, and Tom McLaury in Tombstone, Arizona.[6]

One other killing has frequently been attributed to Doc after he left Tombstone. Johnny Ringo's body was found beneath an oak tree on July 14, 1882, in Morse's Canyon, just east of Tombstone, where it had lain approximately twenty-four hours prior to discovery.[7] He had last been seen in Galeyville on July 11, drinking heavily. Doc was mentioned among the possible murderers, as were Wyatt Earp, Buckskin Frank Leslie, Johnny-Behind-the-Deuce (John O'Rourke) and a man hired by Captain Henry Hooker, from whom Ringo had often rustled cattle. They did have a distinct dislike for each other, but Doc is clearly documented as having been in Pueblo, Colorado, that day. Stranger than fiction, a gentleman helping Johnny Breckenridge interview Wyatt in San Francisco claimed that Earp said that he shot Ringo. Wrong.

Doc is so often charged with the crime, it is being addressed here. The truth, according to John Ringo's biographer Jack Burrows, is that the outlaw actually killed himself.[8] Perhaps sick of the way of life he was living, and unable to deal with it any longer, Burrows presents a fairly solid case for suicide in his worthwhile read to flush out your Tombstone databank. Other books and articles on John Ringo have since been published.

Wyatt Earp intended his remarks about Doc to sum up, as any fair portrayal should, both the goodness and the errors of his friend. He expected the story to stand that way once and for all. Unfortunately, the opportunities for expanded enhancement and further degradation of Holliday were too great a temptation: he could not be left a mere mortal. The story has changed, yet almost never changing, in practically every literary and filmed version since Earp talked to that *Inquirer* reporter. It is interesting that today, even the heroic Wyatt Earp himself has been converted from good man into bad man and is now rounding third, going back to being good. History insists on stirring the brew.

Wolfville, published in 1897 under Alfred Henry Lewis' pen name Dan Quin, was based almost entirely on hearsay.[9] Illustrated by famous western artist Frederick Remington, a copy of *Wolfville* today is priceless. Lewis went on to publish *Wolfville Days* and *Wolfville Nights* in 1902.[10] After meeting with Bat Masterson, however, Lewis published *The Sunset Trail*, ignoring anything Wyatt had said and capitulating completely to the Masterson version.[11]

There is not one word of Earp's synopsis that has not since been emphasized and retold. Until about the 1990s, however, Holliday biographers generally chose to pick only the worst points of his character to reiterate: a drunk, a gambler, and a killer. Further articles in the *Examiner*, coupled with careless news reports in the last decade of the twentieth century, placed Doc on several imaginary adventures. None were accurate. *The Kansas City Journal*'s attempt to set the record straight produced such a pallid and limp figure as to be more unbelievable than the darker image.[12]

Doc Holliday was actually resurrected in the twentieth century by a man he most disliked in life.[13] Bat Masterson's article in a 1907 *Human Life* series presented what would become the Holliday stereotype that haunts him to this day. A few chosen phrases show the majority of what Masterson, who often claimed only to have "put up with Doc for the sake of Wyatt Earp," had to say: "Of mean disposition, ungovernable temper, and a most dangerous man. If there was anything Holliday loved better than a poker game, it was conflict."

Masterson depicted Doc as a weakling who resorted to weapons for defense. He declared Doc much given to drink and very disliked "among men who did not fear him." He went on to state that Doc already had the reputation of a killer when he arrived in Texas. This is untrue, as pointed out earlier. Masterson based this on his exaggerated account of the swimming hole incident in Georgia before young John Henry left for the West. The article further accuses Doc of murdering a man in Dallas and another in Jacksboro, Texas.

Doc's killing inclinations are heightened in Masterson's account of the Kid Colton shooting in Trinidad, and the fact that Doc "shot dead" Mike Gordon in Las Vegas. The Mike Gordon killing had been confirmed by Wyatt Earp, but it is doubtful that Doc had any kind of reputation when he arrived in Dallas (within three years, however, he was well on his way to being considered a thoroughly bad case). Texas law was not so slack as to have allowed him to come in and out of their state had he been suspected of frequent homicides. Masterson's only good words on the deadly dentist regarded his unswerving loyalty to Wyatt Earp ("his whole heart and soul were wrapped up in Wyatt Earp") and the announcement that he was "picturesque." Bat must have choked at having to say anything good about Doc.

One point of interest is that Masterson is the first recognized reference to what later became known as "the vendetta ride." It receives little or no attention until almost the next century: "After Wyatt and his party had run down and killed nearly all their enemies in Arizona, Holliday returned to Denver, where he was arrested on an order from the Arizona authorities, charged with aiding in the killing of Frank Stillwell."[14]

Masterson's article sported what was then the only known photograph of John H. Holliday. It was allegedly taken by Fly's Studio in Tombstone. It is the best recognized by western buffs but in the twenty-first century its provenance would come into serious question. The writer of an unidentified article in the Frontier Museum reflects much of what would prove true of Doc's legend: "half truth ... fabulous truth and untruth."[15]

Several claimed photographs of John Henry have been proven false but historian and author Robert G. McCubbin believes the one used by Masterson and Lake is an authentic Doc Holliday.[16] The provenance of another well-recognized likeness came under close scrutiny during the twenty-first century when it proved to be a Tombstone mining engineer.

By 1907, then, John H. Holliday had been clearly identified by two men of prominence: one who claimed him as a loyal and trusted friend; the other disliked him immensely. Unfortunately, it is the discrepancies of these stories that have completely muddied Doc's image and given him a multi-faceted appearance throughout remaining history.

Neither Holliday nor many of his companions had risen to fame during the glory days of the dime novel, yet it was this sensationalized form of fiction, viewed as fact by many of its readers, that created much of what then, and still today, is perceived as "The Wild West." This mass-market fiction inevitably pictured the gambler as icy, with the mounting tension of a card game ultimately resulting in some type of killing.

This typecasting etched Doc's image in the American mind long before he personally appeared in literature or movies.

Doc in the Roaring Twenties

Conjecture can only imagine what Doc Holliday would have made of the first twenty years of the new century. Women got the vote, immigration quotas were set, and buying on credit became an American way of life. He might have returned in desperation to his native South to become a part of the Ku Klux Klan, possibly driving one of Henry Ford's new $290 automobiles. He conceivably could have joined the gangster mob control in the north, or turned back to renewed interest in the arts and literature of his childhood, leading the quiet life of a gentleman. The rise in illiteracy may have escaped his attention but he could not have avoided noting the technology explosion with radios, cars, and movies.

By the 1920s, another strong factor in the return of frontier values was the renewed public and government interest in America's national heritage. The restoration of many historic battlefields, the Mount Rushmore sculpture, and attempts to maintain the homes of American heroes, led directly to a renewed interest in our frontier and the values it reflected.

Otherwise, lacking a nineteenth century literary godfather of William F. Cody's Ned Buntline stature, or the publicity of Davy Crockett's almanacs and stories, Doc got off to a late start in the literature department. Walter Noble Burns' *Tombstone: An Iliad of the Southwest*, followed in close order by William B. Breckenridge's *Helldorado* and Lorenzo D. Walters' *Tombstone's Yesterday*, were all published in the late '20s.[17]

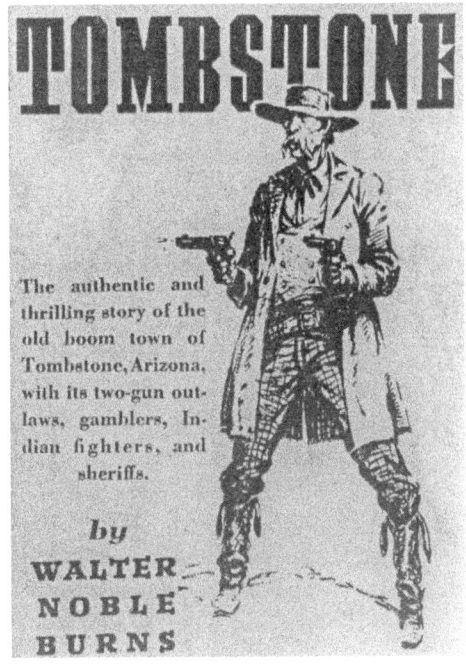

The cover of *Tombstone: Iliad of the Southwest* (1927) by Walter Noble Burns, the first book on the Doc Holliday legend.

Burns, through their mutual movie star friend William S. Hart, had approached Earp about writing his biography. His hopes were based on previous luck with his Billy the Kid legend. Unfortunately for both, Wyatt's friend, John H. Flood, Jr., had just written a "biography," which he was attempting to circulate, also with the help of Hart. Earp, therefore, declined Burns' offer. He was tricked yet again into thinking the author would write on his friend, Holliday. Interestingly, the Flood manuscript had dropped from sight, and when later unearthed, proved it likely would have done Earp more harm than good.

Burns added to what Wyatt had told him by going to Tombstone, interviewing survivors and researching the records. His book set the Earp story on the road to fame, and established a plausible description of Doc. It mentions the "witticisms of the humorous doctor, as agreeable a fellow as ever looked over the barrel of a gun." Burns further established Doc's bad man reputation, but elevates him to "the fighting ace of the Earp faction and the coldest-blooded killer in Tombstone."[18]

Burns describes Doc as rather tall and extremely slender, with ash-blonde hair and blue eyes. This writer believed Doc was waiting for a bullet to edge out consumption at the wire. *An Iliad* credits Doc with two killings in Texas and another man in Las Vegas, New Mexico. He did not fail to include the Bud Ryan and Kid Kolton [sic] incidents. It follows Burns' practice of sticking to the facts as much as possible. With many of the old-timers involved still living, however, he faced problems the modern author does not. Burns missed a few of the salient points, but the book is a good read to begin your life with Doc Holliday.

Burns is one of only two early authors to mention the so-called "vendetta ride." That appears in Chapter 14, "The Red Road of Vengeance," much of which was picked up from Wyatt's interview with *The Examiner*.[19] Keep in mind, however, that Burns was more familiar with Al Capone than the Badlands, and that is how he presented his tale. West Texans, in particular, took offense at being portrayed as the center of Trans-Mississippi mob rule.

Often lost today with the plethora of Kindle, video games, and iPods all taking new generations into different avenues of the Old West, Burns' *Helldorado*, together with his earlier *The Saga of Billy the Kid* and followed by *The Robin Hood of Eldorado*, based on the life of Joaquín Murrieta, are today considered cornerstones of the western myth.[20] His books are still in print after nearly one hundred years.

Breckenridge's *Helldorado: Bringing the Law to the Mesquite* is the only first-hand account of the dispute between Doc, the Earps, and the Cowboys.[21] Sometimes termed Breckenridge's memoirs, it appears almost a brief history of the U.S. West. Despite containing some 150 pages termed "After Tombstone," the author's primary concern in this 1928 effort is apparently self-glorification. Breckenridge was in town at the time of the street fight, and rode with both posses. Because of his stand against the "Law and Order" faction, most Earp and Holliday fanciers make light of his work. However, the version given was accurate, simply from another point of view.

William MacLeod Raine, in his introduction to *Helldorado*, groups Doc with Billy the Kid and John Wesley Hardin as "against organized society ... without respect for the rights of others." He decrees: "They had gone bad — the trend of their lives was toward evil. Apparently they enjoyed taking human life, for the least opposition set their guns smoking." This account goes contrary to the tradition that it was only Doc's friendship with Wyatt that kept him in line. History has established that neither the Kid nor Hardin had such redeeming qualities.

Breckenridge had been one of Sheriff John Behan's deputies in Cochise County, and was assisted by Wyatt in his research. It is suspected, however, that Earp may well have been displeased with the dark picture painted of Holliday. Breckenridge had been in the posse against the Earp faction during their vendetta ride and, like many, disliked the dentist. He claims in *Helldorado* that Doc was "one of the noted fighters and gambling men of Tombstone." Breckenridge is the first to officially question Holliday's role in the Benson stage robbery, although Doc's ultimate acquittal is admitted. The writer is also the first to mention the Holliday–John Ringo enmity, an item much used in later film renditions. Breckenridge is given a good deal of attention in the 1993 film *Tombstone*.[22]

A greatly revised edition of the Breckenridge work was published in the 1990s, but proved fraught with error.[23] The original chapter on John Ringo was replaced by excerpts from his biographer, abandoning the reader to wonder at the egotism of a revisionist changing the words of a man who actually knew and rode with the characters involved. The book also suffers from the omission of many original photographs.

Lorenzo Walters' narrative, published in 1929, is almost impossible to obtain today. It does not mention Holliday until page 52, when it is noted he had "assisted Wyatt Earp in making Dodge City a safe place to live."[24] Doc's disagreements with Ike Clanton play a major role in one of Walters' chapters. He bears the dentist no grudge, and attests Holliday was always loyal to his friends.

Tombstone's Yesterday account of the famous gunfight is among the more accurate of the early editions, and bears a sharp resemblance to the Earp-Lake interviews. It is the first citing that Doc pumped a round out of a Wells Fargo shotgun into Tom McLaury but, thinking it had failed, threw it aside in favor of his six-gun. Walters further reconfirms the Earp-Holliday alliance in the disposition of Frank Stilwell, shot at the Tucson railroad station. He established another part of the legend in claiming that "as one man, they all drew their guns and fired at the cowboy." If this were true, it not only condemns Doc and Wyatt, but Warren Earp, who is often unmentioned, together with the remainder of the riders, vicariously identified over the years. "Texas Jack" Vermillion and Sherman McMaster were certainly a part of the contingency, as was Turkey Creek Jack Johnson.[25] This suggests that although five are usually portrayed in this death-dealing group, there were, in fact, six. The mysterious "Dock Stillwell" named by Walters would have made it seven.[26] He has never been identified. The work was republished in 1968 with added pages from the *Epitaph*, and a collection of photographs.²⁷ Twenty-first century historians would update identity and vital statistics of the actual vendetta riders.

In the interim, a sideline take on Doc Holliday appeared in the April 6, 1926, *Tucson Star*.²⁸ It carried a two-page obituary of Anthony O'Donnell, a native of Ireland who had come to Arizona in 1878, following a stint as a Canadian Mounted policeman. He and his brother Pat operated a cattle- and horse-raising ranch in the Huachuca Mountains until 1889 when, according to an article by his daughter, O'Donnell "took an active part in subduing the Apache renegades." This information, and reminiscences of his stories, was furnished directly by Patrick's granddaughter Catherine Ann Curry. They offer a decidedly different picture of the Tombstone situation than is usually portrayed.²⁹

O'Donnell, by his account, "knew Johnnie Ringo, Wyatt Earp, Doc Holliday, and Curly Bill Brocious." Although containing a few discrepancies, this previously unheard of source makes it worth mentioning:

> Doc Holliday was a dentist and he came out of Georgia — killed a couple of soldiers. He had Bignosed [*sic*] Kate who went everywhere with him; she saved him and they came to Tombstone.
> He didn't care what he did as he had TB. Johnny Ringo ... met Doc Holliday who said, "Here's my handkerchief."

Those last three words have frequently been incorporated into one scene or another in movies; the meaning goes over the heads of most twentieth and twenty-first century readers and viewers. It was called *duel au monchoir* in early France: Two combatants holding the ends of a handkerchief in their teeth, sliced away at each other with knives until, usually, both were dead. On rare occasions, the duel was ended upon the draw of first blood. It gives a cold look at the true meaning of "personal" combat, and was always a matter of honor.³⁰

In 1927 young Stuart N. Lake wrote Wyatt Earp suggesting that he ghostwrite the lawman's memoirs. Lake, a former *New York Herald Tribune* reporter and campaign press agent for Theodore Roosevelt, promised Earp he would write the truth. Between 1924 and 1929, Earp and Lake met on many occasions. Although a study of Lake's notes creates total confusion with their rambling style, no one has seriously questioned much of the truth found in Earp's reminiscences.

Lake's book devotes "Two and Three for Morg" to the events following Morgan Earp's murder. Lake lists the only participants known for nearly a hundred years as Doc Holliday, Warren Earp, Sherman McMasters, Turkey Creek Jack Johnson, and Texas Jack Vermillion. Warren was repeatedly omitted and McMaster's name misspelled.³¹ Both Burns and Lake use Wyatt's admission to the *San Francisco Examiner* that he shot gunned Frank Stillwell at the Tucson railroad depot in retribution for killing his brother. Doc is always credited with helping him, but two blasts at close range hardly needed any assistance to finish the job. The mystery remains open to conjecture.

This lengthy life story of Wyatt Berry Stapp Earp, including Lake's five years of interviews with Earp, surprisingly follows Masterson's versions. *Wyatt Earp, Frontier Marshal* seems to involve Holliday in the Benson stage affair, but ends the account without pointing a finger.[32] On other topics Lake is clearly influenced by Earp, referring at length to Doc's loyalty to his friends. Lake's book also deals with the feud between Holliday and Ike Clanton,

The cover of *Wyatt Earp, Frontier Marshal* (1931), Stuart N. Lake's biography of Wyatt Earp.

and to Doc's taking the shotgun from Virgil Earp just prior to the street fight. Billy Claiborne's statement before the grand jury that Doc fired first is repeated. This is upheld in *Frontier Marshal*, although Earp stated emphatically that he shot first (after being fired upon, or simultaneously with, Billy Clanton.[33])

Frontier Marshal, Lake admitted, was more a compilation of what others told him, yoked with "invented dialog." Wyatt would tell him nothing directly. Microfilm copies of the notes bear this out. Unless it is known where the questions are attempting to lead, they can only be labeled as "ramblings." Although the book is touted as having come straight from Wyatt's mouth, it is anything but.

Lake also had problems with "what to do about" Wyatt's wife, Josephine Sarah Marcus. She had actually come to town as Johnny Behan's sweetheart, had been "no better than she should" with other men. This romantic shift to Wyatt had been a part of the entire conflict. The lady's character, which Lake decided to leave untarnished, has, in later years, become better known. Wyatt and Josephine's forty years together after Tombstone, however, speak for themselves.

Lake's *Wyatt Earp, Frontier Marshal*, published in October 1931, was what catapulted both the marshal and the author to fame. A three-part *Saturday Evening Post* series, shortly after Earp's death, dealt primarily with the Kansas years, but insured that the book itself was an immediate success. Wyatt did not live to see the book dedicated to his life. He died on January 13, 1929, in a rented Los Angeles cottage. While being proclaimed the most definitive work on Earp for nearly seventy years, *Wyatt Earp, Frontier Marshal* goes far to establish Doc Holliday's reputation as well. For sixty-six years it served as the primary literary odyssey on both Wyatt Earp and Doc Holliday, setting the bar for ensuing novelists. It resulted, on its own, in the screenplays for four films and a television series.[34] Although only the three brothers were shown on the original cover, Doc was added in later editions.

Interestingly, moving pictures became a minute reality the year Doc Holliday died. They were not, however, a public conveyance until 1893, when Thomas Alva Edison's "peep show" was unveiled at the Columbian Exposition in Chicago. Amazingly, all were westerns, most taken from William F. "Buffalo Bill" Cody's Wild West and Congress of Rough Riders show. They included Annie Oakley, the Ghost Dance, and Buffalo Bill firing a rifle. Edison mistakenly believed his entertainment would be a losing venture, appealing only to the masses, and failed to get the proper patents. It cost the business individuality and artistry, but soon fulfilled the worst fears of social workers as people flocked to the theaters.

A young entrepreneur, Edwin Stanton Porter, realized the potential and convinced Edison there was no sin in viewing *motion*. Stanton set about creating what would seem a news clip today. His first western, the two-minute *The Capture of the Biddle Brothers*, was released in 1902.[35] His prominence was established the following year with *The Great Train Robbery*, starring soon-to-be western star Gilbert M. "Broncho Billy" Anderson.[36] Porter went on to direct Edison's new studios in Manhattan and in the Bronx until 1906.

Porter's films also derived inspiration from what was happening in the "real" west: train robberies. Butch Cassidy and the Wild Bunch, the James Gang, and Kid Curry's failed attempt to rob the Denver and Rio Grande all created eastern headlines and captured film audiences. As early as 1910, however, "Bronco Billy" (Max Aranson) had realized that galloping horses and Indian attacks were vastly enhanced by outdoor filming, and that the West furnished the best scenery. Aranson's silent films were the first to deliberately depict a good man-bad man image. Bronco Billy filmed several westerners in the Denver area in 1907, and later in New Mexico and Wyoming. It was the fact that so many cowboys, and real Indians as well, settled in and around Niles, California, that determined Hollywood as the ultimate site of the film industry.

Thomas H. Ince left vaudeville that same year and was hired by one of the many independent studios making its fame through the use of "stars." The Hollywood Cowboy was born in 1911, brought to the screen by Ince. Ince, a giant in early silent film, began directing in 1911. He partnered with D.W. Griffith and Mack Sennett in Triangle Film Corporation and built Culver City Studios, which became the legendary MGM. Thus began the assembly-line system all studios would eventually adopt. When Biograph Studios refused to let Griffith make films longer than two reels, he resigned to go with one of the more modern-thinking film companies. Both these directors added some confusing western symbolism, such as the noble savage versus abused humanity, and "glorious" as opposed to barbaric military. Both played a vital role in the rise of film popularity. Griffith's 1915 epic *Birth of a Nation* is considered the beginning of American film as art.[37]

Ince directed the bulk of his early productions on the 20,000 acres of seacoast where he built a studio. It was abandoned in 1918 when Ince built the antebellum administration building in Culver City. The grandiose structure was later taken over by David O. Selznick, then by Desilu, and, more recently, by Grant Tinker/Gannett Productions, which failed in 1990.

Although Ince directed eighty films between 1911 and 1923, he was particularly known for his westerns. William S. Hart was his first star. Hart set the precedent of the strong, silent, somewhat rough-about-the-edges Western hero. Always true to a peculiar code of honor, the initial image of the cowboy had not been a positive one. Dime novels and magazines such as *The Police Gazette* usually portrayed him as a rowdy, unscrupulous drunk, prone to shoot up cattle towns.[38] Cody's Wild West Show, together with Owen Wister's novel *The Virginian* and western artists such as Frederic Remington and Charles Russell, changed this persona.[39]

Hart, a New Yorker by birth, had traveled west as a child, but returned to his native home and become an actor. An accomplished Shakespearean actor, he won acclaim for his role in the 1899 stage version of *Ben Hur*, but gave up theater to work for Thomas H. Ince.[40] His first western movie with Ince was declared "awful!"[41] However, although stoic and expressionless for the most part, his intense acting and production work is said to have projected the mythic West on the screen more authentically than anyone before. Hart became good friends with Wyatt Earp, who often visited his Horseshoe Ranch outside Newhall, California. According to

Ronald L. Davis' *John Ford, Hollywood's Old Master*, "Earp was concerned about the inaccuracies of his legend, and thought the best way to get them straight was on screen."[42] He is quoted as saying this in a letter to Hart in July 1923, and continued in this effort with various writers until his death.

When sound first came to movies in 1927, studios thought it would be unsuitable for Westerns. They felt "talkies" were inappropriate for cowboys. There was also the technical problem of filming galloping horses and rattling wagons with sound cameras. They were big, noisy, and had to be put into special boxes to prevent their noise from interfering with what was being picked up on the microphones. Further, whereas silent cameras had been easy to move, and what were called "tracking shots" could be made with the camera moving along with the action, this was no longer feasible with the bulky camera "boxes."

Raoul Walsh decided a sound western must be made, and when he saw a Fox Movietone newsreel that interviewed a longshoreman in motion, he brought his idea to Fox. The executive is said to have asked, "Are you drunk?"[43] Walsh insisted, however, asking for the Movietone wagon, which filmed the first western with sound, In Old Arizona.[44] The film won an Oscar for its star, Warner Baxter, and induced Paramount to cast Gary Cooper in *The Virginian*, solidifying a place for sound westerns forever.[45] *In Old Arizona* also won the Best Picture of the year, plus four other Academy Awards.

A Walsh movie was living adventure and usually began with an escape from something real or imagined. His movies were based on his Irish fantasies and, like him, his heroes and heroines had neither book learning nor ancestry. They had only themselves, youth, and bravado. Walsh directed over 120 films during his long career, many still familiar to late night viewers.

With their success, studio technicians devised an even more convenient method of filming outdoors, a revolutionary process called "Grandeur." This was a 70mm film with a picture twice the size of the normal 35mm, and in widescreen. The first bold venture utilizing this medium had Walsh again directing, and was called *The Big Trail*.[46] Although the film was something of a box office flop, it was John Wayne's first starring role, but that's another story.

Wyatt Earp's appearance in the 1923 *Wild Bill Hickok* is verified in an article by noted historian and western film authority Paul Andrew Hutton on blog.truewestmagazine.com.[47] Hutton cites three little-known sources that possibly identify Bert Lindley in the role. He goes on to state: "Thus, this must also be the first appearance of Doc Holliday in a film (although we don't know the actor)."

This studio photograph of *Wild Bill Hickok* (1923) includes Wild Bill, as portrayed by William S. Hart (tall man in light colored hat). The other characters and actors are unknown, although the film is said to have starred Ethel Grey Terry as Calamity Jane, Jack Gardner as Bat Masterson, and an uncredited Bert Lindley as Wyatt Earp. In a 2012 *True West* article, Paul A. Hutton mentioned that *Wild Bill Hickok* was likely Doc Holliday's first film appearance, but the actor remains unknown (courtesy Paul A. Hutton).

The gist of it is the growth of film popularity coincides with the evolution of the Great Depression. Americans had a desperate need to escape their daily lives and were eager to enter into the world of fantasy and imagination that Hollywood offered. The American dream had become a nightmare, and Hollywood offered an escape from despair.

THREE

The Great Depression

America in the 1930s was basically broke and unhappy. Gang rule and killing in many major cities contributed to the misery. Board and parlor games became popular. People gathered around the radio to hear their favorite baseball team win or lose. An era of complexity and contradiction, the Thirties began with the Depression and ended with the onset of a modern age. The mystery novel flowered. Riding high on the wave of entertainment, and soon to outstrip them all, was the motion picture.

America continued to rediscover Doc Holliday in the 1930s with William Riley Burnett's third novel *Saint Johnson*, which made it to Hollywood.[1] Burnett, primarily a gangster novelist, had screenwriting credits for *Little Caesar, Scarface, and High Sierra*.[2] In addition to his work with Hollywood's most prestigious directors, he worked with famous western actors John Wayne, Steve McQueen, and Clint Eastwood. His associates were horrified when he became fascinated with the Tombstone saga after reading Burns' account. He remained undaunted, and admitted that one of the characters in *Saint Johnson* is based on "Doc Holliday, gambler, gunfighter and wit."

Burnett's book alters names as well as location, with Doc appearing as "Brant White" and Wyatt Earp as "Wayt Johnson." *Saint Johnson* also places Doc and Earp, by intimation, together, and in gunfights in Dodge City, Kansas, and Trinidad, Colorado, prior to arrival in Arizona. This novel reiterates Doc's penchant for gambling and drinking, and exaggerates his killer instincts. Doc's use of the ever-popular shotgun as a weapon is magnified, and he is glorified for having been nicked by a bullet in the temple and shot through the body while engaged in law enforcement.

Burnett was the first writer to call attention to Holliday's expensive clothes and meticulous appearance. Doc also evidences a certain misguided sense of humor throughout *Saint Johnson*, and rides out of town alive.

This book offers everything for Depression-ridden America, torn by political and social complexity, but little in the way of romance. A first edition, in board covered cloth, sells for over $1200.

Tombstone Pistoleers, a novel published in 1936 by Graham Cassidy, links the Earps and Clantons, again under assumed names, with the rustling-robbery incidents and cowboy–Mexican conflicts along the border.[3] The Holliday character makes his immaculate broadcloth appearance as "Doc Benson." Known more for his clichés than wit in *Tombstone Pistoleers*, the character seems intended for conversation and intimidation rather than action. In a reference to the Bud Ryan cutting, he is revealed as having to "end a card game dispute with a Bowie knife." A love affair with "Arizona Kate" is eulogized, and Holliday's handiness with a derringer is questionably introduced. Cassidy's book makes several references to the gambler as an older man, possibly attributing to his continued depiction in film as such. Holliday is killed in a Skeleton Canyon shootout, attempting to save a friend.

Another effort at presenting the legend appears in the purely fictional *Boom Town*, published in 1938.[4] Big Nose Kate becomes "Big Mouth Moll." Doc is christened "Keith Bagby, a regular sawbones" and a Civil War veteran from South Carolina. This is not the only time such discrepancies in profession, age and background occur. Jack O'Connor, however, manages to keep some of the names straight. *Boom Town* gives details of the trouble between Doc and Ringo, but falls prey to an attempted assumption of what might have happened to Holliday had he lived. Obviously that is anybody's guess.

Two magazine articles and one newspaper write-up from the 1930s have also survived. The September 1933 *Oral Hygiene* shows a blonde Doc Holliday portrait to accompany "Celebrating a Holliday."[5] Dentist Frank A. Dunn attributes the story of several frontier incidents to Doc, the majority of which happened to other notorious characters. Incorrectly identifying Holliday's place of birth and education, a common mistake of the day, Dunn's article shows a vast reading background with little attention to detail. Holliday is identified as fast and fearless, a man who "seemed to court danger and death." That same month the *Dodge City Globe* resurrected Doc with "Dodge's First Dentist Was a Pistoleer."[6] It reads so closely to the *Oral Hygiene* piece as to smack of plagiarism.

Surprisingly, the first film based on Wyatt Earp's life was not based on Stuart Lake's more famous work, but rather on Burnett's hard-edged 1930 *Saint Johnson*. This 1932 Universal film, John Huston's first screenwriting attempt, contains much of the dark moodiness that prevailed in the 1930s and would haunt the Doc Holliday image for decades to come. It was directed by the prolific Edward L. Cahn. Although his work is uneven,

Cahn's visualization was people oriented and this, together with his use of frontal shots, is strongly indicative of more systematic principles, possibly resulting in his a B-Movie director. Perhaps his greatest claim to fame is the 1933 *Emergency Call*, one of the few American-made films in which one man makes an explicit declaration of love for another man.[7]

Huston's father, Walter, stars as the Wyatt Earp figure, Frame Johnson. Harry Carey, a seasoned actor who starred in numerous John Ford films, portrays the Holliday character, renamed Brandt White.[8] As in literature, Doc is cast as a man older than the Johnson (Earp) brothers. Additionally, although Carey was familiar with expected behavior of the western hero, he lacked a true insight into the Holliday character. *Law and Order* permanently attached Holliday to a shotgun, which he is usually brandishing, sleeps with, and asks to be buried with. Carey portrays Brandt White as a hard-drinking gambler from the onset. Repeal of Prohibition made liquor on the screen now acceptable.

Huston's script clarifies familial ties early on as Brandt and the three brothers (Walter Huston as Frame Johnson [Earp], Russell Hopton as Luther Johnson [Earp] and Raymond Hatton as "Deadwood" Johnson [Earp] appear seated around a campfire. After they sing (with amazing harmony) "My Pretty Quadroon," various bits of moralizing and memories from Dodge City are exchanged, which bring the audience up to date on where the current action is taking place.

A romantic element is introduced when Doc looks at his watch encasing the portrait of a thirties-type blonde beauty, inscribed "With love, Lotta." This alludes directly to the oft-repeated conjecture of his involvement with Lottie Deno, the infamous lady gambler and entertainer of Fort Griffin and points west.

Gambling enters the film early when Brandt suggests "one hand of Showdown" to determine their destination. When one brother draws the famous "Wild Bill" Hickok "Dead Man's Hand," the audience is led to expect dark days ahead. This is one glaring historical mistake in the screenwriting, for in a later scene it is suggested that Bill Hickok would like the job of marshal. Since the aces and eights death hand refers directly to the one Hickok was holding when gunned down in Deadwood, South Dakota, some four years before our boys ventured into South Arizona, the two lines are definitely out of sync.

Three "Clantons" make their appearance as the Northups. Ralph Ince plays Poe, Harry Woods is Walt, and Richard Alexander portrays Kurt. A thin Andy Devine does an amazing take on Johnny O'Rourke (Johnny Kinsman). An uncredited appearance is made by Walter Brennan, who would become almost a household name.

Law and Order (1932) Harry Carey (in top hat) is cast as Brandt White, the Doc figure, while the Johnson brothers are based on the Earps, here, from left to right: "Deadwood" (Raymond Hatton), Luther (Russell Hopton) and Frame Johnson (Walter Huston) (courtesy Paul A. Hutton).

Although the Doc character shows no sign of ill health in *Law and Order*, champions of his drinking habits are horrified at the small sips he takes of what is established as his favorite, "sangria." His meticulous dress and grooming is basic black complete with a silk top hat. There is no evidence of a classical education in his speech, or of musical ability. Efforts to convey the famous Holliday wit are perceived by modern-day viewers as more buffoonery than caustic.

The dangerous nature of the man is clearly in evidence, however, with such pronouncements as, "I'll take ya," "I'll murder you!" and, "The only way to clean up this town [is] lemme turn loose with my shotgun!" This is 1930s gangster language, which Burnett was accustomed to writing. Although Brandt White accepts a badge from the Wyatt figure, it is evident he has no intention of upholding the law. Threatening epithets more in sync with the late 1880s would have made the film more convincing.

As in many of Doc Holliday's first films, he is killed prior to the gunfight. However, in *Law and Order*, he is given a rather prolonged deathbed scene in which he bequeaths his money to pay a madam and a bar keep; his guns go to Frame; his ring, saddle and "fixings" go to the two other Johnson brothers. He also orders his boots removed, saying he promised his mother he would not die with them on. This line has been attributed also to Billy Clanton and various other western outlaws but was doubtless the farthest thing possible from the mind of 14-year-old John Holliday's dying mother. The action does, however, number Doc among the loyal and honest men.

Jon Tuska's comprehensive study *The Filming of the West* (1976) condemns *Law and Order* as "a concentrated glimpse of human brutality."[9] In a fairly recent interview with Harry Carey, Jr., himself a veteran of more films than one would dare to count, he pondered, "Why didn't Dad portray Doc the way he really was?"[10] The answer lies in the fact that nobody knew the answer then, nor is it known today.

Stuart Lake sold his story to Fox for $7,500. He gave half of it to Wyatt Earp's widow, who had hated Burnett's version. The studio planned a more biographic production to be entitled *Wyatt Earp, Frontier Marshal*, but was stymied by Josephine (Sadie) Earp's strident defense of her husband's reputation (or was it her own?). It was ultimately released as part of a George O'Brien series of budget westerns; the title of the first film allegedly based on Lake's book was *Frontier Marshal*.[11]

O'Brien had started his career as a stuntman. He and his horse Mike were a steady Top Ten box-office attraction during the Thirties. This second effort at portraying the boys in Tombstone was directed by Lewis Seiler.

Frontier Marshal stars O'Brien as Michael Wyatt, who rides into a lawless frontier town and butts heads immediately with the crooked town boss "Doc" Warren (Alan Edwards). Mounting tension leads to the inevitable showdown, in the local saloon rather than the corral. A dance hall girl takes a fatal bullet intended for the hero. Although it was the first of several "official" versions of Lake's book, any resemblance to the real people is purely coincidental, and true history suffers intolerably. Russell Simpson, a staple in many B movies, appears again in a Tombstone telling, this time as the editor. Ward Bond makes his film debut in a minor role; this was his first of three Tombstone stories. Irene Bentley and Ruthie Gillette play the two women in conflict, with no further relationships identifiable.

In Charles Vidor's *The Arizonian* (1935), there is a dramatic personality change for Doc.[12] The script was by Dudley Nichols, winner of an Academy Award that year for John Ford's *The Informer*, Nichols later wrote the screenplay for *Stagecoach*.[13] The character portrayed by Preston Foster and christened "Tex Randolph" is the first and only suave, debonair gambler Doc. Drinking, flirting, and briefly dancing converts a morose Doc to one of near-caballero status. The demeanor is of a different tone but most of the underlying stigma remains.

The Arizonian places blame directly on Tex Randolph for the "Yellow" (Benson) stage robbery. Although an unresolved issue that some recorders tend to artfully skirt, it has caused much controversy for Holliday researchers to date. Wyatt wrote Burns in 1927, "Doc never did such a thing as rob stages in his life." It still leaves doubt in the mind of most readers as it might be said Earp "doth protest too much." Doc commented that if he had been involved, he would have shot one of the lead horses and been successful in the attempt. This smacks of the truth, as our gambling dentist was not one to mince words, or to fail at much of anything involving cash.

Seemingly unknown to each other at this film's onset, Randolph and Clay Tallant, the Wyatt Earp figure played by Richard Dix (yes, again), are initially at odds when crooked Sheriff Jake Mannen (that's John Behan, in case you don't recognize him), played by Louis Calhern, hires Tex to kill the newly appointed marshal. Following a confrontation involving much dashing of wine into faces of innocent bystanders, Randolph tells his employer that he has "called Tallant the wrong color, it's not yellow, but white." Shortly thereafter, the new friends save each other's lives in a barroom showdown with a gang of cowboys. This, of course, comes from the Dodge City recounting of similar ilk.

Doc wears the storied ivory-handled revolvers. It is gratifying to note that Doc shows no inclination whatsoever toward a shotgun. A delight to fans, his sarcastic wit makes its early appearance; after which it disappears from film for some sixty years. Although the judge (Edward Van Sloan) condemns Tex for "having killed three men in this county," Foster plays a lighter, less deadly Doc Holliday, and his dress code is certainly a cut above most of the cast. Also, as in the two earlier film appearances, Doc shows absolutely no evidence of having tuberculosis. This could have been a concession to the all-too-awful truth of '30s audiences. He is undeniably a stagecoach robber, albeit a jovial one, laughing fit to kill. He makes his play only seconds after the Earp character has chased off his cronies. Still indicating not a single cough in all that dust, Tex Randolph is just entirely too robust to be a lunger. He does his fair share of heavy drinking. His dying words to Wyatt are, "Did we get 'em?"

There is no love interest for the Holliday character in *The Arizonian*; he shows an actual reticence to associate with the ladies. Interestingly, this is the only Earp-based film prior to 1993's *Tombstone* to even hint at rivalry over a girl.¹⁴ Kitty Rivers is played by Margot Grahame, and portrayed as one of the factors in the Tallent-Mannen (Earp-Behan) conflict. As prostitution would have been distasteful to 1930s audiences, this love interest is labeled "an actress," which, in fact, Josephine Sarah Marcus was.

Only one Tallant-Earp brother appears, Orin, played by James Bush, with several of the cast recognizable from other Tombstone films: Francis Ford, Hank Bell, D'Arcy Corrigan, Art Mix, and Russ Powell. Willie Best and well-known Etta McDaniel, sister of Academy Award–winning Hattie McDaniel of *Gone with the Wind*, also appear in *The Arizonian*. The movie is lost among many low-budget westerns of the day. But Foster's Doc Holliday is refreshing in its charm and good humor. The film was remade by RKO in 1939, but with decided less attention to casting.

Two film productions in 1937 played off the Wyatt Earp theme but managed intolerable versions of what may have been intended as Doc Holliday figures.

Law for Tombstone was a Buck Jones production, co-directed by Jones

The Arizonian (1935) Preston Foster played Tex Randolph, the first representation of a handsome and witty "Doc," embraced here by Richard Dix as Clay Tallant, a.k.a. Wyatt Earp (courtesy Paul A. Hutton).

and W.B. Eason.[15] Mostly forgotten today, Buck Jones was a star in good standing during the '20s and '30s. Raised in Montana, he learned his roping and riding skills honestly, honing them during a stint with the U.S. Cavalry. He brought them up to show standards with Miller Brothers 101 Ranch Wild West Show, and later with Ringling Brothers Circus. Much of his fame stemmed from the fact that he performed all his own stunts astride his famous horse Silver. He remained a B-western star until his untimely death in the 1942 Cocoanut Grove nightclub fire in Boston, where he was guest of honor.

Law for Tombstone starred Jones as the Earp figure, Alamo Bowie, and Harvey Clark as Doc Holliday. Unfortunately, nowhere in the film is he addressed as anything other than "Doc" and he is dirty, overweight, obviously drunk, and decidedly disreputable. Again an older man, Clark is eventually identified as one of the "good guys," but only after secret messages pass between the hero and him, enlightening the viewer of the drunkenness as a disguise. Would the real Doc have been amused at portraying a "make-believe" alcoholic? A minor character at best, Doc's credibility is certainly questioned when he fires wildly at several of the miscreants, and is asked by Alamo if he can "handle" one man. He's a dubious drunk who never gambles, can't shoot, has no female interest, is on the back side of fifty, and looks like a bum; the only resemblance to the Doc Holliday we revere, in *Law for Tombstone*, is his loyalty.

This movie in reality is a Texas Ranger tale, raising the question of what they were doing in Tombstone, Arizona. The story involves a frequent stage robber (nobody ever forgets the Benson Stage) called "Twin Gun Jack." It falls one song short of being a singing cowboy saga but is, however, the first film appearance of a Nellie Cashman, the "angel of Tombstone." Frances Guihan, the screenwriter, also knew enough history to include a Clanton for the first time in film with Alexander Cross' "Bull" as dastardly a villain as ever crossed a B-movie screen. He is shy his infamous father or any brothers, but it is commented, "Everybody is afraid to cross him." There is no gunfight per se in this film.

Music, of course, had been unavailable for silent westerns, other than the local theater's piano, organ, or phonograph. Music soon made its way to horse opera.[16] The soundtrack for 1932's *Law and Order* is upped a notch by campfire singing, common with many B westerns of the era. *The Arizonan* goes a good bit further with a solo by "Miz Kitty" and the mournful lament of "Roll Along Covered Wagon, Roll Along" by a black seamstress. "Departure" music had additionally become somewhat of a mainstay for several decades of O.K. Corral stories, with more of vaudeville, traveling theater groups, and saloon girls adding rhythm to the storyline.

Let us count ourselves fortunate that, unlike the saga of Billy the Kid, made into a ballet by Aaron Copland in the '30s, and the Alamo stage production recognized by that historic foundation, the Tombstone story had not yet been endowed with musical qualities.

The second awakening of how film was affecting, and affected by, public opinion dawned on Hollywood in the late 1930s. Despite social realism portrayed in crime and war movies, a condition now in full swing on the continent, the western continued in much the same vein as before. Although the popular medium of noise, any kind, was certainly an increasing part of the horse opera, developing dialogue had little impact. Hoofbeats, gunshots, and mooing constituted the bulk of the sound track.

Late in the 1930s, directors began a search for heroes somewhere between the dark portrayals of earlier westerns and the now popular singing cowboys. MGM was the first to find a replacement for stalwarts Bill Hart and Tom Mix, an all–American football star, Johnny Mack Brown.

Never the success John Wayne would become after John Ford's 1939 *Stagecoach*, Brown would become standard fare for generations of B-westerns and hero of the Saturday matinee crowd. His films, together with those of Hopalong Cassidy, Gene Autry, Roy Rogers, and other B-heroes, emphasized the value of cooperation. This accent on teamwork would have a strong impact on what America needed to call on at the beginning of World War II. It was also the reason for the B-western's failure at the end of the war, when the demand for national cooperation was no longer required.

Johnny Mack Brown's serial *Wild West Days* did not overlook the Tombstone crowd.[17] It was advertised as "thirteen roaring chapters of pioneer days," with opening credits declaring that the film series was based on W.R. Burnett's *Saint Johnson*. Any similarity is difficult to discover. The majority of episodes joined the popular trend of referring to "Injuns" who "sometimes howl like coyotes," and contained numerous other remarks now considered politically incorrect. As was also the case in many budget and singing cowboy films, there's only one woman, Lucy Munro (Lynn Gilbert), sister of the victimized rancher. Lucy is no softy, however, handy with a rifle and ready to ride with the boys whenever duty demands. This serial's one claim to originality is the discovery of platinum, rather than the usual gold mine.

In Early Arizona (1938) cannot officially be identified as a Tombstone film.[18] Screenwriter Nate Gatzert joined with director Joseph Levering and producer Larry Darmour in Bill (not yet "Wild" Bill) Elliott's first effort for Columbia Pictures. Although clearly based on the life of Wyatt Earp, the film did a careful two-step around the copyright then being held by 20th Century–Fox, with only the town of Tombstone as public domain lending itself to some understanding of the film. Whether Earp's name simply carried little significance, or due to Josephine Marcus Earp's continued determined efforts to protect his image, Wyatt again appeared under a pseudonym in this production.

Opening frames of *In Early Arizona* proclaim the film is "based on historical fact," admitting to fictional names, but specifically mentioning Wyatt Earp, Bat Masterson, Doc Holliday, Wild Bill Hickok, the Clantons, McLaurys, Johnny Ringo, and Curly Bill. ("So there!" Ms. Earp and Fox Studios!) Reference is made to the "ever increasing" control of federal government as the "only way to law and order." The old Union song "Rally 'Round the Flag" ups the beat about midway of the film and a dance hall girl's rendition of "My Darling Clementine" reminds the Tombstone researcher of better days to come.

That such blatant bureaucracy should be in westerns is not shocking for the late '30s. America had gotten over the Depression, the economy was good, and Roosevelt's fireside chats comforted all, while the golden age of radio and good mystery writers added to Americans' entertainment. It would not be the last time U.S. citizens were duped by our cherished media.

A character called "Doc" (Lester Dorr) by the hero and greeted like an old friend, is easily recognized despite wearing a silk top hat. Fairly young, thin, and well-dressed, this figure exhibits little personality and none of Doc's characteristic deadliness. Kate is called Lil (not in the credits) and their being "on yelling terms" is reflective of their turbulent relationship. Reference is made to friendships in Dodge, the character has a sharp wit, and he spends a good deal of time gambling and drinking. His loyalty to the Earp figure is not overlooked as he is shot dead rushing out the saloon door to help his friend.

The Earp character appears in *In Early Arizona* as Whit Gordon, who rides into Tombstone to keep the peace and becomes a target for every fast gun in the territory. Harry Woods gets a shot at portraying "Bull" (Clanton) while Jack Ingram appears as the marshal. Slim Whitaker plays the sheriff.

George O'Brien's *The Marshal of Mesa City* the following year offers so little in the way of innovation it would be difficult to find an original thought. Despite being touted as "sudden death in his barking guns bringing excitement every minute," it does little other than play its role in strengthening the theme of loyalty as a primary part of Doc Holliday's character.[19] It was intended as RKO's remake of *The Arizonian*, and directed by David Howard. Leon Ames is featured as the slick Sheriff Judd Cronan, running the town until the arrival of O'Brien's Cliff Mason, the

Earp character. Cronan's lawlessness and unwanted attentions to the local schoolmarm, Virginia King (Virginia Vale), are thwarted by Mason, who sends for backup in the form of Duke Allison, the Holliday character. Again young, almost a teenager, slim, dressed in black, and with the inevitable ivory-handled revolvers (a figment of someone's imagination, as has been explained), Duke, played by Henry Brandon, does a Holliday-worthy amount of drinking. Despite being made deputy marshal, he is identified as a notorious murderer. Several scenes show him at the bar but neither he nor anyone else summons a single cough, even during a severe fire. As with the Foster depiction, this Doc Holliday is ill at ease with women and holds them at a safe distance during the dance. In the 1930s, only the hero got the girl.

When the fog and smoke of the gunfight (which one critic declares "an inspired scene") clears, Doc dispatches the last bad guy standing while asking with his dying breath, "Did we get 'em?" (Is that an echo?)

Harry Cording, Joe McGuinn and Frank Ellis represent the three other henchmen (possibly Clantons) with Lloyd Ingraham cast as Mayor Sam Bentley. The supporting female role went to Mary Gordon, as Mrs. Dudley.

Nineteen thirty-nine is viewed by many movie buffs as the greatest year in film history, premiering *Gone with the Wind*, *The Wizard of Oz*, *Stagecoach*, *Wuthering Heights*, and *Gunga Din*, among many other notables.[20] Not among the Top Ten was Allan Dwan's *Frontier Marshal*, his first sound western, in which both Wyatt Earp and Doc Holliday finally appear under their own names.[21] They had been heavily fictionalized in *The Arizonian*, although the portrayals were relatively on-target. Dwan, who came to Hollywood in 1911, is still remembered as a screenwriter, producer, and director. A true innovator, Dwan filmed a few western series, but was most famous for his Mary Pickford, Douglas Fairbanks, and Shirley Temple movies. One of his best-remembered films, *Sands of Iwo Jima*, is still often seen on television.[22]

Frontier Marshal is the second of three films based on Stuart Lake's book. Its greatest attraction was Randolph Scott using Wyatt Earp's own name, although still flying in the face of Josephine Marcus Earp's violent objections. Twentieth Century–Fox produced this 71-minute black and white film.

Despite opening frames indicating the film is based on Lake's story, screenwriter Sam Hellman consistently misspells Doc's surname as Halliday. Cesar Romero, who at the time (and for the same studio) was playing the Cisco Kid, makes a surprisingly good Doc. While incredibly unbelievable, he is certainly threatening. Once again young and well-dressed, he continues to be a doctor, not a dentist. Depicted as from Illinois he loses any chance at a Southern accent.

No audience could miss the silence that follows Doc's first entrance into the film, at about eight minutes. The whispered words, "That's Doc Halliday," casts its immediate pall, and are followed by those spoken aside to Earp, "Coldest killer in these parts; always looking for trouble." The lawman makes his own judgments, however, and stops a double-dealing gambler who pulls leather on Doc when he, at last, goes into a coughing spasm. It is amazing, after having been totally ignored since 1932, that Doc's poor health is almost overplayed in this film. Scott is an excellent solid and stoic Wyatt Earp.

Doc's present-day adherents will be appalled at his drinking milk in Dwan's rendition, worse than the sangria of Harry Carey's very first recognized Doc in film. However, the unquestionable friendship is sealed when Doc shows Earp his hardware — originally a Buntline special: "Had the barrel cut down about two inches and the trigger smoothed." Notably, neither of the guns is ivory or pearl-handled.

Conversational love is again only evidenced between Doc and his female counterparts, two in this venture. The Kate figure, played by Binnie Barnes, is a typical saloon girl who considers herself Doc's property. Sparks fly when Sarah Allen, played by Nancy Kelly, a former nurse-fiancée of the doctor, arrives. Doc's penchant for evil is clear in his statement of, "I'm a killer, what of it? Life is nothing." His milk-drinking days end the day Sarah arrives (that is what a good woman will do for you). He does manage, however, to temporarily desert his binge to help Earp rescue Eddie Foy (played by Foy's son) from a rival of the Bella Union saloon. Curly Bill Brocious, played by Joe Sawyer, had kidnapped Foy. Doc returns directly to the bottle, stares moodily into the mirror and coldly states, "I don't like you," firing the only shot discharged by the deadly dentist in the film. If the director is suggesting seven years' bad luck, Doc did not have that many left after Tombstone.

Ward Bond makes his second Tombstone appearance in the role of the town marshal with Harry Hayden as Mayor John Henderson and Dell Henderson as Dave Hall. "Ben Custer," played by John Carradine, always a dandy villain, leads the oft-mentioned stage robbery in Dwan's *Frontier Marshal*, assisted by a very dark Curly Bill. Wyatt and Doc, who is shot, foil the attempt. Despite his injury, Doc manages to bring the horses to a halt. He is nursed by the ever-faithful Sarah, who proves she is no softie by physically throwing Kate out of the room. He somehow revives long enough to perform miraculous arterial surgery on Pablo, a wounded boy (Ventura Yberra). He is completely thwarted from attending the O.K. Corral confrontation when a bunch of bad guys hurrahing the town gun him down. The last we see of Doc is both women mooning over his prostrate body on the barroom floor. Dressed in black with a string tie, Doc carries few surprises in dress, and speaks with neither wit nor deadliness. *Frontier Marshal* presents the closest to a reformed Doc we may ever see. There is no vendetta ride, and a final frame shows Boot Hill with a tombstone inscribed "John Halliday, 1848–1880." Yes, even the dates are wrong.[23]

Cesar Romero as a deadly Doc in **Frontier Marshal** (1939), the first film to use Doc's and the Earps' real names (courtesy Paul A. Hutton).

The question remaining for 1930s film viewers is whether the inebriated doctor in John Ford's Oscar-winning *Stagecoach* was intended to be a Holliday character. It is often conjectured but remains a controversy. Jeff Morey, Holliday film expert, believes a better argument could be made that Hatfield, the gambler, was inspired by Doc, an opinion supported by other writers. The film was remade several times with the answer never clearly defined. The 1939 *Stagecoach* doctor (played by Thomas Mitchell) is neither Southern, sexy, nor stealthy. With no hint of gambling, only his title and affinity for liquor give some hint of any intended identity. John Ford aficionados believe he had no thought of Doc Holliday. The 1966 and 1986 remakes will be discussed later.

FOUR

The War Years

The 1930s ended on a sad note for Doc Holliday, although not for the United States. The early '40s foretold good things, although the American public would not know for nearly another two years the tragedy that decade would bring. Despite Hitler's activities in Europe, Hollywood continued to turn out top movies while the Third Reich invaded Scandinavia and France, and through the Battle of Britain and the bombing of London. *The Grapes of Wrath* earned Henry Fonda acclaim, as Charlie Chaplin ridiculed Hitler in *The Great Dictator*, and Disney hit his stride with *Fantasia*.[1] The United States was in denial and calmly read Hemingway's story of the Spanish Civil War *For Whom the Bell Tolls* while listening to Woody Guthrie, Charlie Parker and Dizzy Gillespie.[2] Nor did it miss a beat when the Luftwaffe extended the Blitzkrieg north into Scotland, the homeland of so many Americans.

Perhaps one of the more interesting, although questionably informative, documents concerning John H. Holliday during this time was a letter written on March 18, 1940. Originating at the Pioneer Home in Prescott, Arizona, its author was none other than "Kate Elder Cummings" (aka Big Nose Kate).[3] It was written to her niece, Lillian Lane Raffert. Kate was 89 at the time and died two years later. She always showed a remarkable memory for detail, despite her dates being a few years off. It is suggested she be given due consideration.

Based on subsequent findings, her telling is strongly in line with most of the facts as we know them. She begins the relationship between Doc and Wyatt in 1875, making no mention of their having been together in St. Louis. She places herself and Doc in Arizona in the fall of 1881, insisting throughout that they were married. Wyatt says it was the spring of 1880 and does not mention Kate. As he fails to mention the arrival of his brothers' women, the fact they simply were not important is obvious. It is also noteworthy that 1880 is when Wyatt, Jim and Virgil arrived in Tombstone from Prescott. It has been established that both Morgan and Doc arrived later. Kate claims Doc slept in the morning of October 26, 1881, perhaps accounting for his appearance in his underwear (*Tombstone*, 1993), horrifying some Holliday fans.[4]

According to Kate, Doc "got a man with every shot he fired." Does this mean he killed Billy Clanton and both McLaurys? She also states, "[S]omething was wrong with [Doc's] rifle." No other reports mention a rifle in connection with Holliday or the street fight (except the one Tom McLaury tried to reach). The same paragraph alleges, "Virgil and Morgan Earp were killed," but ends with, "Virge and Morgan [did] get well." Of course, both were wounded in the gunfight, and both recovered. It would be two months, three days after Christmas, that Virgil was crippled by a shotgun blast, and five months before Morgan was fatally shot in the back as he played pool.

Two novels with a Tombstone theme appeared during the war years but dealt only marginally with the crowd we are accustomed to encountering. *The Blue-Eyed Kid* (1944) is fictional, but contains a more fairly accurate history of Tombstone and its major players than many so-called biographies.[5] The author makes that fatal mistake of so many, however, declaring Doc "wore" a sawed-off shotgun.

The postwar *Guns of Happy Valley* (1947) mentions Doc Holliday twice, with a surprisingly unique, but probably accurate, description: "A walking skeleton whose guns were second only to Earp's in speed.[6] Once he'd been a dentist: now he drilled with smoking lead."

Universal took another shot at *Saint Johnson* in a screenplay by Sherman Lowe and Victor McLeod, again titled *Law and Order*, with the subtitle of *Man from Cheyenne*.[7] Johnny Mack Brown is cast in the easily recognized Wyatt role of Bill Ralston. Fuzzy Knight is cast as "Deadwood" (echo from the first *Law and Order*) and one of the brothers. James Craig plays a fine-cut Doc ("Brandt White," another return to the 1932 version). As in other films, his death is the catalyst for the gunfight. The Kurt Daggett (Ethan Laidlaw as Ike Clanton) gang attack Ralston and Deadwood's stage. Brothers, Poe (Harry Cording) and Walt (Ted Adams) join in. They are angry with a third party on the stage, the gambler figure. The incident puts a quick end to Ralston's ("the man from Cheyenne") plan to settle down in Ryolite. The Wyatt figure, as always, despite being urged by Judge Williams (William Worthington), refuses a badge. When local rancher Cal Dixon (Harry Humphrey) is gunned down, leaving his two children to fend for themselves, Bill has no choice. James Dodd and Nell O'Day play the two youngsters, Jimmy and Sally. The kids are about the only departure from the usual telling; there is no female lead. Earle Hodgins gets the role of Sheriff Fin Elder, with Robert Fiske as Ed Deal. George Plues plays the stage driver.

Just a year before the Detroit race riots, a screenplay "based on Walter Noble Burns' *Tombstone*" was filmed under a similar name. The 1942 79-minute black and white Paramount movie was billed as *Tombstone: The Town Too Tough to Die*.[8] Staying fairly close to the book in its general events and correct characters, using all the real names, it heavily distorts people and events. Kent Taylor portrays Doc (again Halliday). Richard Dix is given a second chance at the Earp character, this time with a wispy mustache. Some of the action takes place in a first-mentioned Galeyville, Arizona.

Doc is fairly young, but bears a darker persona than in his earlier appearances. Wyatt introduces him as "the greatest gunfighter and best Faro dealer this side of Texas." Wyatt never said Doc liked Faro, he indeed felt it foolish to "buck the tiger," and believed poker was a true gentleman's game. That did not mean his keen mind prevented his being an expert dealer when the occasion arose. When the issue of deputizing Holliday comes up, Earp laughingly comments, "Give you a badge and there'd be a gunfight every night."

Doc's health is not an issue, but is mentioned when he jokingly tells Wyatt, "The doctors tell me that fine Arizona air you get in pool halls and saloons might do me some good." Steady appearances at poker games leave no doubt he is a gambler and no smoke obscures the brief shoot-out where Virgil (Rex Bell) and Morgan (Harvey Stephens, uncredited) are wounded and three cowboys killed. Director William C. McGann and producer Harry Sherman do not fail to carry out Burns' indictment, and later-founded truth, that Doc carried a shotgun on that occasion and blasted one on the opposing side. For the first time in movies, Doc not only makes it to the gunfight, he survives unscathed. When Wyatt leaves for California, Doc is staying on in Tombstone declaring himself "better at producing aces than oranges."

For pure enjoyment, Edgar Buchanan's portrayal of Curly Bill gives the film an almost comical side. He apparently has a serious problem keeping his pants up. Victor Jory, always juicily evil, appears as Ike Clanton and deserts the street fight, as subsequent research would reveal true. He is joined by his brothers Phineas (played by Donald Curtis) with James Ferrara as Billy, both parts uncredited. The only love interest is between a boyish Johnny Ringo (Don Castle) and his girl from Kansas. The McLowerys [sic] are mentioned as being in Curly Bill's gang for the first time, casting Dick Curtis as Frank and Paul Sutton as Tom (both uncredited).[9] The film is somewhat lighthearted in theme, perhaps because of the war looming dark in the audience's mind. Indian Charley shows up (Charles Stevens) with Emmett Vogan as John Clum. Frances Gifford has the main female lead of Ruth Grant, with Queenie Fontaine as the "bad" girl, played by an uncredited Beryl Wallace.

Music, continuing primarily as background, consists of some singing and a vivacious rendition of the can-can. The Queen of the Barbary Coast (Queenie) later gives vent to "A Man Was the Cause of It All," throwing an aging fallen angel into a fit of weeping into her beer. The best musical rendition in *Town Too Tough to Die* is Queenie and a barbershop quartet harmonizing "I Will Take You Home, Kathleen." New freedom in women's wear permits all the girls' skirts to be shorter than in previous films.

Frank Gruber's story "Peace Marshal" was produced in 1943 by Harry Sherman as another Richard Dix strictly Wyatt Earp film entitled *The Kansan*.[10] Forrest Taylor plays a doctor, but no serious consideration has been given that he is our Holliday. This film received an Oscar nomination for its original score. As with many of the older films, *The Kansan* (known as *Wagon Wheels* in the UK) can be viewed on the Internet at www.Internet Active, a part of Wikipedia.[11]

Up to this point in westerns, certainly in the Tombstone sagas, there appears to have been an all-out obsession with stagecoaches, holdups, runaways, wrecks, and long chases. The plots begin to improve considerably by the mid-1940s and storyline replaces stagecoach. No telling of the Doc Holliday story will ever be complete, however, without some reference to his alleged involvement in the Benson Stage robbery and murders. This may be due to the fact the mystery has never been resolved. Research and discovery notwithstanding, you are permitted your own opinion in this matter.

The remainder of 1940s western literature and film continued to follow what Richard Aquila terms "pseudohistorical pageants" of American folklore.[12] Once focused on national progress or frontier heroes, directors soon grasped the attraction of more lawless and ruthless elements, and senseless violence became more popular during and after the war. With public and media opinion upholding authority figures, this myth found difficulty taking its place in the western until at least a decade later. It continued to confirm self-determination coupled with responsible freedom, but gradually began to recognize science and technology as problems to be confronted in man's relationship with nature. Still clinging to the ideals of Theodore Roosevelt, the American western maintained its effort to salvage individualism and, considering its sustained popularity, this ideal has succeeded admirably.

Howard Hughes' *The Outlaw* is a prime example of such individualism in film production.[13] As the first American film to defy the Production

Doc (Walter Huston) defends Billy the Kid (Jack Beutel) against Pat Garrett (Thomas Mitchell) in *The Outlaw* (1943), which is considered by some to be Howard Hughes first "adult" western (courtesy Paul A. Hutton).

Code of the Hays Office, which dictated what could and could not be shown on screen, the 116-minute film was first released in 1943. Banned, it was then re-released in 1946. It is strongly recommend you take your sense of humor along if you get a chance to view this oldie.

Possibly the most historically inaccurate variation of the legend ever on celluloid, it remains outstanding as one of the first "adult" westerns.

To this point, westerns had steered clear of any sexual scenarios, but Hughes blew this precedent wide open in his clearly Doc Holliday story with Walter Huston playing the lead. Other than using real names, any similarity to fact is purely coincidental. Character actor Ben Johnson made his debut in *The Outlaw*, in an uncredited role as a deputy. The tale wanders far afield, taking place in Lincoln County, New Mexico, which would be more than happy to claim the event had it been true. Doc's friends are Pat Garrett (played by Thomas Mitchell) and Billy the Kid (Jack Beutel in one of his few Hollywood performances). Not one other of the Tombstone crowd is mentioned and only one from the Lincoln County Wars: Emory Parnell is called "Dolan."

Hughes, evidently not a connoisseur of Holliday's more outstanding characteristics, offers him up dressed in baggy, checkered pants and black frock coat, but with an ornate concho hatband. Hughes' Doc is full of homespun quotes and philosophy. He displays a much keener interest in a roan pony, over which he and Billy constantly quibble, than any woman. He is restored to wearing the ever-popular pearl-handled revolvers. Doc is vilified for past crimes but ultimately glorified by goading Garrett into gunning him down.

Early in the movie, a backroom shooting interrupts Holliday and Billy's poker game. Doc intervenes with the Kid's arrest by Garrett, his flashing twin revolvers killing two deputies. Doc leaves town with the wounded Kid, arriving at a small rock hacienda where he delivers a lengthy medical diagnosis and treatment plan to the voluptuous Rio (Jane Russell, the reason for Hughes shooting the film). Rio is obviously Doc's girl. Following a parting kiss he sternly admonishes her to "do your best by that boy." She follows his instructions to the letter.

An interim scene shows Doc with a lathered-up roan, which of course he took from a wounded and defenseless Kid. Using a rifle with deadly precision, he kills two of the pursuing posse and doubles back to the hacienda. He and Billy engage in yet another controversy over girl versus pony, with Doc again choosing the horse. The pair head for Fort Sumner, but are halted midway due to lack of water, an outstandingly geographic fact. Garrett arrives on the scene and arrests them both but, miraculously, they again escape. When the two reunite, the inevitable argument continues, still over that darn pony, and Billy offers Rio in exchange for the horse. Doc's comment is, "Cattle don't graze after sheep." Nothing in *The Outlaw* is favorable to the feminist cause.

Doc shows great wisdom in Indian ways, erasing their tracks by trailing mesquite as the trio makes a run for Fort Sumner. Whoever taught Doc failed to mention the cloud of dust a blind man could follow, and one that Garrett and his posse do. The chase scene is accompanied by a rollicking musical rendition of "Bury Me Not on the Lone Prairie." Garrett gives Doc and the Kid their guns, demanding a solemn promise they are to be returned. "Yeah, bet me," is probably going through the mind of the entire audience. They take refuge in an abandoned cabin. The roan pony is once again up for grabs. In more of a "talk-out" than shoot-out, Doc nicks Billy's hand, then ears, in well-aimed shots. This may be another obvious play to the idea Doc preferred death before dishonor. The Kid refuses to throw down.

In an exaggerated emotional scene including numerous teary epithets by Garrett, Doc outdraws but deliberately lets his old friend kill him. He slumps to the floor, declaring he had always feared dying in bed. He is buried in a grave marked "Billy the Kid," possibly adhering to yet another myth: that Billy was not killed but lived to a happy old age in Texas (or Mexico, or California, or wherever).

Despite constant ownership changes, the roan pony appears as somewhat of a wonder horse and winds up turning in one of the better performances of the film.

Hughes produced the film, but it was directed by Howard Hawks, who had thirty straight award-winning films to his credit, several starring John Wayne. It was filmed in 1941, Russell's assets prevented it passing the censors, despite aircraft pioneer Hughes' brassier engineered for the occasion. It was the first sex western. Hughes ultimately released it without approval in 1943, making it a *cause celebré*. Despite its lack of depth and spelling, it was the beginning of the end for the outdated Hays Code. *The Outlaw* finally reached the American public in 1946, but was banned in many theaters. You may recognize Joe Sawyer and Ethan Laidlaw from prior Tombstone films.

The Outlaw can't be beat for a fun evening with a bag of popcorn and a good friend. But truer history, finer actors, and certainly greater directorship were soon to follow. Proving once again America's fickle public unpredictability, *The Outlaw* became one of the most popular westerns of the 1940s, grossing over three million.

It is fair to say that the world of entertainment was poised on the brink of a new world.

My Darling Clementine was John Ford's second film after his return from World War II.[14] Only his second sound western, the first being the award-winning *Stagecoach*, it was his third of four with Henry Fonda. Ford claimed to have heard the story "straight from Wyatt Earp" in the early 1920s, but was primarily intrigued with the idea of a climactic gunfight. If Ford really got any data from Earp, or had read Lake's book, on which the 20th Century–Fox film is said to be based, it is little evidenced in what has, nonetheless, become an O.K. Corral classic. Scriptwriter Winston Miller declared, "We made it up as we went along," and it is, indeed, the mythical power of *My Darling Clementine* that marks it as one of the best tellings of the Tombstone saga.[15] UCLA film archivists in 1994 discovered a note from Daryl F. Zanuck, demanding the movie be cut, seemingly wanting more music and less action. Ford's reply was to leave in most of the action and shoot the gunfight in dead silence. A brief documentary on the story is included in a recently released DVD. Many leading western historians consider *My Darling Clementine* the best classic rendition of the legend.

Following her victories in the Atlantic and Pacific, America had once more turned to its nostalgic past and that free-spirited man who answered to no one but himself. The death of Josephine Earp in 1944 paved the way for Ford's use of all the actual names with no legal problems. Also, when Ford filmed *My Darling Clementine* in 1946, women, who were the major filmgoers during the war, had proved they could be self-reliant and responsible, capable of running their own lives without the help of men. *Clementine* continued the western film rite of passage from budget (B) level entertainment into the heart and soul of American viewing for the next fifteen years.

Zanuck, swearing he wanted the third telling to be charmed, had promised Ford a good cast, and he delivered. Henry Fonda turned in an excellent portrayal of the fighting marshal, while Victor Mature got the back-up role of Doc Holliday. The swarthy and over-healthy Mature, however, proved too morose and belligerent to become popular. It might have been due to Ford's constant off-stage reference to him as "liver lips." It was, however, perhaps Mature's best performance of his career. Ward Bond and Tim Holt played Morgan and Virgil Earp. Many of these seasoned actors had, and would again, appear in the Tombstone odyssey.

Despite this distinctive casting advantage, and but for the arrival of the Earps with a cattle herd, the first ten or fifteen minutes of *My Darling Clementine* are reminiscent of *Law for Tombstone* and *Frontier Marshal*. The line "What kind of town is this?" reverberates through all three films and while never cleaving to just the facts, screenwriters Sam Engel and Winston Miller invent numerous additions and storylines. A major contribution of this picture is a more believable Doc Holliday character than seen previously.

"Doc Holliday owns the gambling," is conveyed to Marshal Earp. There is little question as to Holliday's clout when he arrives on the scene, obviously trail-weary and wearing a five-o'clock shadow. The Victor

Mature Holliday seems near lethargic in most of the film and the two men are neither friends nor acquaintances in Ford's version, with the concept of loyalty never fully developed. Doc's prior legendary stays in Deadwood and Denver are further established, but with no mention of Texas or Kansas. Identified as being a doctor from Boston, Holliday is decidedly educated and even has some Biblical background, asking Earp if he is "delivering us all from evil." A classical education is confirmed when he completes Hamlet's soliloquy for a drunken actor, Alan Mowbray's Granville Thorndyke. Doc's dress code varies throughout the film, but the viewer is so caught up in the simple but direct dialogue and Ford's almost ballet-type action that it seems to matter little. Doc engages in limited card-playing throughout *My Darling Clementine*, but definitely indulges in more than his share of spirits, shifting from champagne to whiskey as his troubles increase.

Unable to resist some reference to Doc and a stagecoach robbery, Ford places him as a shotgun rider on the "Tucson" Wells Fargo line carrying bullion. Several frames show Doc screaming and brutally whipping the horses to more and more speed. The viewer wonders if he is running to or away from something. Perhaps both.

Ford's Holliday has frequent violent coughing attacks and his tuberculosis is confirmed when the "good girl" from his past, Miss Clementine Carter, played by Cathy Downs, arrives. Chihuahua, the good/bad girl, with Linda Darnell in the role, is visible early on, singing, pouting, and leaving absolutely no doubt whatsoever that she is Doc's property. Holliday's mood swings from telling her to go away to ordering a bridal breakfast. Chihuahua's lying to Earp concerning an amulet removed from the body of an alleged young James Earp (John Garner) murdered early in the film, reflects on Kate's actual lying about Doc's involvement in the Benson stage robbery. Doc manages to sober up long enough to perform delicate but unsuccessful surgery when the saloon girl is shot by Billy Clanton. Doc's final words concerning the unquestionably unfaithful Chihuahua are, "She was a brave girl." We are not surprised at her death; bad girls always had to die in 1940s filmdom.

The showdown is much different under Ford's direction. Virgil is killed at the outlaw ranch when he pursues Billy, leaving Doc to face down the Clantons with Wyatt and Morgan. Old Man Clanton, in reality long dead by the time of the street fight, has survived eternally intact, portrayed by Walter Brennan. The others are John Ireland as Billy Clanton, Grant Withers as Ike, Fred Libby as Phin and never-heard-of-before-or-since Sam Clanton, played by Mickey Simpson. Brennan and his whip do more to denounce child abuse than had or would be seen in film until the reality

Victor Mature as Doc in *My Darling Clementine* (1946) (courtesy Paul A. Hutton).

era. Doc is not questioned when he involves himself with the fight preparations, taking a huge shotgun from the law office gun rack.

"The walk" is excellent filming, dead quiet but for the barking of a dog. Unable to resist some cloud upon the scene, the fight is begun in the haze raised by a racing stagecoach, leaving Doc dead before the dust settles. The fight is true to the degree that it is quick, with the remaining Earp brothers surviving. Doc has saved Wyatt's life, leaving a bloodstained handkerchief fluttering on the fence rail.

Although Ford declared *My Darling Clementine* to be exactly the way Wyatt Earp had told him when he was young, the crowd to whom we have grown accustomed is not present. There is no John Behan to compete with Wyatt for the hand of the fair maiden, in this version originally Doc's sweetheart. There is no Johnny Ringo, no Curly Bill Brocious, and no McLaury brothers. Neither does Ford hold with frivolity in hurrahing the town, theatrical performances, or permitting the Victor Mature Holliday one iota of wit. Accepted morals and political values of the day are clearly evident resulting in *My Darling Clementine* being almost a Bible story with Ford's declaration it did not end as it should have, nor as he wished.

To those who would grumble at the lack of historical accuracy, it should be remembered that both Ford and Zanuck were interested in entertainment, period. In both this and later films, directors tended to play off what knowledge they expected the audience to already have. No aim of enlightenment was in mind. Other credited actors are Roy Roberts, Jane Darwell, Grant Withers, J. Farrell McDonald, and by now well-known Russell Simpson. Ford's brother, Francis, is cast as "Dad, Old Soldier."

Cyril Mockridge does new and interesting things with the music for *Clementine*. He begins with a mournful version of the song; the old west theme is initially identified by credits cut into weathered barn wood signs. Chihuahua's first song about ten thousand straying cattle clearly defines Earp's anger, but the pace soon picks up with "Camptown Races" and a piano rendition of "Oh, Them Golden Slippers." Seemingly a favorite of the director, "Shall We Gather at the River" is heard in this as well as several other of his films. Ford does, however, utilize dead silence at exactly the right moments, and his dialogue is simple and straight to the point.

My Darling Clementine was the forerunner of 1950s westerns, but still held many of the older themes such as rocking chairs and porches. Whereas scenery had been merely a backdrop in earlier westerns, with Ford they became part and parcel of the story. A review of the film places much of its value on Fonda's performance, and although his talent cannot be discounted, it is to Ford's genius that Doc Holliday, the Tombstone saga, and the O.K. Corral owe much of their accelerated interest to the American public.[16]

Future writers and filmmakers would take full advantage of that curiosity.

FIVE

The Glory Days

Despite its start with three years of war in Korea, and ending with a rumble of the impending Civil Rights issues, the 1950s are irrefutably the best decade of the century insofar as westerns are concerned. The wonder years for many, they are still considered the Golden Age of Hollywood. Rock music disrupted the romantic lyrics of the 1940s, but crooners like Nat King Cole and Frank Sinatra were still popular. Leisure for the working class came into existence. Teen idols and television made the 1950s a time of individuality and happiness.

America felt good about her past and her future. With much of the remaining myth virtually untouched, Doc Holliday was no deviation. Except for exaggerated emphasis on the more unenviable aspects of his stereotype, Doc's reputation underwent little alteration until very near the end of the decade.

More than fifteen books, including notes or stories concerning Holliday, were joined by magazine articles in everything from western pulp fiction to dental journals and newspapers. In literature, popular historian John Myers Myers tackled the subject twice, first in his 1950 *Tombstone's Early Years: The Last Chance.*[1] Much of Myers' information is taken from *The Tombstone Epitaph*, a newspaper published during the Earp-Holliday era in southern Arizona. John Clum, friend, editor, and member of the Law and Order Party, edited it.[2] It was identified as a "popular history"; no evidence of footnotes prevents its falling into an academic category. Among several errors are that Wyatt wore a sheriff's badge. While he may have been a deputy sheriff briefly, rumors of his assuming Virgil's U.S. marshal badge after he left Tombstone are questionable. *The Tombstone Nugget*, spokesman for the cowboy faction and strongly Democratic in its politics, was blatantly anti–Earp in viewpoint.[3] *The Nugget* began publication in 1879 and only survived the *Epitaph* by five days. These newspapers reports, at exactly the beginning of the Tombstone saga, were sufficient unto the day in many cases. Both offer new insight into the words and deeds of Doc, although the majority is hearsay. Several of Doc's epithets have become common fare of his persona.

Tombstone's Early Years is primarily what it states and has more bad than good to say about John H. Holliday, despite proclaiming that his only virtue, aside from courage, was loyalty. Myers declares Doc totally indifferent to public opinion, making strong note of his success in the gambling profession. *Tombstone's Early Years* is quick to assert Doc's possible involvement in the killing of Bud Philpot during the Benson stage holdup and his confrontations with Ike Clanton over that same issue. Myers quotes a *Nugget* account that Holliday rented a horse for "seven or eight days," claiming he did not return until ten o'clock the night of the holdup. This is a greatly embellished version of Wyatt's story. Doc never denied his friendship with Bill Leonard, a strong factor with those who would implicate him. Myers takes care to admit that Doc was officially cleared of all charges involving him in the Benson holdup and murder but, like many others, once offering up the topic, never completely abandons it.

Finally, after thirty years of accounting, Myers is first to accurately describe the location and events of the gunfight, and correctly. He places Doc in his flanking position on Fremont. Myers writes of Doc's having Virgil's shotgun, but states later he "was not fond of the weapon." Considering Doc's attested weight at the time (between 120 and 130 pounds), weakened by tuberculosis, this should come as no surprise to any who maintains he used the weapon mercilessly on various killing sprees.

Myers further vilifies Doc in *Tombstone's Early Years* when he suggests a mouthy bystander be shot "just for luck." The author takes little notice of Doc's dress in his first look at the Tombstone crowd, but comments on the contrast between his blonde hair and the tawny hue of the Earps. Myers contends, "They were all tanned by the Arizona sun," leaving us to wonder if they had sunlamps in the Oriental. The writer lends Holliday a jocular note in mentioning his whistling on the walk (a quote from Wyatt) but also emphasizes his coolness under fire.

Myers' first book of the decade declares Doc a killer wanted for shootings in a variety of places. Doc's final words "This is funny" first appear in *Early Years* and have become a popular part of the Holliday legend. They are very possibly true. Myers' date of Holliday's death is not, however; he places it eight years later than it actually happened. He further falls prey to a myth of the time, that Lotta Crabtree and Jenny Lind sang at the Bird Cage Theater in Tombstone. When all is said and done, *Tombstone's Early Years* captures the boiling blood and hot lead that made the town a legend.

Several works appeared between Myers' two books, all dealing with Holliday, the Earps, and the Tombstone years. Tom J. Hopkins' 1951 *Trouble in Tombstone* maintains Doc's friendship with Wyatt but questions the honesty of them both.[4] Doc is termed a cold-blooded killer who had turned outlaw, killer, and gunman extraordinaire. This work is little known and rarely found today, although amazon.com occasionally has used paperbacks.

Prolific writer Clarence Budington Kelland also tried his luck with the boys in the 1952 *Tombstone*, published in mass-market paperback.[5] Author of the Mark Tidd and Scattergood Baines books, Kelland emphasizes Holliday as a Southern gentleman, astonishing the reader with his gallantry in saving various ladies from all sorts of impending tragedies. Kelland plays heavily on Doc's tubercular condition and loyalty to Wyatt, calling him Earp's "shadow." Although presenting a new viewpoint of Doc, Kelland's book offers a somewhat mixed account of the Tombstone events. It does not fail to include four Clantons who, with the Earps, are joined by an unknown woman and man to comprise the love ingredient for the Tombstone setting.

Will Henry, pseudonym of the late Henry Wilson Allen, who obviously knew the Tombstone story in fact, myth, and legend as it existed at the time, published *Who Rides with Wyatt* in 1954.[6] The back cover calls Tombstone "the Sodom of the Sagebrush" and attributes its taming to Earp. Although Doc does not arrive until mid-book, a great many of the characters and situations are highly colored by the writer's imagination. The story is easily recognizable, however, to anyone familiar with the tale. Award-winning Henry is the first to use the term "cowboys" as the anti-law faction, previous writers having resorted to "ranch hands," "rustlers," or simply, "the wild bunch."

W.R. Burnett, whose *Saint Johnson* had been made into three Tombstone movies, returned to the subject in *Bitter Ground* the same year.[7] A trip to Arizona in 1930, where he met living witnesses to the O.K. Corral incident, gave some of his writing a western bent. In *Bitter Ground* he again uses fictitious names, but the Doc character makes possibly both his and Burnett's opinion clear when he declares that law and order was "ruining" the west.

John Myers Myers touts his second effort at the theme, *Doc Holliday* (1955), as "not stock biographical fare," and goes on to prove it.[8] Myers continues to build on the gambling dentist's previous infamy in simply more imaginative ways. Basically, it is not much of a biography at all, as a good deal of the writer's story plays fast and loose with the facts. True, Myers wrote *Doc Holliday* before much had come to light on him, and he writes it well. The book is, however, more about the times, for which Myers had a great feel, rather than the man. Myers made excellent use of available primary sources in both Georgia and Arizona during the early 1950s. To this he added his expertise at myth and legend, which flutters throughout the work.

Myers argues that Doc came west merely to survive. Although this allegation appears in many accounts and opinions, the truth is that Holliday turned a one-year death sentence into fifteen years of fairly full living, hardly a lesson in defeat. During one fanciful moment of musing, Myers equates Doc with Abraham Lincoln, Robin Hood, and Billy the Kid. His comparison of the four figures argues they were all credited with both good and bad they never did. One must surely contemplate the same could be true for all actors on the stage of life, in or out of the U.S. West. *SAGA: True Adventures for Men* contained further "authentic" information from Myers.[9]

The latter half of the 1950s began, frighteningly, to point toward the increasing trauma that would become the 1960s. Primarily disruptive were the radical 1954 rulings regarding separate but equal education for all. Rock and roll reigned supreme in the world of popular music, Barbie and Ken were introduced to little girls, and Slip 'n Slide became backyard fun for everyone. Leakproof ballpoint pens and the first copy machine made their appearance early in the decade. The year 1955 brought the great medical discovery, Dr. Jonas Salk's polio vaccine. It was quickly overshadowed by Russia's Sputnik I and the resulting satellite race. All would soon to be lost among the sobering facts of increasing Cold War tensions. The world of music suffered the tragic loss of three celebrities, Buddy Holly, Ritchie Valens, and J.P. "The Big Bopper" Richardson in a plane crash. As the upbeat "Music! Music! Music!" of 1950 descended into "Mack the Knife" in 1959, America stood poised on the brink of an entirely different world.

Doc along the Texas Fort Trails, in a book by Carl Coke Rister, was received with enthusiasm in 1956.[10] Richard O'Connor's work *Bat Masterson*, (1957) had a great deal to say about Doc.[11] Holliday is termed "a suicide-bent renegade," and his relationship with Kate is given some notice. However, like most of his counterparts, O'Connor found little that was endearing about Doc Holliday. This mass production paperback sells today for upwards of $200.

A well-researched work is Pat Jahns' 1957 *The Frontier World of Doc Holliday*.[12] Jahns presents her research as history, and while it proves a chronically precise work of western non-fiction, too many later-discovered facts prevent its being a true biography today. The author's primary-sourced story does include quotes from newspapers of Holliday's time, but falls victim to conjecture. On occasion Jahns submits her characters to psychoanalysis, detracting further from its academic worth. While introducing too much personally, Jahns uses many of the same old songs, albeit with a few new verses. One new theme in this work is the purported love affair with a Georgia cousin, a story that family descendants adamantly deny but which has stuck like glue.

Jahns is the first writer to include Warren Earp as one of the "vendetta" riders. She also includes Sherman McMasters [sic], Turkey Creek Jack Johnson, and Texas Jack Vermillion. Research in the late 1990s and early twenty-first century would clear up much of this dilemma. Although an excellent history of the nineteenth-century frontier, Jahns' book deals more with Holliday's world than the man himself, yet remains a cut above many of the attempts to that time.

Douglas Martin, in 1958, edited the first ten years' records of the *Tombstone Epitaph* in a fairly accurate account of the story.[13] To the author's credit, he uses data from the rival newspaper, *The Nugget*, as well. *Tombstone Epitaph* is basically another story of "how Topsy grew." It presents elaborate accounts of sporting parlors and saloons, as well as mentioning some of the concerts and social events taking place. Although not filled with extraordinary writing, Martin's book vividly portrays the life and times that were the silver boomtown. He includes an eyewitness account of the street fight reporting, "Doc Holliday was as calm as though at target practice and fired rapidly." Martin also reported Holliday was hit in the left hip, but kept on firing. This later proved to be a near miss, the shot hitting his scabbard and resulting in a few days' limp. California historian Jeff Morey would draw a crystal clear picture of what happened that day in a 2001 article.[14]

In the *Epitaph* records, Cochise County Sheriff John Behan allegedly talks about a nickel-plated pistol, but repeatedly denies knowing to whom it belonged, saying he "thought" it was Doc Holliday. This account led to many nickel-plated revolvers in subsequent films. Morey's article answers that question with clarity as well.

That same year saw a similar telling in Leslie Scott's *Tombstone Showdown*.[15] Although advertised as a history of Tombstone, some have called it "the tale of the recklessly brave, amazingly cultured man who drew a gun as other men."[16] Mixed in with the usual crowd, and stating John Ringo was the only man Wyatt Earp feared, Scott describes Doc Holliday as "gaunt and consumptive," with the added notation he was "a born killer."

Oakley Hall's *Warlock*, published in 1958, is a parody of the Tombstone legend, and completely rewrites the traditional story.[17] The book was a finalist for the Pulitzer Prize while the film emerged as something of a libretto for the opera based on Wallace Stegner's *Angle of Repose*.[18] Stegner's story is that of a highly dysfunctional family and centers around a disabled young man trying to survive in a less than normal world. It appeared at the height of the McCarthy era; it is difficult to form an opinion of Hall's work as it opens as comic, although raw. The viewpoint is utterly devastating, with the film presentation belonging more in the genre of '60s debunking. It is inevitable, however, that the reader becomes entrapped in what evolves into the first modernistic telling of the Tombstone legend. Neither the Wyatt or Doc characters are presented as heroes, an interesting new take. It just misses converting into an American Camelot of clearly defined heroes and villains. *Warlock* additionally deals with every possible faction in town at the time—miners and politicians, both corrupt and honest, complete with gunfighters both good and bad. All are forced to face the ultimate factor of law and order. The novel received tremendous reviews, comparing the author with Henry James and Mark Twain, and the book with Walter Van Tilburg Clark's *The Ox-Bow Incident*.[19]

Warlock clearly portrays the Holliday character, Tom Morgan, as evil and self-centered. Both he and the Earp figure are shown as warped personalities with a hinted homosexual relationship. The basis for character analysis lies primarily in the conversations Doc has with himself. His declaration that money is his second priority, and friendship with Wyatt primary, is refuted by his actions. Before the book's end, everyone seems to hate Doc, labeling him "a son of a bitching gambling man." He is blamed for the death of competing henchmen, his own piano player, the man on the stagecoach, and "at least one or two innocent bystanders." As the story culminates, Doc appears to sink deeper into self-pity, despite Kate's scathing accusation that Doc killed himself for Wyatt Earp. The book was scripted and filmed the following year with similar implications regarding the dark side of Doc Holliday.

The Gunfighters (1959) boasted both paintings and text by Lea F. McCarty.[20] Doc Holliday appears in this rendering between Wyatt and Clay Allison, and is said to be "a chronic killer." McCarty attempts to prove this by citing five shooting deaths in Texas and one knifing, adding three murders in Denver and Wyoming. He adds two dead by Doc's guns in Dodge and three more in Santa Fe, although crediting him with only the one in Tombstone. Other errors leave the reader with an impression that the writer of *The Gunfighters* did not do his research. The worst fallacy from this writer is that the Earp brothers, including Wyatt, in the statement, "did not like him." The foreword by A.M. King, "Once Wyatt Earp's Deputy;" makes the rather startling statement, "About ninety-five percent of all the gunslingers were blue-eyed." He blames the rise of gunfighters in general on the Civil War, Negro police, and railroad towns. King labels the gun and scabbard "the waistband of death," and says that any boy would rather hear of the deeds of Wild Bill Hickok than read all the books ever written on George Washington or Abraham Lincoln. The history in McCarty's book is far off the mark, but his paintings of outlaws and lawmen are quite good.

The Glenwood Springs Historical Society contains two 1950s newspaper articles on Doc, one in Denver's *The Rocky Mountain News* and another in *The Dallas News*.[21] The first, dated July 26, 1953, reads "'Doc' Holliday Gained Fame with His 'Fast Draw.'" He is credited with killing 23 men and quotes the *Denver Republican* article published shortly after Doc's death, admitting he was "perhaps ... not after all such a bad man." It goes on to relate how Holliday "and his crowd killed 13 cowboys." The Dallas article mentions that few in the city knew of Doc's history. It repeats the usual errors concerning his education and the killing of the Negroes in Georgia, and continues with a few of the facts, albeit in the wrong sequence. One statement would have made both men cringe: that he and Bat Masterson were "friends." "One Dallas Dentist Rightly Forgotten" had little good to say about Doc, calling him a "cold-blooded killer" in the first sentence.[22] It is incorrect in stating Holliday's name was never in the Dallas city directory and goes downhill from there. Apparently the *Dallas News* was sadly short of material on that day.

Film renditions of the Holliday story during the Fifties were more rewarding than much of the literature. The three earliest told vastly different stories and are often overlooked.

Future President Ronald Reagan plays Frame Johnson in a 1950 adaptation of Burnett's novel, another version of *Law and Order*. It continues to use several names utilized in the 1932 film.[23] Alex Nicol portrays brother Lute, with no sign of Deadwood (Johnson). Popular actress Dorothy Malone got the female lead of Jeannie. These screenwriters give the sheriff's badge to Fin Elder (Barry Kelley), with Chubby Johnson playing the Doc character, Denver Cahoon. Friendship is about all to be recognized between the characters, Johnson getting nowhere near the amount of action Harry Carey had in the Thirties version. There is a Doc. Holly (Watson Downs), although evidently not our Doc. Preston Foster shows up in another Tombstone film as Kurt Durling, accompanied by Maria Durling (Ruth Hampton), with Dennis Weaver as Frank Durling, and Bart Durling played by an uncredited Don Gordon. The Durlings are obviously the Clantons. Jack Kelly as Jed is a better-recognized member of the cast, but despite the film being declared an "adaptation," it takes a huge imagination to recognize it as the Tombstone story with which we have come to know.

Powder River, a 1953 20th Century–Fox production, is another alleged attempt at a Stuart Lake lookalike. Director Louis King casts Cameron Mitchell as the gambling dentist in a drama of drink and depression.[24] It can at best be called a half-hearted attempt at the well-known story, with dull contrivances slung together with little rhyme or reason. Mitchell plays a schizophrenic young doctor, Mitch Hardin, with Rory Calhoun cast in the unbelievable role of his sheriff-keeper, Chino. When Chino's best friend is gunned down, he takes up with the Doc character to clean up the town. Although screenwriter Sam Hellman inserts two women of dual personalities and a sprinkling of gun forays, the film is almost unrecognizable as a Tombstone recounting.

Corinne Calvet is believably cast as Frenchie Dumont with Penny Edwards in the Debbie Adams role. Nobody wants to admit that Doc, once he left Georgia, never had more than one significant woman in his life, whether they were in love or not. Cousin Martha Anne Holliday was too much a lady to have ever visited. Although she did not enter a convent until after his Tombstone days, screenwriters seem obsessed with adding her to his troubles. The Clanton brothers are Loney and Harvey Logan, played by Carl Betz and John Dehner, which is as far as any recognizable characters from Arizona are concerned. James Griffith, who went on to star as Doc Holliday in a film the following year, is cast as Mac, the hotel clerk. Watch this on your PC at www.TelevisionFanatic.com.

Despite his rowdy reputation, Rory Calhoun was something of a heartthrob. He returned the following year in Universal-International's 80-minute *Dawn at Socorro*, a tale spun with action between Lordsburg and Socorro, New Mexico.[25] Although a gambler and imbiber in this George Zuckerman screenplay, he is also a gentleman to warm the heart of any woman. One cannot miss Doc's Southern heritage by his name, Brett Rutledge Wayde, and he plays classical piano almost as well as he does poker. The screenwriter uses both of Doc's characteristics to bring the story together: Wayde is a retired gunfighter, turned to gambling for his livelihood.

A tense poker game with appropriate animosity and fistfights takes place, but despite performances by David Brian, Piper Laurie, and Edgar Buchanan, *Dawn at Socorro* barely makes it as well-oiled western fare. Doc is once again a real gentleman, trying to save the good-bad girl from a life of wickedness. "Old Man Tom Ferris" (played by Stanley Andrews) and his sons Tom and Earl (played by, Richard Garland and Lee Van Cleef) are likely the Clantons, but none of the usual Arizona names appear. George Sherman, a prolific director of thirties B-movies, went on to direct more memorable films, two starring John Wayne.[26]

Cameron Mitchell (left) portrays Mitch Hardin, a thinly disguised Doc Holliday, in *Powder River* (1953) while Rory Calhoun plays Chino Bull, who strongly resembles Wyatt Earp (courtesy Paul A. Hutton).

Cast names do appear with which we have become familiar, or certainly would in the near future. Skip Homeier, a Clanton-Ferris in this film, later played Doc on television. Others of the cast include Kathleen Hughes, Alex Nicol, Mara Corday, and Roy Roberts. *Dawn at Socorro* is available on DVD at several sources.

Masterson of Kansas (1954), an excellent, but often overlooked, Doc figure appears in a story by screenwriter Douglas Heyes.[27] A confusion of historic information has Doc and Wyatt as adversaries, losing sight of Doc's most redeeming grace. He is again clearly shown as a doctor when patching up Virgil. James Griffith is an excellent choice for the Holliday role as he looks the part and brilliantly conveys the sarcastic wit for which Doc has now become well known. It was produced by Columbia Pictures; its direction by William Castle should have made it a bigger hit. It has been said that Castle's films were like going to an amusement park, you were always entertained. Many of his movies are still being shown on television, but for some reason this western doesn't seem to have made it. A shame, Doc fans, if no others, would love it.

Masterson of Kansas takes place after the gunfight in Tombstone and casts George Montgomery as an almost anonymous William Barclay (Bat) Masterson with none of the devotion to fancy dress for which Bat was famous. Wyatt and Virgil Earp, played by Bruce Cowling and Donald Murphy, are somewhat nondescript, and no other names associated with the Arizona crowd are included. Doc's character is something of an amalgamation of how others view him, varying from the defense of a lady, played by Nancy Gates, being vastly philosophical, to declaring that anyone fast enough to kill him would be doing him a favor. This, of course, was the rumor concerning his attitude at the time. He dies while saving Masterson's life. A lot of history is lost in *Masterson of Kansas*, but the idea of putting the three together is interesting, and the miracle James Griffith pulls off in playing the role is well worth the watching. It is available on your computer at www.TelevisionFanatic.com.

Whether Edgar Buchanan's Doc Black is really our Doc in the Golden Globe award–winning 1955's *Wichita* is debatable.[28] If so, it is his second shot at the role. This time he plays a saloon owner who plots to have Wyatt killed. When Wyatt orders him out of town, he returns with badman Clint Wallace (played by Walter Sande) and tough henchmen Gyp and Hal Clements (Lloyd Bridges and Rayford Barnes). There is, of course, a gunfight. Joel McCrea, one of Hollywood's great western actors, does an excellent job as Wyatt, with Peter Graves as Morgan. Keith Watson is cast as Bat Masterson, and if you watch closely you may catch Sam Peckinpah as the bank teller. The DVD of *Wichita* is now available directly from Warner, or watch it on your computer at www.TelevisionFanatic.com.

The best-known Tombstone film, and most popular with the public for at least thirty-five years, was produced from a screenplay by Leon Uris.[29] *Gunfight at the O.K. Corral* (1957) followed in the tradition of films about highly committed heroes. It was directed by John Sturges, the workingman's filmmaker often forgotten in the contemporary time of western sagas; his enduringly popular action-adventure movies are among the best known in America. This 122-minute Technicolor Paramount production presents a high-strung Kirk Douglas as the most cold and deadly, although certainly robust, Holliday to date, in a story running from Fort Griffin, Texas, to Tombstone, Arizona. Doc was not running from anything or anybody in Texas at the time he reached Tombstone. Ad posters for the film declared Doc the most feared gambler-badman of the West, while the opening scenes reveal him as a drunken, bad-tempered abuser of women. Doc's early defense of his family to Kate Fisher, played by Jo Van Fleet, seems to indicate he has fallen as low as his lady-love, and thus needs Wyatt Earp's (Burt Lancaster) good name to maintain his own.

In *Gunfight at the O.K. Corral*, knives as weapons play on earlier referneces to Doc's prowess. As his first actual victim was allegedly "disemboweled," there is adequate evidence to support this. Douglas' speed and accuracy with a six-gun also confirm everything Earp told the *San Francisco Examiner*. Holliday consumes enormous quantities of alcohol and lingers long at the gambling tables, yet Douglas' healthy tan belies his consumptive cough. In depicting some of Doc's worst traits, the movie gives an excellent interpretation of the lawman-outlaw friendship. Following earlier explanations of the legend, Doc behaves as he does only because of Wyatt. Although Uris' script attempts to convince viewers that Doc is afraid to die, greater evidence suggests a fear of life, and in some scenes he almost whines.

Gunfight at the O.K. Corral punishes Doc with a fate worse than death when Earp rides off to a new life in California, with the Lottie Deno figure (Rhonda Fleming) leaving Holliday alone with his liquor and cards. This concept is a repeat of Paramount's ending from *Tombstone, the Town Too Tough to Die*.[30] Uris intimates that Holliday must have the good side of Earp to maintain his honor, while the lawman leans heavily on Doc's killer instincts in his showdowns with outlaws. It is certainly to Uris' credit that this film contains most of the cast associated with the true story, called by their real names.

Virgil Earp is played by John Hudson, given a wife (Joan Camden) and a son he never had, Tommy (Charles Herbert). John Ireland makes his second Tombstone appearance on the wrong side (here as Johnny Ringo) and DeForrest Kelley his first of three (this time as Morgan Earp). James (Jimmy) Earp is played by Martin Milner of *Route 66* and *Adam 12*. As was usually the case, there is no mention of Warren Earp. Of the Clantons there are four: Ike, Finn and Billy, played by Lyle Bettger, Lee Roberts and Dennis Hopper, with Harry Carey's wife Olive appearing as Mrs. Clanton.

Two McLowerys [sic] appear, Tom, (Jack Elam) and Frank (Mickey Simpson). Whit Bissell portrays John P. Clum and George Matthews caught the part of Fort Griffin, Texas, saloon keep John Shanssey [sic]. Kenneth Tobey is cast as Bat Masterson, who actually was in Tombstone until shortly before the gunfight. Lee Van Cleef plays Ed Bailey (whom Doc had "caught just below the brisket" in a knife fight some six years prior, in Texas).

Dimitri Tiomkin's brilliant musical score added to the strong appeal of the film's theme song, rendered by Frankie Laine, which is spine-tin-

Poster for *Gunfight at the O.K. Corral* (1956) (courtesy of Michael F. Blake).

gling. *Gunfight at the O.K. Corral* is still often seen on television and is available from amazon.com and other DVD and movie suppliers.

Warlock is the fictitious name given Tombstone by Oakley Hall's book. Twentieth Century–Fox put a new slant to the old title in the 122-minute film *Warlock* (1959) directed by Edward Dmytryk.[31] Getting past that transgression gains us little, despite a screenplay by Robert Alan Aurthur and Henry Fonda's second appearance as the Wyatt Earp figure (Clay Blaisedell). Richard Widmark appears in the John Behan role (Johnny Gannon). Doc in called Tom Morgan and played by Anthony Quinn who is, by far, the weakest of the three leading male characters. Overall, he is a murderous sociopath, moving from a cool, detached killer early in the movie to a singularly pathetic and suicidal cripple, in every sense of the word, at the conclusion. A return to pseudonyms makes a poor film even worse and more confusing. Dorothy Malone and Dolores Michaels do little to soften the blows.

Doc is disliked from the beginning, with his sardonic wit and chilling chuckle. Quinn's character is devious, crooked, and blood-curdling, as he appears utterly committed to remaking himself into the lawman's image and the possession of people and things. Holliday evidences little warmth or charm although it is not his sarcasm, but his total and complete irreverence that raises the hackles. Many viewers might agree with a closing comment that the Holliday figure is "a dirty, rotten dog." The only dignity allowed Doc Holliday in *Warlock* is the Valhalla-type funeral pyre Earp offers, bordering on the melodramatic, and the accompanying remarks, which offer a modicum of salvation.

Although the film is well laid out and moves with precision to the inevitable climax, Doc Holliday's image departs little from his twenty-five years in pictures. The acceptance of violence in language and action is nearly complete, leaving little to the imagination. Here is the darkest characterization thus far of John Henry Holliday; he is totally depraved in *Warlock*.

Longtime staple Wallace Ford as Judge Holloway and Tom Drake as Abe McQuown do not bring any more clarification than does the appearance of Richard Arlen as "Bacon." It is hoped that DeForrest Kelley (in his second Tombstone film) as Curley Burne, just may be Curley Bill Brocious. The balance of credited actors is equally as difficult to identify: Regis Toomey as Skinner, Vaughn Taylor as Henry Richardson, Don Beddoe as Dr. Wagner, and Bartlett Robinson as Buck Slavin.

The film is, if nothing else, a proper setting for the next three decades of western motion pictures in America.

Television did for the minds and imagination of 1950s America what motion pictures had for the previous generation. Transcontinental television began with a speech by President Truman in 1951 and fast became the audience-preferred medium of entertainment. Television, too, realized that westerns were not dying. Twenty hours of western viewing weekly was available for homes across the nation by 1959. While the total number filmed from the early 1950s well into the 1970s is mind-boggling, TV westerns had almost disappeared by the mid–1980s. Doc became a family name along with many other early western heroes, real and fancied. Although a few turned in unique performances, the vast majority followed the stereotype set by earlier writers and film directors.

Gary Yoggy's *Riding the Video Range* is a vital read for a better understanding of this epic era of the western in television.[32] Yoggy focuses on over 150 television westerns, analyzing why shows succeeded or failed. He covers social, ethnic, gender, and political issues that played a part in the rise and fall of the Western in television.

Cavalcade of America ran from 1952 through 1953 on NBC and on ABC until 1957. It probably carries the distinction of being the first western documentary. It was renamed *DuPont Cavalcade Theater* in August of 1955 and later as a 90-minute dramatization of actual plays, films and books. The series ran until 1961. "Duel at the O.K. Corral" (March 9, 1954) was written by William Rousseau and directed by Wilheim Thiele. It starred favorites of the time, Henry Morgan and Lee Van Cleef.[33] Peter Hansen was included in the cast, as well as Keith Richards, Lyle Talbot and Kenneth Tobey. The UCLA Film and Television Archives have kinescopes of this series and many can be view online.

Kim Spalding got a crack at Doc in Republic Pictures' *Stories of the Century*[34] as a young, well-educated Dr. John H. (Doc) Holliday (he leads a double life as good man/bad man). Matt Clark (played by veteran Jim Davis), investigator for the Southwestern Railroad Company, attempts to end Doc's larcenous career. When a train is robbed, Doc, whom one critic refers to as the "Dr. Jekyll and Mr. Hyde of the Old West," is suspected, and Matt goes after him. It comes closer to the truth than later, more fanciful TV efforts. The series was also known as *The Fast Guns* and, although television had yet to discover the true documentary, *Stories of the Century* did a fair expeditionary job based on official records of many infamous in the West. The series won an Emmy for Best Western or Adventure Series in 1954.

Walter Cronkite joined CBS News in 1950, making his mark as the newly termed "anchor" at both Republican and Democratic National Conventions. Cronkite's contribution to western history came when he hosted the program *You Are There*, which ran for five years (1953–57, 102 episodes). The series used the format of a news report to reenact historical events throughout world history. On November 6, 1955, the inevitable "The Gunfight at the O.K. Corral," aired.[35] It's a remarkably factual story, written and directed by Bernard Girard, with much of the dialogue, action, and characteristics of Wyatt as he had revealed them to Stuart Lake. In light of how far afield the telling would deteriorate in coming years, the account in this television telling is amazingly accurate. Barry Atwater, steely, slim and pale, portrays Doc Holliday and looks appropriately dangerous. An early barroom scene has him accused of having been "run out of Dodge City and Bisbee" and of being no better than Ike Clanton, played by DeForrest Kelly in another of his several O.K. Corral scenarios. The latter comparison has never been verbalized, although his questioned association with the Earp lawmen often has. The error is made of Doc's having been deputized earlier than the day of the street fight, with Doc reluctant to be "interviewed." He simply tells the reporter, "I was pretty drunk" the night of his encounter with Ike. Although his position during "the walk" is correctly shown, next to the buildings, there is no evidence of a shotgun, the object of much dispute before and after this filming. He appears to have been slightly wounded, another matter often discussed.

Robert Bray is cast as Wyatt with John Alderson and John Larch in the Virgil and Morgan roles. Edward McNally plays the only other Clanton, Billy, with only one McLaury seen: Art Reese as Frank. Paul Birch was tapped for the Behan role, joined by Tyler McVey, Robert Karnes, Roy Engel, Cyril Delevanti, Charles Perry, Earl Brown and Tom Hunter.

You Are There, despite being a somewhat accurate filming, made at least two fairly serious mistakes. One is having Wyatt Earp zip his pants (with back to the camera, of course). The zipper was not patented until 1893; this was a common error in many westerns until too many people caught on. Insofar as the gunfight goes, other than Doc's absent ten-gauge, Ike gets off several shots with a revolver and throws it down before retreating. These minor errors do not detract from the Cronkite summary that the Earp brothers and Doc were fully justified as acting in discharge of official duties. The final words condemn all such actions as "among the many that stunted the growth of progress in the far West."

Aimed at young adults and teens, this *You Are There* Tombstone saga is available today on remastered DVD. Although documentaries as we know them today were still in the future, *You Are There* came close.

Harry Bartell portrayed Doc on a CBS radio western of *Gunsmoke*, simply entitled "Doc Holliday," on July 19, 1952.[36] The radio series starred William Conrad as Marshal Dillon and has the town bully picking on a "dude" he assumes to be ill. Doc is, but is in Dodge on a mission to avenge the murder of two family friends. He accomplishes his intentions, of course. Radio often required more real acting than television, and Bartell does a great job of playing a Doc in failing health, but cold steel underneath. These shows can be heard on www.TelevisionFanatic.com.

CBS-TV's *Gunsmoke* began running on September 10, 1955. Almost unbelievably, out of a total 402 episodes, not one Doc Holliday appears.[37] (Almost every other famous or infamous personage of the time showed up in one episode or another.) *Gunsmoke* was a purely fictional western whose first episode was followed in four days by one based on solid history. It ran for twenty years.

The Life and Legend of Wyatt Earp was the first western directly aimed at primarily adult audiences. It ventured from the path of previous western scripts, which had been written to appeal to more general audiences. *The Life and Legend of Wyatt Earp*, introduced by ABC in 1955 and parlayed into a six-year run, was written by playwright Frederick Hazlett Brennan and taken from Stuart Lake's *Frontier Marshal*. The series, with Hugh O'Brian as Wyatt, featured a Doc played by two different actors in 63 of 226 half-hour episodes.[38]

Douglas Fowley first appeared as Doc Holliday in April 23, 1957's "Wyatt Meets Doc Holliday." Doc's first comment was, "I hate good men."[39] When Wyatt sides with Doc against his wife (Kate Holliday played by Carol Stone), they become friends. Again perceived as an older man, the dapper Doc has a sardonic wit that some followers today find cold. The two share five more episodes taking place in Kansas with Fowley in "Wells Faro vs. Doc Holliday."

Myron Healey played a much younger Doc in the 1958-59 season while Fowley did movie work elsewhere.[40] He appeared in, among others, "Doc Holliday Rewrites History" (how prophetic), "Dig a Grave for Ben Thompson," "The Reformation of Doc Holliday" with Collette Lyons as Kate, "My Husband," "Little Gray Home in the West," and "Dodge City: Hail and Farewell." Of corresponding interest is Collette Lyons' appearance in "Little Brother," a pre–Christmas episode, as Kate Holliday, but without Doc."[41] While Healey leaves Dodge in "Hail and Farewell," Douglas Fowley, once more in the Doc role, returned to the set on April 7 and appears in the opening fall 1959 season "Tombstone."[42]

More murky figures are found for Doc's acquaintance and the story takes him to rather far-flung places like Charleston and Galeyville. Although these have rarely been mentioned, they were most likely spots for a good hand of poker. Still well-dressed and cool, Doc's reputation for loyalty is arguable when he openly consorts with Curly Bill Brocious and Johnny Ringo. Some fairly good research was done for the last six episodes, which tell the O.K. Corral story and a part of its aftermath.[43] Had Hugh O'Brian not become somewhat tired of the role and wanted to move on, the show could have easily stood another season or more and ridden with the vendetta band.

Healey and Fowley both portrayed Holliday's respect and loyalty for his good friend Wyatt, but Doc's true deadliness is often only intimated. *Life and Legend of Wyatt Earp* is definitely one cinematic presentation in which the Doc figure does not overshadow that of the Wyatt character. There is no doubt whatsoever as to exactly whose life and legend it is.

In April of 1955, James Griffith appeared as Doc in an episode of the short-lived *Buffalo Bill, Jr.*, produced by singing cowboy matinee idol Gene Autry.[44] "The First Posse" also featured Walter Reed as Marshal Wyatt Earp and Nancy Gilbert as a "Calamity"(not really Jane) who was young Bill's sister. Writer Samuel Newman had enough knowledge to include a Frank Stillwell, played by Lane Bradford. The series only lasted a brief 52 episodes, possibly because of too much misrepresentation.

Gerald Mohr nabbed the Doc role in two 1957 *Maverick* episodes.[45] He managed to look more weary than deadly with his assertion of "The Quick and the Dead" being the only two kinds of people in the West, giving title to another of James Garner's smiling tomfooleries.[46] All the customary elements of Doc's character are relayed before he appears on screen, after having been declared the "meanest and fastest cheap tinhorn" in the West. Maverick claims Doc is afflicted with a "sickness that has no cure, making him mad to see anybody healthy while he really wanted to die." There is sufficient coughing to support the statement. In an episode written and directed by Douglas Heyes, Maverick eventually teams up with Doc to bring some poker players using counterfeit money to justice.

The episodes were filmed shortly after Sturges' *Gunfight at the O.K. Corral*, and Mohr seems influenced by the identical self-pity Kirk Douglas put into Doc's role; his character is less strong than in other TV programs. The positive factors shown are Doc's superstitions about not killing anyone or leaving the game when on a winning streak. An April 1958 episode, "Seed of Deception," finds the dentist in Arizona as the two Maverick brothers are mistaken for Wyatt and Doc.[47] On this occasion he earns the title of a "lawman" and is put in serious trouble by the local sheriff who tries to use the pair to scare off an outlaw gang who is out to rob the bank.

Tombstone Territory is really not about the usual Tombstone crowd, with 92 episodes of fiction starring Pat Conway as Sheriff Clay Hollister. Harris Claibourne (John Clum) adds a touch of reality as *Epitaph* editor and narrator.[48] Acclaimed as set in Tombstone (the town too tough to die), it can't seem to help pulling the old gang in on the script. Gerald

Gerald Mohr (right) played Doc in *Maverick* episodes "The Quick and the Dead" (1957) and "Seed of Deception" (1958). James Garner was Bret Maverick and Marie Windsor appeared as Doc's ladylove (courtesy Paul A. Hutton).

Mohr is again Doc in "Doc Holliday in Durango," and in trouble.[49] With much of the young Holliday's slim, deadly demeanor, this Doc is identified as "the fastest gun in these parts" and "a man with no friends." His penchant for whiskey is undeniable when his flask is found empty and he knocks down the barkeep for not keeping a fresh bottle on the table. He demands manners from others, but shows few himself. No prior friendship exists with the Wyatt character (Clay Hollister). Doc ultimately shows his friendship for the lawman in trouble with a sporty shotgun he seems questionably slow in loading. He and the sheriff (not marshal) pursue and dispatch three Texans, the really bad guys in this episode. Not only do numerous fits of coughing reveal his tubercular condition, he tells Hollister he is a consumptive, a word unlikely to have come from Doc Holliday's mouth. The exaggeration of Doc seeking death is reflected in his comment that relief for his condition is "maybe a bullet some day." Absolute disregard for human life is evidenced in not remembering a man he killed only a month earlier, and indicating he will quickly forget his current shooting. The show is fraught with incorrect dates, names, and a Durango that the residents of that lovely place would cringe to view. Mohr's depiction of Doc is definitely a notch up, and the series itself was more serious and deadly in tone than prior ones.

For purely Tombstone interest, watch this series' February 19, 1958, "Johnny Ringo's Last Ride" starring Myron Healey.[50] Although consistently told as a Ringo legend, the character's terminal health problems, good man/bad man image, and wrongful death are so much Doc as impossible to miss. A dance hall girl with a heart of gold completes a close friendship with Hollister, the Wyatt character.

Lawman's 156 episodes were Warner Bros. productions set in Laramie, Wyoming.[51] Former Marine John Russell stars as Marshal Dan Troop who represented law and order at its most rigid. Peter Brown is his deputy, Johnny McKay, with Peggie Castle furnishing the female interest in the role of Lily Merrill.

To play Doc, director Lee Sholem chose charming Adam West, a strong contrast to the no-nonsense marshal who stood for justice at any cost. In "The Wayfarer," stubborn Marshal Troop wants Doc, who shot a man over the lady he is waiting to arrive by stage, to leave town before he is called out. Television makes much more of Holliday's vicarious love life than either reality or earlier films had. This episode had been intended as the pilot for a new western series, *Doc Holliday*, on which ABC pulled the plug. So thoroughly did they wash their hands of the idea, no Doc appeared during the remaining four-plus years of the show.

Lawman, together with a host of other favorites from the 1950s, is showing nightly on television's Encore Westerns channel. If you like interesting trivia, watch the credits on those old movies and be amazed at how many bit part players made it to big-time Hollywood.

West's second chance at Doc came in *Colt .45*'s "The Devil's Godson," written by James Barnett and Malcolm Stuart Boylan.[52] A 1950s Randolph Scott film was the inspiration for the series. Hugh Benson took the idea, but not the entire plot, to comply with a beer company's request for a western to sponsor. Almost unknown and inexperienced Wayde Preston, a Wyoming park ranger and rodeo rider of unquestioned good looks, was cast in the role. The show ran 69 episodes and included many character actors and actresses. West's Doc is neither a gambling nor drinking gunman, and dentistry is practiced for the first time. Doc makes a filling out of cartridge lead for the series hero, but not before quoting Shakespeare on toothaches. Despite references to his wicked ways and a slim, blonde appearance, the character is just too cussed friendly to pass muster as Doc. The show ran into casting and sponsoring problems and died an untimely death after only two years.

Adam West returned as Holliday in *Sugarfoot*'s "The Trial of the Canary Kid."[53] Doc once more is called on to test his dental education when teeth are needed to identify a twin accused of murder. Seems at one point he had done work on the more legitimate of the two brothers. Series star Will Hutchins plays look-alikes Sugarfoot Brewster and the Canary Kid. The episode is spiced up further with appearances by western series stars Ty Hardin (Bronco Layne), Peter Brown (Deputy Johnny McKay) and Wayde Preston (Christopher Colt). The show lasted four seasons.

Zane Grey Theater, based on the short stories and novels of the famous author, ran from October 5, 1956, until the end of the 1960-61 season. The series was also known as *The Westerners*. Doc Holliday emerged in the frontier justice series in an episode entitled "Man of Fear."[54] Dewey Martin plays a quite respectable lawman type who rescues a young couple from a gang of thieves demanding protection money to keep their ranch safe. Hopes for another spin-off series again fell flat.

Tales of Wells Fargo starred real Oklahoma cowboy Dale Robertson as railroad detective and narrator, Jim Hardie.[55] The series chose a new face, the somewhat sedate and aristocratic Martin Landau, for its "Doc Holliday" episode. He was less than thirty at the time; Landau's silver hair and lean frame gave him the look usually sought for an older Doc. Always considered a bad lot, however, Doc Holliday was, of course, an easy suspect for the train robber Hardie was seeking. Aaron Spelling, like other writers, seem determined to have Doc either rob a stage or a train; they did not seem to much care which. The stigma is always there if not the conviction. The setting for the series is the 1860s gold rush period. *Tales of Wells Fargo* held TV audiences for five years, going from 30 minutes to an hour and color the last season.

"The Frontier World of Doc Holliday" was yet another failed pilot for a series, starring Adam West.[56] It was scheduled to be broadcast as an episode of *Cheyenne*, and entitled "Birth of a Nation." In it, Holliday kills his first man, but does not mind since he is doomed already. The episode was never aired.

Doc Holliday almost made it through the decade unscathed. All in all, the 1950s had been good to him. What would the age of confusion and anger, offset by love and the flower child, make of his controversy?

SIX

The Tragic Sixties

The Sixties, impacted with tragedy, were the start of a delusional and embittered three decades in America. The number of unusual, unnatural, or untimely deaths of random celebrities included the western stars Jeff Chandler, Alan Ladd, Everett Sloane, Montgomery Clift, Eric Fleming, and box office bombshells Marilyn Monroe and Jayne Mansfield. Two Kennedy assassinations, linked with those of Malcolm X and Martin Luther King, Jr., kindled national rage. Anger toward the situation in Vietnam and dishonest politicians created an atmosphere of distrust. The entire entertainment world had been deeply touched by McCarthyism, which would haunt it for years to come. Hemingway committed suicide. Death stalked the land, as doom became the siren song of both literature and film.

During this turbulent decade the interest in Doc's trials and tribulations didn't wane, but the retelling of his biography took on a decidedly critical tone. Published in 1960, *The Earp Brothers of Tombstone* was subtitled "The Story of Mrs. Virgil Earp,"[1] and allegedly dictated by Virgil's widow Allie. Basically a poison pen epistle against Wyatt, Doc, and everyone involved with Tombstone, the book played a vital role in the dark picture painted of Doc and the Earp brothers during the next two decades. Virgil is the exception, of course. Frank Waters is adamant the widow told him several people identified Doc Holliday as having been present at the Benson stage robbery. Waters seemingly did pump the Irish lady, and then so manipulated her story she threatened to shoot him after reading the final draft. The original manuscript was placed in the University of New Mexico archives and was not taken out and brushed off until after the irate woman's death. Many of the author's disparities then became evident. Waters had several Nobel Prize nominations, wrote beautiful children's stories, and was an excellent prose writer. Why he stooped to such chicanery is unknown other than his abiding hatred of Wyatt Earp. The book is considered flawed, but valuable to the Tombstone student.

Vengeance at the O.K. Corral was written by Robert E. Ladd, and published by the Arizona Historical Society in 1963.[2]

Again adding to the Holliday legend, while proving highly controversial, is Glenn G. Boyer's 1966 *Illustrated Life of Doc Holliday*.[3] A maudlin effort at giving Doc's personal point of view, it suggests that the dentist drank for solace and forgetfulness, while terming him "a ghost called Doc Holliday." This and other Boyer books created controversy in the 1990s when the author himself admitted he was "a novelist, not a historian." Untruth is obvious early on when Boyer notes that Doc "said goodbye to his mother" and left for Texas. Those with even the slightest familiarity with Holliday know Alice McKey Holliday died in 1866 when John Henry was but a teenager. The writer further intimates that Doc gained his penchant for alcohol while in dental school, yet anyone with knowledge of the Antebellum South will know that it probably happened much earlier, as did his acquaintance with playing cards and betting on almost anything. The greatest error in *The Illustrated Life of Doc Holliday* is Boyer's statement, "He did not surrender the final spark of life for many years, but he gave up living" (in 1871). If ever a man truly lived, it was John Henry Holliday. This fictional account's descriptive "desperate" offends the soul of every person yearning for Holliday truth.

Boyer's fascination with Tombstone, including a seeming vendetta against all things Earp, is reflected in a multitude of other books following his early attack on Doc. Book stores, reviews, and Internet articles can do greater justice to his flamboyant and numerous writings. Boyer's second falsification of fact, in 1969, *The Suppressed Murder of Wyatt Earp*, has entirely to do with the Earp family's allegedly hidden secrets.[4] Boyer's theory that Wyatt's abandonment of his second "wife" and her subsequent suicide would have led to the ruination of his legend. This is scarcely believable. It is much too good a story to be spoiled by the death of an addicted prostitute.

Joseph G. Rosa's *The Gunfighter: Man or Myth?* is highly recommended when undertaking any study of the West.[5] It extinguishes immediately the possibility of historic accuracy by stating the so-called "Code of the West" never really existed. Its basic worth lies in the description and explanation of so many terms and realities necessary to the student of both film and literature. The book is well documented and footnoted, notwithstanding Doc Holliday's portrayal as a psychopathic killer.

The University of Oklahoma published *Under Cover for Wells Fargo, The Unvarnished Recollections of Fred Dodge* the last year of the decade.[6]

Dodge was a real man who worked fifty years as a Wells Fargo agent. He was allegedly a dead ringer for Morgan Earp, and friend of that faction from the day he stepped off the stage in Tombstone (1879); his journal was discovered and edited by Stuart Lake's daughter. A succinct statement by Dodge lays blame for the Benson stage robbery and murders directly on Holliday. This author's telling of the confrontation with Ike Clanton just prior to the street fight, however, takes place in a different setting than Ike's story. Dodge's other official reference to our subject is, "Graduate dentist turned frontiersman, gambler, killer, what have you." Again, not a work on Doc Holliday (which Dodge spells "Hilliday"), *Under Cover for Wells Fargo* gives an excellent play-by-play account of life in America's late nineteenth century Southwest.

Several musts for reading and understanding what was happening in Hollywood need to be mentioned here. Harris M. Lentz III's *Western and Frontier Film and Television Credits*, a two-volume set, presents a comprehensive account for both the film and television industries.[7] The set covers more than nine decades from 1903 to 1995 of western and frontier entertainment. *From Hopalong to Hud: Thoughts on Western Fiction*, another source guide to written western fiction, contains some great personality analysis.[8] Author Carl Sonnischen notes that while much has been made of western movies, little has been written of the spoken tales and legends.

Although Hollywood had quickly grasped how to tell (and sell) the old story to a new generation, Doc's few film appearances during this decade largely followed his earlier stereotype. *Warlock*'s grim image was temporarily ignored.

John Ford's last film *Cheyenne Autumn* leaves no doubt where the director's sentiments lie. His statement of trying to make amends for the bad image he'd previously given Native Americans might have been more easily believed had he hired real Indians instead of Latinos.[9] Richard Slotkin defines the work as a "counterculture Western" that comprised the new Cult of the Indian.[10] Writers Mari Sandoz and James R. Webb suggest that Native American lifestyles and beliefs might be superior to "civilization," and it was at the forefront of America's re-evaluation of her original inhabitants' history and ethnography.

The movie was, however, a delightful departure insofar as Doc was concerned. Arthur Kennedy plays a wisecracking, devil-may-care Holliday, in a zany interlude in an otherwise serious film. Although Kennedy's Doc presents a blatantly comical side of the gambler, his role obviously ridicules law and order, typical fare for Sixties Hollywood. When questioned as to the placement of the incident amidst a serious, newly emerging Native American image, Jimmy Stewart, who plays Wyatt Earp, declares that John

Ford inserted the skit "to keep the audience from ... going to the bathroom." One of Holliday's amusing lines appearing in this segment: "I'm a dentist ... wait 'til somebody shoots 'em in the teeth."

The U.S. military contingent includes Richard Widmark as Capt. Thomas Archer, Karl Malden as Capt. Wessels, George O'Brien as Major Braden, and Patrick Wayne as Second Lt. Scott. Harry Carey, Jr., and Ben Johnson are cast as Troopers Smith and Plumtree.

A totally unfocused screenplay is the real problem with the film. It cuts from the long trek of the Cheyenne to ridiculous scenes in Dodge City, returning again to the Long Flight (the original film title). Historians and audiences alike may flounder with this purely fanciful Hollywood approach.

Gordon Douglas' 1966 *Stagecoach* came nowhere near Ford's earlier version of Dudley Nichols screenplay.[11] This effort cast Bing Crosby as another oft-debated Doc Holliday with nothing to identify him but the booze. Holliday fans would not consider him as their hero. The role did, however, prove that Crosby could do more than sing. None of the actors had the power that Wayne brought to the screen twenty-six years earlier, although Alex Cord as Ringo does a passable job. The best reason for watching this *Stagecoach* is the spectacular CinemaScope photography.

A year later, another Holliday character provided a new slant in John Sturges' second Tombstone film with a script by Edward Anhalt, *Hour of the Gun*.[12] Jason Robards is cast as a mature, world-weary but wise Doc. Viewers had little difficulty with a Holliday professing to be a Civil War veteran, since he was so often depicted as an older man. Historians knew better. Audiences also accepted the best effort yet of Holliday as a man of wry wit and humor. Playing a Doc not so robust and edgy as others, Robards serves almost as a father figure to James Garner's Wyatt Earp. There is, however, little doubt as to Doc's lack of humanity.

Prior to production, United Artists had made it quite clear to Sturges that none of the primary roles were to be filled by actors who played the same characters in his earlier Earp film, *Gunfight at the O.K. Corral*. UA wanted this film to be distinctive from the 1957 one, and demanded other actors in those roles. Sturges, however, believed that the roles of Virgil and Morgan Earp were minor enough that the same actors could do it again without harming the film's uniqueness. UA agreed and allowed him to cast John Hudson as Virgil and DeForrest Kelly as Morgan. Unfortunately, Hudson had retired from acting in the early Sixties and was unwilling to do the role, while Kelley was currently working on the TV series *Star Trek* and unable to break away (little knowing it would lead him back to Tombstone the very next year). Thus, both Earp brothers were recast

Jason Robards as an older Doc in *Hour of the Gun* (1967) (courtesy Paul A. Hutton).

with Sam Melville and Frank Converse in roles that, in this version, were certainly minor.

Robert Ryan, a classic western actor, is grossly miscast in the Ike Clanton role, with brother Billy played by Walter Gregg. David Perna and Jim Sheppard play Frank and Tom McLowery (misspelled), with Jon Voight as Curly Bill Brocius and Robert Phillips as Frank Stillwell. Other names we now recognize appear: Michael Tolan as Pete Spence, Larry Gates as John P. Clum, William Schallert as Judge Spicer, and Monte Markham as Tucson Sheriff Sherman McMasters (also misspelled). A stab is made at the Vendetta members with William Windom as Texas Jack Vermillion and Lonny Chapman as Turkey Creek Johnson. There is not one female in the cast. James Garner makes an excellent Wyatt, some have said second only to Kurt Russell's in 1993. Unfortunately, this film moves slowly and could use a good bit more action.

Hour of the Gun ends with a look at the aftermath of the gunfight and chronicles the post-gunfight trials. It plays strongly on Wyatt's alleged dedication to revenge, although Morgan was not gunned down until the following March. Hollywood and Mirisch Pictures remained bogged down in the myth.

Television in the Sixties was something you watched, just no longer in amazement. It continued to play a leading role in telling the same old stories to the American public and Doc's image shifted little until late in the decade. For a few years, people at home continued to bask in the sunshine of an almost humorous approach to the Wild West.

Peter Breck's ready smile and dimples made him as clean-cut a Doc as any American mother could want for her child. Appearing in five episodes of the comedy-western *Maverick*, he contributed to its being one of the most popular and best remembered.[13] It often got better ratings than the Ed Sullivan and Steve Allen shows. Always in tandem with brother Jack Kelly's Bart Maverick character, Breck's first appearance in "Triple Indemnity" finds him as Bart's hired backup.[14] Their aim is to help him and the mother of a town bully, while teaching him a lesson against cheating. Although Bart has whipped the man, he wants Doc's bad reputation to help regain his gambling losses and teach the man humility. Alan Hewitt and Charity Grace play the roles of bad man George Parker and his mother. Breck's second appearance as Doc was in "A Technical Error."[15] This episode finds Bart winning a bank way too easily, and then discovering it is missing a pile of money belonging to the locals. The sheriff (Ben Gage) and his deputy (Jake Sheffield) cannot wait to nab the stranger they believe responsible. Bart begs Doc for any help he can offer in getting his money and reputation back. Doc, however, is way too interested in the lady (Jolene Brand) he has met through a lonely-hearts club. Our gambler waxes almost Biblical when he preaches to his lady friend (who also happens to be Bart's bank teller) about too much thinking taking the joy out of life. Bart's statement that only a shotgun would get Holliday to a wedding reminds the audience of that weapon's image still haunting him. Doc willingly abandons his mail order bride to help Bret out of the mess.

"The Maverick Report" finds Bart calling on Doc's support when a corrupt Colorado senator files a $100,000 libel suit against him (which he so graciously splits with Doc).[16] The wisdom of our gambling dentist appears in the statement, "He doesn't give anything, he's a politician." Since the conniving Senator and his sinister boss are Ivy Leaguers, Doc's days in Philadelphia come in handy. Doc's appearance was brief in "Marshal Maverick" the very next week.[17] As ridiculous and riotous an episode as can be found, it makes the heinous error of declaring Wyatt marshal of Abilene, one place he was never a lawman. Although Bart kills the murderer of the town marshal, he is jailed, and only the return of Wyatt Earp can save him. When Wyatt (Med Flory) arrives, he insists that Bart stay on as his deputy. This episode does little to promote Earp's reputation. *Maverick*'s grand finale, "One of Our Trains Is Missing," includes Breck in his Doc role.[18] Aboard Diamond Jim Brady's special express with Bart and brother Brett while headed for the state line to avoid a beating, Doc has his own agenda with yet another lady friend (played by Kathleen Crowley). Not surprisingly, it involves train robbery, with the entire lot being foiled when the car is side-railed by another crook.

The television series *The Tall Man* grasps Howard Hughes' *The Outlaw* misconception and returns Doc to Lincoln County, New Mexico.[19] The 75-episode series, created by Samuel A. Peeples, starred Barry Sullivan and Clu Gulager in "The Rovin' Gambler," a fictionalized story of Pat Garrett and Billy the Kid as lifelong friends. This television series portrays them as Hughes had, and features Robert Lansing as a suitably tall and grim Doc. The storyline follows Kate's (Faith Domergue) betrayal of Doc in Tombstone over the Benson stage robbery. It once more shifts to a further alliance with an ennobled Billy the Kid, who tries to save Doc. Billy knows Doc is innocent of Kate's accusations as they played poker all that night. He thus attempts to prevent a showdown with Garrett.

Bonanza's 1963 story did little to damage his image, although Holliday history continued downhill.[20] Christopher Dark turns in a rather timorous Doc Holliday image against an apparently intimidated Little Joe (Michael Landon) in "Calamity Over the Comstock."[21] Stefanie Powers is an unrealistically beautiful Calamity Jane who teases the two until Pa intervenes. This episode allegedly takes place in 1859, when Martha Jane Cannary was three and Doc seven—neither likely in Nevada. That is the history; this *Bonanza* rendition is pure entertainment except for Doc's cough, clearly in evidence. With regulars Lorne Greene, Pernell Roberts, Dan Blocker, and Landon, *Bonanza* won two Golden Globes and survived fourteen seasons into the next decade.

Dan Stafford played a somewhat ignominious Doc in *Death Valley Days*' 1964 "After the O.K. Corral," featuring Wyatt, Virgil, and Morgan (played by Jim Davis, John Clarke, and Jeff Morris).[22] William Tannen as Ike Clanton and Stewart Bradley as Curley Bill fill out a fairly good cast for a 30-minute episode. Skip Homeier turns in the decade's first barely threatening Doc in the second of two back-to-back Tombstone stories.[23] The

Skip Homier portrays a gambling Doc in "The Quiet and the Fury," episode of *Death Valley Days* (courtesy Paul A. Hutton).

series had been heard on radio for fifteen years and had the longest television run of any syndicated show (twenty-three years). Stephen Lord, prolific writer for multiple other television and film productions, wrote the script. A 1966 episode, "Doc Holliday's Gold Bars" featured Warren Stevens as the deadly dentist, with little further bleakness of the character.[24] Possibly referencing Doc's bunko charges in Pueblo, Colorado, the episode contrives an attempt to bankroll his gambling by conning a banker out of $20,000.

Failing still to find the right actor for the role, ABC turned to Henry Silva the following year for its Doc Holliday figure in a *Wagon Train* episode. Wyatt, Virgil, Morgan (Don Collier, Don Galloway, Michael Burns) emerge with Doc in a flashback story told by Coop (Robert Fuller). "The Silver Lady" tells of a lady killed when a stagecoach loaded with silver is plundered and wrecked. The nearest proximity to Doc and the Earps is the silver.[25]

Midway in America's plunge into complete gloom and despair (Timothy Leary urged its youth to "tune in, turn on and drop out"), the only studio making money was United Artists with their "spaghetti westerns."

UA also snagged the 007 series[26] and the Beatles. Continued efforts to exploit the youth culture emerged in films like *Bonnie and Clyde*, *Wild in the Streets*, and *Easy Rider*.[27] America and Hollywood seemed to maintain its sense of humor and found more comedy in *The Graduate* than lessons satiring materialism or the change in traditional female roles.[28]

For something completely different, take a look at the BBC's John H. Holliday, discovered in the spring of 1966 by *Doctor Who*—listed in *Guinness World Records* as the longest-running science fiction television show in the world. Originally intended to be educational, the English series appeared on prime time Saturday night with the cast roaming the universe in an unreliable old time machine (the TARDIS) that strongly resembles a British police box. The regular cast was comprised of William Hartnell as Doctor Who, Jackie Lane as Dodo Chaplet, and Peter Purves as Steven Taylor. Production Code Z, subtitled *The Gunfighters*, is comprised of four episodes and declared the first British western made for television.

"A Holliday for the Doctor," aired on April 30, 1966. Writer Donald Cotton must have seen the 1939 *Frontier Marshal*: He has Doc Holliday, played by Anthony Jacobs, drinking milk. John Alderson is cast as Wyatt Earp with Richard Beale as Sheriff Bat Masterson. Reed de Rouen, Maurice Good, William Hurndall, and David Cole play Pa, Phineas, Ike, and Billy Clanton. Kate's role is played by Sheena Marshe, who does a good Mae West impersonation. Virgil (Victor Carin) and Warren (Martyn Huntley) appear in a later episode, while Johnny Ringo (Laurence Payne) shows up in the third. Other episodes appearing on May 7, 14, and 21 are entitled "Don't Shoot the Pianist," "Johnny Ringo," and "The OK Corral."[29]

The Clantons are looking for Doc Holliday for killing Reuben, a brother unheard of before or since. The arrival of the time travelers causes them confusion, as they can't seem to get the two doctors straight. Doctor Who, finding himself in Tombstone with a toothache, is shocked to find the only dentist to be the infamous one. His merry band soon join forces with Wyatt *and* the Clantons, however. Despite getting a good bit of action, the Holliday of British lore displays some very nefarious characteristics. One is hoping the other doctor is shot so that he, himself, can be declared dead. Johnny Ringo appears, enlisted by the Clantons, when Earp arrests Phineas for harassing one of the Who gang. Virgil and Warren come to town, although Warren is killed in the Clanton attempt to free Phin. Dodo takes up with Doc and Kate, who plan on leaving town with him. "The OK Corral" comes fairly near the truth but has the odds and most of the characters wrong. Ringo, with Phin, Ike and Billy, face off against Wyatt, Virgil and Doc. The results are incorrect, of course, with all four adversaries killed and none of the "three" good guys getting a scratch. The cast remains the same for all four episodes.

It's riotous British comedy if you appreciate that it does acknowledge John Holliday, the dentist, had a "penchant for alcohol." In one of the concluding episodes, Doctor Who imagines all the members of the Tombstone saga living futuristically "in peace and prosperity." Delightful; England has not achieved the same with Scotland and Ireland, and we seriously suspect the idea might be not quite to our Doc's liking. To be perfectly fair, however, the BBC occasionally waxed a good deal more historically correct than some of Hollywood's efforts, albeit a few of the cast sound straight out of the Royal Shakespeare Company. An interesting aside is that John Alderson, who plays Wyatt, portrayed Virgil in the 1953 *You Are There* O.K. Corral episode. He is the only actor to have been cast in the role of both Earp brothers, and on two continents.

Doc and the Earp brothers fall not only off the continent, but off the planet in "Spectre of the Gun," a *Star Trek* episode. It literally takes him and the brothers into outer space.[30] Ignoring a warning buoy, the *Enterprise* arrives in Melkotian space intent on establishing relations. The secretive race takes offense, and as a form of punishment sends five of the crew (Kirk, Spock, McCoy, Scotty, and Chekov) to a warped version of Tombstone, plucked from the captain's inaccurate memory bank. The set is surrealistic, making the episode offbeat while maintaining a gloomy "ghost town effect." Many of the story's characters are recognizable to the aficionado but the interaction plays the crew (the Clantons, McLaurys and Billy Claiborn) off against near-demonic Doc (Sam Gilman) and the Earps (Ron Soble as Wyatt, Charles Maxwell as Virgil, and Rex Holman as Morgan). Arizona seems overrun with zombies trapped in a western time warp. In a scene that did not make the final cut, McCoy offers to make a deal with Doc in exchange for a tuberculosis cure. DeForrest Kelley thus makes his third appearance in an O.K. Corral filming. He was cast as Ike Clanton in the *You Are There* episode, as Morgan in *Gunfight at the O.K. Corral*, and here in the Tom McLaury role. Spock inevitably saves the day and no one (except Chekov, shot and killed) is harmed. "Spectre of the Gun" should be watched simultaneously with Hughes' *The Outlaw* for an evening of total frivolity and abandoned history.

Doc's last three television appearances of the decade continued in a comedic vein with no hint of desperado except in reference. Don Beddoe's playing of our hero works well with that of Roy Engel as Wyatt Earp in one of the many raucous episodes of *Pistols 'n' Petticoats*.[31] Douglas Fowley confuses the viewer with his role of Grandpa, having become so well known as Doc in the *Wyatt Earp* series. The Holliday and Earp of "Shootout at the O'Day Corral" are characters blundering in and out of situations and called on to catch the murderous Blanton (yes, B) brothers.

Jack Kelly is a handsome, although neither tidy nor clean-shaven, young Doc Henry (read between the lines) in a 1967 episode of *High Chaparral*.[32] As disreputable as possible, he saves Billy Blue in a gunfight and then throws in with Kid Curry against the series' solid rancher (Leif Erickson) who has sent his son to help Doc set up a dental practice in Tucson. Well, that is almost Tombstone. The character redeems himself, but not before proving he is the scoundrel of reputation. This late Sixties appearance had little impact on the wagering dentist's reputation. *High Chaparral* was one of the better westerns, touching on many controversial subjects and ahead of its time on some topics. *The High Chaparral* blog, in 2009, posted a birthday memorial to Doc Holliday.

Holliday and western fans may have been praying for a revival, but found small hope in the last of the Sixties sightings.

Despite its ten years of strong emotion, confusion and anger, the Sixties were also the Age of Aquarius, of individual against the system, of newfound freedom of choice — a rerun of frontier times.

Little hope would be found in the next decade.

SEVEN

The Sinking Seventies

The Seventies sank, unfortunately, and remain a largely under-appreciated and misunderstood decade. American society was reshaped by economic decline, the frustration of Watergate, with cultural despair at home and abroad. It was additionally a time of bicentennial celebrations in which many struggled to redefine patriotism and the national dream as it moved into an uncertain future. Changing gender roles, an increasing mistrust of government, reshaping of the working class identity, and new economic transformation resulted in popular culture and subcultures in conflict. It was reflected in the media and certainly through literature and film.

The Seventies was an age of extremes and Doc Holliday suffered, as did the famous and infamous alike. Cable television was taking control of American home viewing, with the prediction it and videocassettes would ruin Hollywood.

Music in the Seventies reflected general thinking. Songs like "Paranoid" and "I Want to Be Sedated" joined bands with names like Black Sabbath and the Sex Pistols. It was also the decade of the never-to-be-forgotten Rolling Stones and the Beatles. Writers of Western lore did not ignore this display of despair and fatalism appearing at the peak of American rebellion against the system. John Holliday and Wyatt Earp appeared on the literary and cinematographic scene during this era, accompanied by almost every other desperado, lawman, and gunfighter.

Tombstone: 1877–1900 was the first of many paperbacks by Ben T. Traywick in 1970.[1] *The Residents of Tombstone's Boothill* added to his offerings early the following year. Dale Schoenberger, also in 1971, opened the hardback literary parade with *The Gunfighters*.[2] Schoenberger's work, which took a great deal of his life to compile, was the best-researched and best-documented on the topic to date. He presents a biography of every outlaw and lawman even remotely known at the time, and states succinctly it is his intention to erase all the mistakes of past writers and present nothing but the truth. The exhaustive bibliography and index prove his dedication to that endeavor. The author's hero appears to be Bat Masterson, while Wyatt Earp does not fare so well. Chapter Four is dedicated almost entirely to quoted untruths regarding John H. Holliday's Georgia, Texas and Kansas adventures (and others). While offering comparatively little in the way of the gambling dentist, *The Gunfighters* does an excellent job of contributing new information on many Old West figures seldom mentioned previously. It is an excellent addition to any historian's bookshelf.

George Turner's *Book of Gun Fighters* (1972) begins with Billy the Kid and lists Doc Holliday as fourteenth, wedged in the unenviable position between Wyatt Earp and Bat Masterson.[3] Where Turner got Earp's quote of Doc being "the most dangerous man alive" is questionable, yet he does add a few sobriquets others have omitted, such as "lover" and "intellectual." Errors abound, which shall remain unmentioned, except a rather inexcusable erroneous report of Doc's final words.

Nineteen seventy-three also saw Albert Pendleton, Jr., and Susan McKey Thomas, relatives of Doc, publish a limited edition of *In Search of the Hollidays*.[4] It deals with John Henry's genealogy, his childhood and adolescence, including family tradition and hearsay evidence. It was a new approach at the time. Pendleton and Thomas cast an entirely different light on Doc and the hows and whys of his personality and penchants. If nothing else, they refute Bat Masterson straight across the board. A modest excerpt was taken from Pendleton and Thomas' work and published in 1975 as "A Pictorial History of Lowndes County, Georgia, 1925–1975."[5] This would be the last family offering for another twenty years.[6] Traywick's *Tombstone's Immortals* was added in 1973.[7] The "immortals" were one of Doc's lines in the 1993 blockbuster film.[8]

Richard O'Connor's *Iron Wheels and Broken Men* (1974) is a tale of transcontinental railroad tycoons.[9] Doc was clearly evident in these arguments between the Santa Fe and Denver and the Rio Grande railroad over the Raton Pass right-of-way. He did indeed participate, together with the entire first Santa Fe contingency solicited from Dodge City. The book alleges that Doc was "even handier at drilling his enemies than rotten molars." The original riders were followed by an allegedly more law-abiding group captained by Bat Masterson, who got himself made a deputy U.S. marshal, and fortified the entire group in the roundhouse armed with a Gatling gun. They surrendered for a $10,000 payoff. Doc is said to have shot Kid Colton in Trinidad, Colorado, on his way home. Wyatt was not along on this questionable caper, but Ben Thompson, a Texas desperado of fame, was.

A Gunnison, Colorado, publication, *Doc Holliday, Wyatt Earp and Bat Masterson: Their Colorado Careers* (1974) recounted the railroad fiasco yet again, and continued by carrying Doc and Wyatt back to Colorado after the street fight.[10] *Colorado Careers* falls for the story about Doc using a McKey alias at the time he cut Bud Ryan's throat. History continues to bear out the fact that Doc never used an alias, leaving his proponents in jaw-dropping amazement he could stay out of trouble for such a length of time. To make it more gruesome, Ryan had previously been reported as "disemboweled." This is untrue as he lived to cause Doc trouble in later years. Churchill contends that Doc was a con man during that mysterious period from 1875 to 1877. It is almost certain Doc was in Denver at least a part of that time, despite no court records having emerged to charge him with anything under either name. This may be confused with the post–Tombstone diversionary larceny charges in Pueblo, Colorado. This work is chronically out of order and full of misconceptions, and it leans heavily on Masterson in its basically hit-and-miss attempt at quotations and legends. Names are tossed about with reckless abandon but the work could certainly serve as a guide from which future researchers and writers might possibly gain leads to the truth. Keep in mind, however, that Wyatt, Warren, and possibly one or two others, did hide out in Gunnison, Colorado, for a while after the "vendetta ride." Doc was in Denver getting arrested and about to close his most public career.

Eugene Hollon, whose 1974 book attempts a less violent heritage, took an entirely different approach to the American West. *Frontier Violence* is presented with a postmodern slant, more from the victims' point of view than as a fact of the times.[11] Violence is also hinted as being integrally independent behavior to achieve civilization, a theme that plays heavily on the theories of Frederick Jackson Turner.[12] Hollon's book is good reference material presenting both sides of several controversial political and ethnic issues, while permitting the reader to individually decide the right or wrong of things.

Sixteen years after Virgil Earp's widow allegedly told her story to Frank Waters, Glenn G. Boyer, self-confessed novelist, but certainly the research holder of much Southwest Arizona lore, sold Josephine Sarah Marcus (Mrs. Wyatt) Earp's story.[13] Undoubtedly none of the Earp women liked Doc, nor were they always on the best of terms with either the brothers or each other. Taken as verbatim for years, *I Married Wyatt Earp*, published by the University of Arizona Press, proved at the time that the writer had a vast and wonderful imagination. The claim that Doc "emptied his pistol" into Frank Stilwell at the Tucson railway station adds another side to the confusion of that scenario. Sadie's flat statement "After Doc shot Frank

McLaury in the belly..." stops readers dead in their tracks. Josephine's "husband" had never denied he deliberately shot Frank, recognizing him as the most dangerous of the three facing them. She admits that much Wyatt himself had told a much different story in the late 1920s. This book, fraught with error as it is, played the role of a challenging pacesetter in inspiring latter-day research into the Tombstone story and its characters.

Ben Traywick's contributions for Tombstone readers the remainder of the decade were *The Earp Years: 1880–1882*, and *The Wild Bunch: The Most Unusual and Exciting Western Show Found Anywhere on Earth*.[14] For an excellent understanding of the U.S. West, discover Howard R. Lamar's *The Reader's Encyclopedia of the American West*, first published in 1977 and updated several times since.[15] One page of the 1306-page volume is dedicated to Doc Holliday.

Larry Ball's definitive 1978 work on U.S. marshals is the last major published book of the decade to mention Doc Holliday.[16] In a chapter entitled "The Arizona Marshalcy, 1876–82," Ball acquaints the reader with the geographic, economic, and outlawry of that segment of Arizona history. We soon read the familiar name of U.S. Marshal Crawley P. Dake, followed closely by a listing of all the "Cowboys" accused of operating on both sides of the border. Wyatt Earp is said to have had political aspirations, although Virgil gets much better press. Of Doc Holliday, Ball had these words:

> Virgil and Wyatt Earp were ... indignant when the sheriff arrested their close friend, gambler-dentist John H. ("Doc") Holliday, for robbery and murder. [Ball here specifically cites Frank Waters' book on the Earp Brothers]
>
> [Virgil Earp] deputized Wyatt, Morgan, and Doc Holliday as city policemen with the intent to arrest the Cowboys.

These are the only two times Doc is mentioned in Ball's work, yet it gives him the legality his advocates would wish. Ball goes on to state that the gunfight tarnished the reputation of the office, despite Marshal Dake's standing by his man and declaring Wyatt Earp "a good officer." Jeff Morey, O.K. Corral expert, contends that Virgil deputized Doc, Wyatt and Morgan simply by the fact they were recruited to assist in the arrests.[17]

Gary L. Roberts, in the January 1970 *Montana Magazine*, wrote a comprehensive introduction, with annotations, of the letter Justice Wells Spicer wrote regarding threats following the street fight.[18] *Roberts includes a brief analysis of the decision, and a presentation of the letter itself.*

Doc's best press continued to be in magazines and journals devoted to his time in the West. They were largely read by those who would never be swayed in their loyalty to heroes and epic events. A 1971 issue of *Western* magazine published Wayne Montgomery's "A Little Ride with Doc."[19]

Family members Albert Pendleton, Jr., and Susan McKey Thomas presented yet another article on Holliday's Georgia background in a 1973 *Journal of Arizona History*. The unique piece included works from *Memoirs of the Holliday Family in Georgia*, a straightforward genealogy of the Holliday family from its Irish-Catholic beginnings.[20] That author was none other than the lady for whom Doc Holliday allegedly held a neverending love, his cousin Martha Anne Holliday. Her writings neither admit nor deny other than a familial kinship. After her death, many letters Doc had written were found still in her possession. A family member, horrified at the possible scandal that might erupt concerning John Henry and Sister Melanie, burned them all.[21] Doc's historians might wish that person had sacrificed herself on the altar of honor, and left us more insight into his true character.

Truth be told, wild west magazines are neither the Alpha nor the Omega to publish fiction as fact. Indeed, who among us does not enjoy a good fantasized historical read? Taking that thought a step further, how much more of our own belief systems have been more shaped by myth rather than truth?

Glenn Boyer's "John Henry Holliday, DDS" appeared in an *Atlanta Historical Society Journal* in the autumn of 1973.[22] That same year, Zoltan Malocsay finally just came out and said what a lot of people might have been thinking in his "OK Corral: 100 Years of Lies."[23]

"The Legend and the Dentist," was published in Georgia during 1974, and contained an early reference to John H. Holliday's true collegiate affiliation.[24] He graduated from the Pennsylvania College of Dental Surgery, not one in Baltimore. Welcomed as totally new information and well established today, the piece contains several bits of corrected history, welcomed at the time as new evidence. *Westerner* magazine published "Doc Holliday's Girl," with another piece by Wayne Montgomery two years later addressing "the deadly doctor."[25]

"Tom 'Pole Cat' Adams Recalls Doc Holliday" was another Montgomery contribution to the Summer 1975 *NOLA Magazine*.[26] An interesting footnote by Gardner P.H. Foley may not have applied to Doc, but is fun to imagine: "In the wild years of Denver, the crib girls of Holladay Street were wont to rob their paying guests by biting studs from their shirt fronts, or scarf pins from their cravats.... A Denver dentist won a widespread underworld reputation for making steel biters to clamp to the rear of the girls' front teeth."

"Desperate Men, Desperate Guns" by Carl W. Breihan in *Real West*'s Fall and Winter issue contained mention of both Doc and Wyatt.[27] Doc also got a mention in Jane Polley's piece on Bat Masterson which appeared in *Readers' Digest* "American Folklore" in 1978.[28]

Between the previously cited books and articles, Boyer also wrote his "Postscripts to Historical Fiction About Wyatt Earp in Tombstone."[29] It considers a rebuttal by William S. Hart of a "scandalous" account of the Earp faction's activities in Tombstone as cited by John M. Scanland. A former El Paso newsman, Scanland was noted for scribbling wild tales of noted western figures, usually after their deaths. Boyer gets a few things correct about Doc, but not his date of birth. His major sources are Pendleton, Thomas, and his vivid imagination. Many of the citations are Boyer's own, but Holliday expert Gary Roberts clarified a great many of these issues in a 1999 article.[30] The Georgia historian would go on to publish his definitive *Doc Holliday: The Life and Legend* in 2006.[31]

Boyer, in collaboration with Dr. A.W. Bork, published the verbal rendition of yet another of the Tombstone women in a 1977 *Arizona and the West* article.[32] It was later published as Mary Katherine (Big Nose Kate) Harony/Elder/Earp/Holliday/Cummings' memoirs, written to her niece late in life. As pointed out earlier, both she and Wyatt held very biased viewpoints of Doc, with their ages similar at the time of revelation. Although Kate may well have encountered Doc in St. Louis before he received his dental license, the time of their relationship was about the same. Considering Kate's propensity for infidelity, however, her version may be viewed with a jaundiced eye. Some of Doc's consort's accounts are in direct contradiction with those of Wyatt, some concur, and others are just off the wall. Read them and judge for yourself.

Hollywood drop-kicked the dentist from Georgia into infamy early in 1971 with Frank Perry's *Doc*.[33] *Doc* was not content with merely debunking the by-now revered cast of the Tombstone scenario; had their names been withheld from Pete Hamill's original screenplay, it is doubtful they would have been recognized. Despite heavy symbolism, no psychological reason is ever given for the violence. The movie was understandably rated R. Stacy Keach's performance obliterated any romantic, myth-ridden Doc Holliday as both he and Wyatt (Harris Yulin) appear in a foggy, drug-addicted and obviously homosexual relationship. Perry had seemingly been confused by past films for in lieu of the usual Cowboys, there is "The Kid," played by Denver John Collins, and gunned down by Doc.

Hamill's bizarre presentation was allegedly a statement against Lyndon Johnson, the Vietnam War, and a national self-righteous spirit. Doc and Katie (Faye Dunaway) jar the viewer with obscenities and brutality. Drunken debauchery and cold-blooded violence dominate the film, concluding with the slaughter of seven almost innocent clan members. The Benson Stage scenario is laid squarely on Doc. The film has a stableman stating that Doc rented a fine horse the day of the robbery and rode out with a Winchester and a six-gun. Lou Rickabaugh (Everett L. Browney), never before or since heard of around southern Arizona, contradicts this suggested indictment by declaring Doc was playing cards all that day at the Alhambra. Clearly depicting national despair, Doc rides off alone. Filmed in Spain, this effort decidedly does not favor Doc Holliday's reputation, nor is it his finest hour.

CBS's *Appointment with Destiny*, a David Wolper television production, gave a new, realistic and unique version of "Showdown at O.K. Corral" in 1972.[34] The audience is reminded in an opening statement, "America relives the legends of its youth not by the facts of our past but by the myths we weave around them." The episode remains true to most of the names and characteristics of those associated with the story. It was touted as a "news documentary" narrated by Lorne Greene, Tim James played the Holliday part. Although slim, blonde, pale, and described as "ill-tempered ... quarrelsome and unpredictable," the Holliday character gets few lines and little action in this film focused primarily on Wyatt Earp (David H. Vowell) and Ike Clanton (Thomas Hunter).

Kate, in a most blatant misportrayal, is called Doc's wife, and an attempt is made to cast her as "a fresh young woman soon bruised by the frontier." A further attempt at making Kate look pathetic comes with the statement that Doc was charged with the Benson stage robbery "based on accusations by [his] own wife who later recanted." Doc is described as a gentleman, although one who had become a "brawling gunman" who is "fighting death with rage and alcohol." A Nellie Cashman figure (Gay Molloy) defines Holliday as "the kind of man you crossed to the other side of the street to get away from."

The writer's character analysis of Doc is, "Sometimes I think Doc would rather get himself killed in a gunfight instead of dying an inch at a time." Regarding the ever-prevalent stage robbery, Wyatt stated, "Doc was gone all day, returning late, and went directly to playing cards." Although Doc exchanges his cane with Virgil's Greener ten-gauge, his late arrival and lack of mention regarding the street fight is disappointing to his devotees. He does cut down Tom McLaury, but is not further mentioned other than being dramatized as the deciding factor in the event. The show stuck to the truth as it was fast becoming known in the early '70s but Greene's comment that such history was being "re-invented" is well taken. The closing comments on Doc Holliday include, "He gambled, drank, and quarreled until his death." With such fanfare, no wonder he got such a bad reputation.

Television's series offering was a complete one-eighty in the comedy western *Alias Smith and Jones'* somewhat bland renditions of the many western characters it attempted to portray.³⁵ The theme of newcomer regulars Ben Murphy and Pete Duel, who play two relatively unknown outlaws trying to go straight, tended to go flat. Despite narrative by Roger Davis, even appearances by several well-known actors of the decade did little to boost the series as the West lost its thrill for the remainder of the 1970s. Bill Fletcher captured the role of Doc Holliday in a February 10, 1971, airing entitled "Which Way to the OK Corral?"³⁶ He returned in the 1972 episode "The 10 Days That Shook Kid Curry."³⁷ The death of Pete Duel, resulting in a change in actors early in 1972, hastened this show's demise. The BBC played off the title for a taboo-breaking late night comedy, *Alas Smith and Jones*, not to be confused with the last western television series of the decade.

Stacy Keach as a true gunman in *Doc* (1971) (courtesy Paul A. Hutton).

Sesame Street #7.19, broadcast on Christmas Day 1975, had a voiceover of Doc Holliday right there with Kermit, the Mad Painter, and Fred the Wonder Horse.³⁸ Frank Oz was the man behind the voice and you can hear it yourself on IMDb.

NOLA Magazine, new to the scene in 1975 but soon a mainstay of the wild west historian, offered an account by someone who had spent research time with, and missed Doc. "Good-bye Old Friend" appeared in 1979, written by Bob Palmquist, one of the more knowledgeable people on Holliday-Earp matters of the time.³⁹

EIGHT

The Ignoble Eighties

The Eighties watched as the Berlin wall came down, the *Challenger* crashed, and Ronald Reagan in the Oval Office played a decisive hand in ending the Cold War. Liberals, nevertheless, have labeled it "the decade of greed" and the "Me Generation." Young people were "walking like Egyptians," while the Rolling Stones were being topped on music charts by newcomers Madonna and Duran Duran. As the major networks lost their monopoly to cable, a melee of soap operas, detective shows, and sitcoms became popular. Soap operas ruled 1980s television with shows like *Dynasty*, *Miami Vice* and *Hart to Hart* big viewing favorites.[1] The Eighties brought a resurgence for Hollywood as a decade of mergers and takeovers boosted studio profits and big star wages.

In a more serious vein, on November 13, 1982, a National Memorial was dedicated which carried the plaque: "Let all know that the United States of America pays tribute to the members of the Armed Forces who served honorably in Southeast Asia during the Vietnam Era." It had been twelve years and six months since the Kent State and other protests against that war.

Literature in the 1980s began with Alford E. Turner's resourceful but questionable *The Earps Talk*.[2] In this work, all three brothers tell their stories in interviews and testimony about the O.K. Corral gunfight. Doc Holliday and Big Nose Kate (Fisher in Turner's version) speak up as well. Leaning toward the melodramatic, Wyatt refers to Doc as "my dear old comrade," and much of his San Francisco interview about Holliday is repeated. Turner, however, goes far beyond anything Wyatt said to the *Examiner*, and includes much of what Masterson and numerous others had since imagined. Its reliability is verified by a Glenn G. Boyer introduction. Boyer himself published *Wyatt Earp* that year using a strange pseudonym.[3]

W.R. Garwood's story *Ringo's Tombstone* has the lead player an innocent, and a secret Ranger to boot. Ike Clanton labels Doc as "meaner than a turpentined coyote." Such flights into fantasy go far to confuse any possibility of truth.[4] The writer harks back to the mistake of Doc's preferring a shotgun, previously addressed. The dentist wears those ever-popular pearl-handled revolvers, but in the end brandishes Wyatt's Buntline special. In a countdown of errors, Doc's gun hand is shattered in the Tucson shooting of Stillwell and he exits on the train. Alford E. Turner edited *The O.K. Corral Inquest* as part of *The Early West* series.[5] Glenn Boyer helped illustrate.

Jack DeMattos annotated and illustrated the chapter on Doc in the *The 75th Anniversary of Famous Gun Fighters of the Western Frontier*.[6] A reprint appeared in a 1984 *Real West*.[7] In 1982 Ben Traywick contributed *A Town Called Tombstone*.[8] "Celluloid Lawman: Wyatt Earp Goes to Hollywood," written by Paul A. Hutton and featured in *American West*, could not fail to include Doc Holliday.[9] Hutton notes the famous friendship between Wyatt and Doc and quotes Paramount Pictures' "The strangest alliance this side of heaven or hell."

Ben T. Traywick, who has spent most of his life in Tombstone, published a first edition of *Tombstone's Deadliest Gun: John Henry Holliday* in 1984.[10] Traywick is well versed on the subject and obviously has a great deal of fun with it. Traywick also published *Tombstone Outlaw Album, The Gunfight at O.K. Corral and Incidents Following*, as well as *Wyatt Earp: The Lion of Tombstone* the same year.[11] *Marshal of Tombstone Virgil Walter Earp* (1984) was another Traywick book.[12]

Outlaws of New Mexico, from Santa Fe's Sundown Press, made much to-do over quite a few of the infamous.[13] "HOLLIDAY, JOHN H. alias DOC, notorious gunman. Once ran a saloon in Las Vegas," however, held few surprises. Traywick's 1985 contributions were *The National Tombstone Epitaph*, and *Marshal of Tombstone Virgil Walter Earp*.[14] Jack De Mattos' "Gunfighters of the Real West" was reprinted in *Real West*.[15] *Western Legend* presented a good overall read the same year.[16]

Jon Tuska's definitive *The American West in Film: Critical Approaches to the Western* examines the fantasies as they play off against actual historical evidence.[17] While taking a look at the structure of western film, the authoritative Tuska considers several greats who have figured prominently in the genre. It is a must for any student of the western or popular culture. During an investigation into narrative, directorship, and the evolution of myth and legend, Doc Holliday is appraised in Chapter 12, along with Wyatt Earp. Tuska suggests the best way to determine the value of any Western is by separating it into three distinct parts: Purpose, Passion, and Perception.

Forty Years on the Wild Frontier contains limited coverage of Doc. It's allegedly based on the diary of co-author Wayne Montgomery's grandfather; the writer genetically traded his own Ohio ancestor for a John Montgomery who really did own the O.K. Corral.[18] The charge of the book being "a huge edifice of pure baloney" stood up in a court of law.

A Dynasty of Western Outlaws by Paul I. Wellman rolled off the presses in 1986.[19] Richard Maxwell Brown's foreword clearly identifies the outlaw as an outstanding figure on the stage of American crime and offers a concise study for the student of badmen in the West. The book's focus is the time period between 1860 and 1930, and primarily deals with Oklahoma, Arkansas, Kansas and Missouri. *Fort Griffin on the Texas Frontier* picked up from his 1956 answers regarding Doc's years there.[20]

Popular and versatile western writer Loren Estleman tackled Doc in *Bloody Season* in 1987.[21] Granted access to many of the most hallowed documents in Cochise County and seizing uniquely upon many traits of the times not previously mentioned, Estleman chose to play off raw courage, political intrigue, and coarseness. He was well aware of the revisionist movement taking place against all prior "heroes" of the west and takes a fair stand between the two. Despite his gripping first words of, "He was dying faster than usual that morning," Doc Holliday fans may not be intrigued unless they, too, are willing to take a new look at the story and the people. The book received both wondrous and horrific reviews. Estleman has since become one of the most prolific and celebrated western writers of our time. He received the Western Writer's of America's Owen Wister Award (Winner for Lifetime Achievement) in 2012.

David Everitt's 1988 *Legends, The Story of Wyatt Earp* did not fail to make mention of the dentist, although its focus was Wyatt.[22] *History of the Discovery of Tombstone Arizona as Told by the Discoverer Edward Lawrence Schieffelin* is probably by Ben Traywick.[23]

The very nature of John Holliday's profession assured him a place in Joseph Rosa and Waldo Coop's *Rowdy Joe Lowe: Gambler with a Gun* (1989). The book, while not about Doc, offers up much information on the life of a gambling man during that time period. *The Lady and Doc Holliday*, a Preston Lewis book, offered a uniquely different approach to the gambling dentist that same year.[24] The only possible lady is Lottie Deno, again fantasized into Holliday's life, but add Kate and a murder to the brew. It was touted as comedic but the Holliday fan will find little amusement. *Equivocation at the O.K. Corral* was also written in 1989 but never intended for publication. It was deposited in the Arizona Historical Society Archives the same year.[25]

As a return to the western hero and legend began to accelerate late in the Eighties, one work added immense insight into how the story would be told in the future, and why. *And Die in the West* tackles the question of murder or self-defense in the Gunfight at the O.K. Corral.[26] Paula Mitchell Marks' tremendous effort to explain the "real complexities of the western frontier experience," while viewing the political, economic, and social conditions surrounding Tombstone, is well done. Noting the town was not unusual in its dilemmas, the work was unquestionably the most thorough to its time. Marks' two strong points are her very well set scenes of the society in which Doc was living, and her careful avoidance of taking sides. It is a well-referenced and indexed volume that does a good job of grasping the soul of the era. Her critics will declare the book a "rehash" while many readers claim it contains much new and insightful information.

It was through movies made for television that America got its few looks at Doc Holliday during this decade. One, a TV mini-series turned into a three-hour video, should not be missed, despite the fact if you blink you will miss the Holliday appearance. *Wild Times* is so filled with familiar faces from western history and its movies that you will feel right at home.[27] Sam Elliott does an excellent job as real-life frontier hero and showman Colonel Hugh Cardiff in this "blood and thunder extravaganza." Ben Johnson, Harry Carey, Jr., Bruce Boxleitner, Cameron Mitchell, Pat Hingle, and L.Q. Jones also turn in excellent performances. Filling out the cast are Timothy Scott, Trish Stewart, Buck Taylor, Geno Sylva, Gene Evans, Sheryl Brown, Russ Cox, Jr., Chuck Hayward, and Eric Sundt. Don Balluck and Brian Garfield wrote the series with Richard Compton directing.

The purpose of Dennis Hopper's cameo appearance as a Doc Holliday out-manned and outdrawn by a fugitive Cardiff is questionable, but not the fact he is Doc Holliday. We must ponder what he was doing in Mexico, as the only other time that is suggested appears in Ford's *My Darling Clementine*, and whoever mentioned Doc as a bounty hunter? Obviously nothing is deemed too dastardly for our John Henry.

To make a case for the action's taking place during the Grant administration, as the storyline goes, it could coincide with the two-year period in which Doc was *in absentia* (from Texas, at least). Holliday's bad press continues in *Wild Times* when he actually fumbles his draw, is shown with an arrow in his back, and appears on a "Wanted Dead or Alive" poster. Hopper's appearance in the role of a falling-down-drunk Doc Holliday was made during Hopper's return as a major Hollywood actor and director after having been deemed its first "drug dropout."

Wild Times, which reviewers considered reminiscent of Louis L'Amour, has survived to delight many late-night western television fans despite a

New York Times movie review almost ignoring Elliott, who indisputably steals the show.[28]

Damon Runyon's Pueblo was a semi-period TV documentary about the famed playwright's early life in the turn-of-the-century West.[29] Raised in Colorado, Runyon became one of the highest paid short story writers of his time. Doc Holliday was played by Tim Abrhamsen, with William Campbell as Bat Masterson. They are the only denizens of the West with whom we are familiar. Eric Austin is cast in the role of Runyon.

Michael O'Herlihy's 1983 telefilm *I Married Wyatt Earp* of course has a Doc Holliday figure.[30] Based on Glenn Boyer's 1976 controversial work, it is allegedly the story of how "a young opera singer from San Francisco" became the wife of Wyatt Earp. Marie Osmond is cast in a screenplay by I.C. Rapoport, which focuses almost entirely on the singing voice of a pretty young girl lacking much of the pizzazz that the real Josephine Marcus possessed. Despite many of the familiar characters making an appearance, not even Bruce Boxleitner as Wyatt has much to say. His brothers, Ron Manning as Virgil and Josef Rainer as Morgan, seem almost tongue-tied. Doc, played by Jeffrey DeMunn, barely gets a word in edgewise. John Bennett Perry gets the role of John Behan, with Charles Benton and John Assalone as Ike and Billy Clanton. Earl W. Smith is cast as Frank Stillwell with Frank and Tom McLaury played by Randy Wells and Joe Corcoran. Sherm Mc-Master is played by Kirk Koskella. The Earp wives are all present and portrayed as if on sewing circle friendships: Allie didn't like any of them and none of them wanted Josephine around. Dee Maaske is cast at Wyatt's Mattie; Allie is played by

Dennis Hopper as a bounty-hunting Doc in *Wild Times* (1980) (courtesy Paul A. Hutton).

Donna Brown, with Linda Rae Jurgens plays the role of Morgan's wife Louisa.

I Married Wyatt Earp is basically a western soap opera and, tossed in between so many truly greats, not a good one at that. It suffered the fate of being made into a musical in the next millennium.

Which leaves Willie Nelson to turn in the most believable Doc of the decade. It's a third attempt at remaking John Ford's classic *Stagecoach* and Willie's Doc is possibly the best thing in it.[31] Reportedly Nelson, when asked to act in the film entrenched with fellow musicians, refused the role of a character named "Joe." When told he could be Doc Holliday, as he is indeed billed, he agreed with alacrity and even became an executive producer. The stage is boarded in Arizona Territory but is headed for Lords-

Willie Nelson was Doc (here with Elizabeth Ashley as Dallas) in *Stagecoach* (1986), the third version of John Ford's 1939 classic (courtesy Paul A. Hutton).

burg, New Mexico. Heavy drinking is the major similarity to be seen to the gambling dentist, and film reviews include words like "sad," "horrendous," and "a waste of money."

Go ahead and see the 1986 *Stagecoach*, throughout which you will keep waiting for Johnny Cash, Waylon Jennings, Kris Kristofferson, and Willie to break into "I'll Be Around." They never do.

But forget your film snobbery, grab a copy of it, *The Outlaw*, that episode of *Star Trek*, an appropriate beverage, and have a good time with your Doc Holliday buddies. Matters get serious from now on.

The Eighties marked the end for TV serial westerns, however, only three remaining from 1959's thirty-two: *The Young Maverick*, *The Chisholms*, and *Bret Maverick*.[32] None featured a John H. Holliday. Just because *Dallas* and *Yellow Rose* were about Texas do not qualify them as westerns.[33]

Actually, the *very* last television appearance of Doc Holliday, in voice only, was another *Sesame Street*.[34] Again with Kermit the Frog and a "Frantic City Gent," Frank Oz did the honors.

In Hollywood, the western, which had been steadily declining since its glory days in the Fifties, staggered back to its feet in 1985 with Clint Eastwood's *Pale Rider*.[35] It finally stood erect again in 1989 with screenwriter John Fusco's *Young Guns*, another favorite still being aired on television, in the video stores, and now on Netflix and Red Box.[36] Hollywood's Eighties will also forever be remembered for its *Indiana Jones*, *Die Hard*, *First Blood*, and *Lethal Weapon* sequels.[37]

For Doc Holliday, Wyatt Earp and the O.K. Corral, however, the best was definitely yet to come.

NINE

The Legendary West at the Turn of the Century

Violence remained a Nineties way of life with the Gulf War, military intervention in Haiti, twenty thousand troops deployed to Bosnia, and air strikes against Kosovo. Nothing emphasized the trauma in our own cities more viciously than the huge death toll when the Alfred P. Murrah Federal Building in Oklahoma City was blown apart by an American citizen. There was also rioting in Los Angeles, the bombing of the World Trade Center, at least fourteen incidents of high school shootings, and the Branch Davidian horror in Waco. Americans sat glued to their televisions watching their football idol, O.J. Simpson, go on trial for the murder of his ex-wife. Despite a booming economy and debated (but unresolved) reforms in health care, Social Security, and gun control, literature, media, and film reported the major theme of the nation: death.

The Old West was right at home. Both it and Doc Holliday held their own.

The Nineties, however, was also the electronic age. The World Wide Web began in 1992, and within two years three million Americans were online spending their money, communicating, and discussing the controversy of the boys in Arizona. As the Internet gave the home researcher new horizons, thwarted western writers crawled out of the woodwork. Never before, and perhaps never again, has so much misbegotten lore been written, nor with such a plethora of errors. Amazingly, by the end of the decade, expanded excursions into the truth had sorted out much of the previous one hundred–plus years of myth, with the Wild West emerging just as wild, yet bearing an altered cast and hue.

To make your own determination of what search engines have made of the West's infamous gambling dentist, it is suggested that you seek out the multitude of published articles and ascertain the truth or error of their ways. The entire Tombstone entourage did, however, become a great favorite among the writers of the age. A Link to Tombstone History Archives contains copies of much published-elsewhere material.[1]

Richard Brown's *No Duty to Retreat* (1990) cast western heroes in a decidedly different light.[2] The author took a critical look at violence and values in American history and society. Brown points to the interesting American-only phenomenon of shooting first and asking questions later, a direct contradiction to human conflict in earlier history, when a man's honor demanded his back be to the wall before his sword was drawn. The author makes extensive reference to both the Magna Carta and "the common man" who, in European history prior to the nineteenth century, had few rights under the law. Although Brown does not raise the issue, it could be suggested that just such a lack of self-defense in their homelands might have accounted for the new attitude in America. It would then follow with the author's premise that guns, as opposed to hand-to-hand conflict, might have rendered running even less of an option. Several judicial rulings deemed it downright cowardice to flee, although political and ideological concepts have faded over the years. Ben Traywick made his first contribution of the decade the same year, with *The Chronicles of Tombstone to a Lady Called Red Marie*.[3]

It is not surprising that Doc's early literary appearance published prior to the two great films of the decade, was in a tale of Fort Worth, Texas, *Hell's Half Acre: Life and Legend of a Red Light District*.[4] Richard F. Selcer's book concerns primarily the topic as stated, but does not fail to note "the acre attracted such well-known knaves [as] Doc Holliday."

The Truth About Wyatt Earp, a result of extensive research by retired criminal defense attorney Richard E. Erwin, was published in 1992.[5] Using archival, museum, court, and newspaper records, the author inquires into several rarely addressed incidents. Although root causes of the street fight have been rehashed fore and aft, Erwin takes a rare look at the arrest of the seldom-mentioned Shanghai Pearce, and gives some attention to Earp's days in Dodge City. Despite little focus on Holliday, the book is a good read of how things played out for both the gamblers, and was something of a pacesetter at the time. Addressing a time of which little had been previously known is *The Frontier World of Fort Griffin....*[6] While not about Doc, it gives a clear picture of where Doc spent much of his time before heading further west.

Richard Slotkin's *Gunfighter Nation* is a classic textbook for any student of the western myth.[7] The author declares it "a cultural history showing the connection of material and political processes of social existence with imaginative projection, symbol-making and interpretation." Slotkin feels the concept of myth a major contribution to the process of ideology, and to how society explains history. The author points to the frontier myth as encompassing the basic elements of regression, separation, conflict, and violence. Chapter 12 suggests that "progress" might be an often-used excuse of mere survival. "The Cult of the Gunfighter" talks about a "renaissance" Western that provided two story forms evolving between 1950 and 1953. Addressing the problem of social justice, and its balance between the individual citizen and the law, the work cites how films like *My Darling Clementine* offered a progressive answer in the form of a town tamer. *Gunfighter Nation* goes on to show how the hero's character is sacrificed, as violence begins to dominate. Slotkin's offering is an academic read, but offers insightful thinking into how and why our western films have changed from the days of yesteryear.

Doc Holliday reappeared in 1992's *Western Lawmen: The High Sheriffs of New Mexico and Arizona*. This look at law and lawmen in the southwest is by one of its more research-oriented writers.[8] Larry Ball's narrative is a definitive explanation of lawman terminology, and is a well-told story of the forty-seventh and forty-eighth states, containing pertinent facts of many well-known western characters. A sequel to Ben Traywick's *Chronicles of Tombstone* looked at some of Southwest Arizona's legendary characters and was also published that year.[9]

Unforgiven, a film directed by and starring Clint Eastwood, paved the way for a 1990s rebirth of the western movie.[10] It led to a dramatic change in the content and nature of all westerns, certainly Tombstone-related literature and film forever after. It was impacted by later stunning scenarios of the films *Tombstone* and *Wyatt Earp*; the three films so dramatically altered the viewpoint and accelerated the number of publications as to demand the story be henceforth studied from a different point of view.[11] With this in mind, let us then proceed with the rogues' gallery of literature that followed in hot pursuit.

Three books, possibly already in progress, came out in 1993, the same year as *Tombstone*, the movie. Ben Traywick's *Hell's Belles of Tombstone* and *Legendary Characters of the Southwest* led the lineup. He collaborated in 1993 with Glenn Boyer on *Wyatt Earp's Tombstone Vendetta*.[12] The Earp book, with a Doc presence, was viewed by some as a narrative of the ongoing feud between various factions of Earp history, as much as the Tombstone story itself. Both writers remain popular, and continue to have a wide audience.

The fourth J.R. Roberts novel in his Gunsmith series was entitled *Trouble in Tombstone*.[13] In a Texas border town, ex-gunfighter Dallas

Stoudemire relies on Wyatt Earp and Doc Holliday to protect his interests from "the Wild West's most notorious killers." "Wyatt did admittedly not write My Friend Doc Holliday," as the author states up front.[14] It remains an enchanting and different slant on the friendship between Doc and the Earps.

Don Cusic published what is termed *An A–Z Guide from the Chisholm Trail to the Silver Screen* in 1994.[15] Both Doc and Big Nosed Kate get a mention, but the book makes an erroneous statement that Doc "left" home in 1867–68. Were this true, his biographers would be left with yet another mystery timeframe. The fact is he was still but a teenager. Cusic's account of Doc's travels is woefully out of sync. Virgil Earp was Don Chaput's focus that same year in *The Earp Papers: In a Brother's* Image.[16] He quotes Ike on Doc's abuse of him, shows the picture now questioned as actually being Doc, but writes accurately concerning the shooting of Frank McLaury by Doc and Morgan near the end of the gunfight. With ample footnotes and several well-placed references, this is a good read.

Two 1994 books devoted specifically to John H. Holliday were written by Sylvia Lynch and Emma Walling. Lynch's *Aristocracy's Outlaw*, while spending some time on the speculated relationship with his cousin Martha Anne (Mattie) Holliday, still relates the story of a determined man striving to play out the hand life had dealt him.[17] Two truths are that the two maintained a close friendship that lasted until his death, and that she kept one of his graduation photos throughout her life. So scandalized was the family at Sister Mary Melanie's image being tarnished, they burned all his letters kept by the cousin. This left historians utterly bereft of facts in the matter. Mattie did not, however, join a convent until after the street fight in Tombstone, certainly not when they were young. *Doc's Colorado Trials and Triumphs*, by Emma Walling, is a collection of thirty-one retyped newspaper articles from 1882 through 1887.[18] While the bulk of Walling's work deals with Doc's post–Tombstone adventures, she uses myth, opinion, and downright fabrication to tie her newspaper clippings into a delightful read describing his tribulations and vindication in Colorado.

Tombstone's own Ben Traywick contributed three new works in 1994, the first being *The Chronicles of Tombstone, Historical Documents* and *Photographs of Tombstone*, joined by *Tombstone Clippings*.[19] Traywick's third was a second edition of *The Chronicle of Tombstone*.[20] Glenn G. Boyer added *Wyatt Earp's Tombstone Vendetta* in large print that year.[21] *The Gunfight at O.K. Corral and Incidents Following* was published as a paperback by Paul Beck.[22] The Department of Archives that same year published its second edition of *A Guide to Public Records in the Arizona State Archives*.[23] The book is well indexed and valuable to any serious researcher.

For fun and entertainment, pick up Bob Boze Bell's *The Illustrated Life and Times of Doc Holliday*.[24] Bell uses some original photographs, together with maps and much of his own colorful art for this unique approach to our favorite gambling dentist.

Books were precious few during the middle of the decade. *The Loser's View of the O.K. Corral*, co-authored by Gene Autry, was one of several mass-market paperbacks appearing in a Wild West series.[25] *Doc Holliday's Woman* by Jane Candia Coleman is yet another version of Doc's love life, in an alleged telling by Kate.[26] Doc is almost a person aside in this publication, with emphasis placed more on the female figure than the gambler himself. Coleman uses a great deal of material found in Kate's 1930 writings. Doc Holliday made a 1995 appearance in the series of children's books *Outlaws and Lawmen of the Wild West*.[27] H. Sheffer's *Gunfight at the O.K. Corral* also appeared that year.[28]

Nineteen ninety-six continued a good year for Doc with the long-awaited publication of George Whitwell Parson's private journal.[29] Although little is known of Parson's previous life, his journal revealed his own private insights into the people and incidents of Tombstone during the seven years he spent there. If a definitive work on Tombstone and Cochise County exists, Parson's journal is it. The brief time Doc Holliday spent there, however, is but a punctuation mark in the fifty years of Arizona history edited by Carl Chafin.

The Killing Season and *The Autumn of the Gun*, also published in 1996, are volumes Two and Three in Ralph Compton's trilogy of vengeance.[30] Nathan Stone, the hero, seems to encounter every outlaw and gunman in the West, while engaging in every major event. The author's announcement in *Killing Season* that Doc Holliday felled Mike Gordon with one shot is wildly imaginative, but does not deter from the narrative's painting Doc as a legend of death. Volume Three is accurate when including Doc as a participant in four major gunfights between 1880 and 1884. Any conflict arises with what one terms "major." *Mix-Up at the O.K. Corral*, by Preston Lewis, is fun whether you like westerns or not, although a sense of humor is definitely recommended.[31] The author lays the Benson Stage squarely on Doc Holliday and has very little good to say about Kate. One of three invented "memoirs of H.H. Lomax," *Mix-Up* is an excellent parody of famous outlaws. Leon Metz, with scholarly authority and a storyteller's passion, included Doc Holliday in 1996's *The Shooters*, an account of many famous gunfighters.[32]

Ben Traywick made two further original contributions with his *John Henry (The "Doc" Holliday Story)*, much of which was covered on *American West* Internet pages.[33] Traywick's *The Clantons of Tombstone* could not have passed muster without mention of Doc.³⁴ This site should be accessed for other topics of interest. *OK Corral Gunfight Symposium*, consisting of two audiotapes, gave a different approach to telling the story. This new educational tool held rather confusing authorship.³⁵

Casey Tefertiller's definitive *Wyatt Earp, The Life Behind the Legend* was the biggest and most vital news in 1997.³⁶ The author acknowledges many sources and people who aided in what Gary L. Roberts, noted western and Doc Holliday historian, has termed, "the first really serious documented biography of Wyatt Earp to be published." It contains a good bit of Holliday information, but essentially stays faithful to its subject. *The Life Behind the Legend* is a must for any student of the U.S. West who wants the facts, and well-written. It would be nine years before Doc Holliday got "equal time." Tefertiller is among the first to record Doc and Wyatt's last meeting at Denver's Windsor Hotel in late 1885 or early 1886.³⁷ The author comments early on, "No one really quite knew what to make of Doc Holliday."³⁸ True, but still we try.

Doc Holliday from Matt Braun's Gunfighter Chronicles series contained coverage of the gambling dentist.³⁹ Braun is very popular in the UK for "faction" westerns, or novelized history, usually attractive reading with some historic accuracy. Bruan has been accused of sounding too much like his own earlier *Tombstone*, as well as the film of the same title. Braun's book portrays Holliday as a man of dignity and pride who tolerated insults from no one. With Doc, the author falls prey to many misconceptions which had been proven incorrect by the time the book was published. Doc comes off as a man determined to survive against all odds. He is called a man who spoke softly and carried a lightning gun, certainly a succinct relation to the Doc Holliday America had come to recognize in recent years.

John Clum's autobiography made it to the presses in 1997, told in the subject's own words and edited by Neil B. Carmony.⁴⁰ *Apache Days and Tombstone Nights* chronicles the Indian agent–entrepreneur's life, while telling a story of the old Southwest from Geronimo to Los Angeles. Generally portrayed as an older man, Clum was one month older than Doc. He was a pallbearer at Wyatt Earp's funeral. Doc was encompassed with the Earps by Clum's friendship while he was editor of the *Tombstone Epitaph*. *Western Gunslingers in Fact and on Film: Hollywood's Famous Lawmen and Outlaws*, Buck Rainey's contribution in 1997, needs a look.⁴¹ *A Texas Frontier: The Clear Fork Country and Fort Griffin, 1849–1887* goes further in giving the advocates of Doc a better image of his haunts after Dallas.⁴² The author makes a terrible *faux pas* in saying that Doc and all the Earps left Arizona for good when the arrest warrants were issued for the street fight killings. Doubtless Virgil and Morgan may have wished they had.

Glenn G. Boyer added three more Earp tales in 1997, *Those Marryin' Earp Men, Suppressed Murder of Wyatt Earp,* and *Trailing an American Myth.*[43] The latter was a new edition of the author's 1967 release containing extensive genealogy and photographic "finds" of Wyatt Earp and his family. In the six volumes comprising *Wyatt Earp, Family, Friends and Foes,* Boyer offers up a series of events in Cochise County that includes Morgan Earp, Big Nose Kate, John Behan, Curley Bill Brocious, and John Ringo.[44] *Outlaws and Lawmen of the Wild West,* a 1997 slick packed with pictures and many tidbits of information, included Doc, this time between Virgil Earp and Newman Haynes "Old Man" Clanton.[45] Compiled from data in several state archives, the publication had little new to say about Doc, but did declare Kate his "only love interest." The authors make him the victim of vigilante justice over the murder of Ed Bailey in Fort Griffin, Texas.

Doc Holliday: A Family Portrait (1998) is exactly as advertised.[46] The author, Karen Holliday Tanner, is a family member who utilizes never-before-seen photographs, together with a succession of real Holliday and McKey history. Tanner gives an entirely new and interesting slant on the man previously portrayed from only one point of view. No genealogist with a Doc Holliday leaning should miss it. TV honored the bulk of her new material on Doc in a twenty-first century documentary.

The Fourth Horseman by Randy Lee Eickhoff takes a blue ribbon for the best-ever title for a Doc Holliday book.[47] A great deal of dialogue is taken from the *Tombstone* film. Several other books that year were devoted to Wyatt Earp, but all contained mention of John Henry. Allen Barra's *Inventing Wyatt Earp* is something of a mythic extension of the previous years life of the lawman.[48] Although the book begins with Barra's termed "odyssey," he offers some new perspective on how the legend grew. *Outlaws and Gunfighters of the Old West* is by Phillip W. Steele,[49] who has written extensively on the Civil War and other notables of the west, including Jesse James and Belle and Pearl Starr. The *Gunfighter* edition is complete with an audiocassette in collaboration with country western musician John D. Levan.

Wyatt Earp Speaks! is yet another account alleged as written by the lawman himself "with contributing author Bat Masterson and real interviews with Doc Holliday."[50] Editor-compiler John Richard Stephens uses this means of utilizing the abbreviated bibliographic material and declares his hope to further clarify the facts. The book is dedicated to the memory of Doc Holliday. With over seventy illustrations and pictures, plus an index, it should not be overlooked as a serious effort, despite several contradictions to the Tefertiller book. *Wyatt's Woman: She Married Wyatt Earp: The Life and Times of Josephine Sarah Marcus* discloses yet another attempt at touting the voice as the real author.⁵¹ Earl Chafin wrote the manuscript and in Chapter 13 repeats the story of the couple's having met up with a dying Doc in Denver. Knowing that none of the Earp woman had a kind word to say for the dentist, it is difficult to imagine that Josie found one. Read carefully, it appears still another contrivance to glorify her husband. Ben Traywick published *Wyatt Earp's 13 Dead Men* in 1998.⁵² Buck Rainey's *Western Gunslingers in Fact and on Film* makes several mentions of Doc.⁵³

Larger volumes evidently having temporarily exhausted the topic, little else in the way of books appeared in 1998. Kathleen Chamberlain published a collection of Richard W. Etulain's papers, *Wild Westerners*.⁵⁴ This source continues to prove invaluable.

Roy Young's *Cochise County Cowboy War* contains much more material of interest than the title suggests.⁵⁵ The compiler includes place names, a chronology, and a bibliography of Earp–Cochise County era sources. *Tombstone Paper Trails*, edited by Ben T. Traywick, was also published in gratitude to the many people who had contributed to Tombstone research over the years.⁵⁶ Alfred H. Lewis uses Bat Masterson to tell essentially the same story he had in 1907 when editing *Gunfighters of the Western Frontier: A Memoir of the Old West*.⁵⁷

As the clock ticked off the last year of the century, Richard Etulain and Glenda Riley's *With Badges and Bullets* proved just how thin the line between lawman and outlaw could be.⁵⁸ Chapter Five is dedicated to Doc, with Wyatt and a host of other well-known men of the times coming to life in these fascinating stories. Etulain and Riley, devotees of truth, take out much of the myth behind many western legends, leaving a remarkably lucid, while still extremely readable, volume of mini-biographies.

Street Fight in Tombstone by Michael M. Hickey was also published that year. Complemented by beautiful paintings, illustrations, interesting maps, and a guide to "the language of the gunfighter," it adds a new look at the Old West.⁵⁹ It finally got the location right while referring to Doc's "homicidal work." Hickey's book contains several references to Holliday, and in some cases corrects prior published errors. He still makes the mistake of saying Doc fired first with his "nickel-plated revolvers" while hiding Virgil's Greener shotgun under his coat, quite a feat if it had been accomplished. The primary drawback to the work is the absence of an index.

Journal and magazines joined with book publishers in making great note of the gambling dentist. Although Doc Holliday, true to character, suffered by the Nineties' confusion, he was also blessed by its perplexity. A 1990 article by J.R. Kirkpatrick discussed his "missing grave."⁶⁰

One article published by *The NOLA Magazine* almost simultaneously

NINE : *The Legendary West at the Turn of the Century* 131

with the premiere of the movie *Tombstone* addressed, "Doc's trusty shotgun."[61] The weapon in question, a street howitzer, was allegedly given to Father Downey, the Catholic priest in Glenwood Springs, by Doc in 1886, just shortly before his death. The piece loses impact with an opening reminiscent of Bat Masterson and very early-day Holliday reporting. Chuck Parsons discussed Doc's statistics, profession, and grave in *True West*'s January, February, and June, 1993, issues.[62]

Two articles in *True West* and one in *Wild West* carried the journalistic load for 1994.[63] The latter chose to take the "deadly dentist" approach. The third piece, Glenn Boyer's "Tombstone's Helen of Troy" (July), suggests Doc was a possible marriage prospect for husband-hunting Josephine Marcus.[64] While "Josie" did not need a rich man, she very likely considered health a major factor. Boyer wisely gives Holliday credit for being more sophisticated and better educated than his friend. Toward the end of the year, *NOLA* featured Jeff Morey's reply to the perplexed Earp buff's lament of, "All the lies about Wyatt Earp are true!"[65]

No less than six tomes appeared that year in exaltation of either Doc Holliday or western figures in general, including some new reference material. Leo Banks' article about Wyatt, featured in the July 1994 *Arizona Highways*, should be read.[66] It is a little-known pacesetter in dealing with Wyatt and Doc in Hollywood, questioning the veracity of several photographs, and generally looking at a lot of questions not heretofore approached and certainly unanswered. Terry "Ike" Clanton added something new on the scene with an audiocassette entitled "Wyatt Earp Murdered My Cousin."[67]

For the best article of the decade on the O.K. Corral in film, read Paul A. Hutton's "Showdown at the Hollywood Corral" in *Montana, the Magazine of Western History*.[68] Although subtitled "Wyatt Earp and the Movies," with scant attention paid to Doc Holliday, it is as good a Bible to both Wyatt and Doc in the cinema as you could want. The article is complete with pictures and told in a professional, picturesque fashion.

Numerous newspaper and magazine articles appeared that same year with Randy Lee Eickhoff's "A Young Doc Holliday" beginning the parade.[69] This piece appeared in the March *True West* and every sentimental Southerner will enjoy it. The October *Wild West* featured Dana Shull's "The Losers View of the O.K. Corral," covering the McLaurys, Clantons, and much Tombstone lore of the time.[70] *True West* added notations by Eickhoff and Chuck Parsons in June and October of 1995.[71]

Only two articles have been unearthed for 1996. *The Arizona Republic Life* in March asked, "Did loan play role at O.K. Corral?" and concerned a record of Ike Clanton and Johnny Behan having co-signed on a $500 loan.[72] More expert witnesses would discuss this matter at greater length in the next century. Chuck Parsons addressed "Doc Holliday's Life" in his column that October.[73]

Nineteen ninety-seven was something of a banner year for Holiday article writing, with nine sprinkled throughout by some new and some familiar writers. Ben Traywick, Victoria Wilcox and an interesting medical approach by Dr. Sylvia Wittels appeared in the April *True West*, which was a Doc Holliday special.[74] This issue contained Rick Cartilage's "Doc Holliday and the Whipet Gun."[75] Randy Smith that summer addressed Wyatt and Doc as "The Stuff of Legends."[76] The remaining four pieces of the year began with P.A. Mallory's tale addressing matters in Dodge City.[77] That summer Robert F. Palmquist wrote on the "Careers of Bob Winders, Charley Smith and Fred Dodge, 1879–1888."[78] Paul Cool also contributed a great find in clearing up the spelling of Sherman McMaster (not McMasters).[79] A most impressive and informative article is Gary L. Roberts' "Trailing An American Mythmaker" which appeared in the Spring 1998 *NOLA Magazine*, and was reprinted in booklet form.[80] A column of Old West memories appeared in *The Sunday Oklahoman*.[81]

In *True West* and in *Old West*, Chuck Hornung wrote of Wyatt and Doc's New Mexico adventures while Karen Holliday Tanner's "Vision of a Legend" appeared in *NOLA*'s September issue.[82] Gary L. Roberts' "The Real Tombstone Travesty" in the Fall *WOLA Journal* wound down the year, almost.[83] New-to-the-scene Australian Peter Brand discussed Sherman W. McMaster(s) in the winter *WOLA Journal*.[84]

On December 9, 1999, *The Arizona Daily Star* published a piece stating the University of Arizona was contemplating cutting ties with one of their top-selling books, *I Married Wyatt Earp*.[85] The reason given was "conflicting statements from the author."

Television in the Nineties did not ignore Doc or any other gunslinger, good or bad. A&E, early in the decade, attempted a change from the previously over-romanticized picture of the West, with a guideline of official documents, journals, and documents. *Real West*, hosted by Kenny Rogers, was eventually shifted to the History Channel and is now available on DVD.[86] Never an effort at historical accuracy, *Real West* did feature commentaries by leaders in the profession to bring its accounts into perspective. In whole, and in bits and pieces scattered throughout other documentaries, it remains popular today, proving again the myth of the west still fascinates America.

"The Ten Most Wanted Outlaws," its fourth segment, included John H. (Doc) Holliday, whose advert placed him with Jesse James and Billy the Kid "on the fringe of society." It was documented primarily by Paul A. Hutton who commented that Doc had come west for his health which was "bad for everybody else's health because he had a bad attitude" and "seemed to court death." Howard Bryan's words were more stinging when mentioning Holliday's time in Las Vegas, New Mexico.[87] "People considered him a shiftless character who was not above robbing coaches or even stealing sheep." This is almost a direct quote from the July 1881 *Las Vegas* (New Mexico) *Daily Optic*.[88]

Gunfighters of the West, a special five-part documentary series, brought several pivotal, legendary gunmen of the Wild West to the fore.[89] It was narrated by Brian Dennehy and aired originally on the Learning Channel; Doc and the Tombstone story appeared in May 1998. These tapes are interesting, but difficult to locate.

Legends of the Wild West, as it was also called, presented the new approach of having commentators tell both sides of the story. Different viewpoints was not general knowledge at the time but the screenwriters did a masterful job of relating them both without actually coming to blows, at least not on film. Words did get a little edgy. Both anti–Earp and anti–Holliday factions were on hand, as well as strong advocates of those generally considered the losers. With a surprisingly new and good cast seemingly unworthy of mention for their roles, both sides presented new and insightful information to the audience. Doc is named early on as a gunfighter who "tried to pick a fight with Ike Clanton." He is affirmed "a dentist by trade, a gambler and gunman by conviction." The militaristic term "ally" is thrown around declaring that Doc was "seen riding away" (but not from where) on the day of the Benson Stage robbery. He is once again declared "a man few cared to know," something Holliday's later life and legend would prove to be at odds with. There are also at least two alleged pictures of Doc, which are not him. Other mistakes encroached.

Jeff Morey, Holliday aficionado, comments that Wyatt enjoyed Doc's sense of humor but "to the rest of the world his only redeeming grace was that he would soon be dead." Frederick Nolan, author and decidedly an anti–Earp and anti–Holliday historian, had refuted Morey's claim the story was not a black-and-white picture. Nolan claimed the Earps (and Doc by association) used the cowboys as a vehicle to make them look good. His slur that Holliday "did not give a damn about any man alive or dead" accompanies further defamation that "Doc concealed" a ten-gauge shotgun. The filming of the cane-shotgun exchange almost bears this out, however, but with no explanation as to the gambler's unusual behavior. Doc was pretty much a "what you see is what you get" kind of man. Another filming error shows Doc first firing with a revolver, then the shotgun.

The narrator's ending comment that Doc, among others, was dead within two years was way off. Doc died in November 1887, more than six pain-wracked years later. The greatest truism spoken may well have been, "There were no real winners." Questionable if you care to exclude over a century of fame and controversy, for which many may have yearned. It is doubtful that Doc Holliday did.

Which brings us to possibly Hollywood's finest hour where Doc Holliday (and, indeed, all the famed of Tombstone) is concerned.

As the Twentieth Century accelerated to its inevitable end, Hollywood paid little tribute to the Tombstone crowd, in general or specifically. It remained an occasional reference in some network effort to revive the western as a genre. In the early Nineties, however, two true epics based on the Holliday and Earp legends appeared and can be likened to the resurrection of the golden years of Hollywood westerns. They are of course *Tombstone* and *Wyatt Earp*.[90]

Tombstone (1993), the more popular and lasting of the two, presents the most authentic cinematic Doc Holliday characterization ever, and was the catalyst for this book. Experts consider Kevin Jarre's screenplay more faithful to history than the film, which remains the most accurate ever. Jarre also directed the scenes with Charlton Heston, without credit." He was originally signed as director but was fired and replaced by George P. Cosmatos. The plot further thickens when, after Cosmatos' death in 2005, Kurt Russell claimed *he* actually directed the film, but agreed to give the seasoned veteran the credit during his lifetime. Some of Cosmatos' direction has been likened to John Ford's, a high accolade indeed. His career began as assistant director to Otto Preminger on *Exodus*; his only other popular movie was *Rambo: First Blood Part II*.

Tombstone featured a voice-over by popular Robert Mitchum, with an all-star cast including Kurt Russell as Wyatt, Val Kilmer as Doc, Sam Elliott as Virgil, and Charlton Heston as rancher Henry Hooker. Bill Paxton got the Morgan Earp role. Excellent casting played an overall role in its success with Harry Carey, Jr., appearing as City Marshal Fred White, in honor of his father's having played in the first O.K. Corral film *Law and Order*.[91] Also featured are Michael Hooker as Sherman McMaster, Peter Sherayko as Texas Jack Vermillion, Buck Taylor as Turkey Creek Jack Jackson, and Jason Priestly as Billy Breckenridge. More familiar characters appearing are John Behan played by Jon Tenney and editor and mayor John Clum played by Terry O'Quinn.

Powers Booth presents the coldest and most authentic Curly Bill Brocious yet to be seen. The Clanton brothers are cut short with only Ike and Billy in sight, played by Stephen Lang and Thomas Hayden Church. John Philbin and Robert John Burn fill the roles of Tom and Frank McLaury, with the surname at last spelled correctly. Michael Biehn does an excellent

NINE : *The Legendary West at the Turn of the Century*   135

Wyatt (left, Kurt Russell) and Doc (right, Val Kilmer) standing over Johnny Ringo (Michael Biehn) in *Tombstone* (1993) (courtesy of Michael F. Blake).

job as Doc's nemesis, Johnny Ringo. Billy Bob Thornton and Frank Stallone play Johnny Tyler and Ed Bailey, who get the worst of it from Doc and Wyatt.

Dana Delany is as feisty a Josephine Sadie Marcus Earp as has yet flickered across the screen, with Joanna Pacula in the role of Doc's infamous Kate. Dana Wheeler-Nicholson is cast as Mattie, Wyatt's ill-fated partner upon arrival in Tombstone. The roles of Virgil's wife Allie and Morgan's wife Louisa are given to Paula Malcomson and Lisa Collins.

Val Kilmer accentuates Doc Holliday's deadliness with a suave, dissolute charm with his proverbial hot temper muted ever so slightly through a pallid sheen, bloody cough, and red-rimmed eyes. Steady gambling and hard drink in no way compromise Doc's loyalty to Wyatt Earp. Nor does Holliday's steadfastness deter from Kilmer's depiction of a nervy, Southern gunfighter. True to the code of the west, Doc knows his time is undoubtedly up when he tells Earp, "I don't want to play [poker] any more." Several film critics have called Kilmer's character the finest Hollywood Holliday to date and an effort was made to have him nominated for Best Supporting Actor that year. His lines from the film can still be heard in almost any Holliday aficionado gathering.

Advertisement for Val Kilmer's nomination for Best Supporting Actor for his portrayal of Doc in *Tombstone* (1993) (author's collection).

Wyatt Earp (released in 1994), one of nine films directed by Lawrence Kasdan, was more a life story than an incident in time. Optimistically, Wyatt's real life was more exciting than

Kasdan and Dan Gordon's script portrayed him, although it bordered on almost as long.

Kevin Costner is cast in the starring role, and Dennis Quaid lost 43 pounds to portray a rail-thin Holliday. Gene Hackman portrays Nicholas Earp, a real-life half-brother not appearing elsewhere in filmdom, together with Virgil and Morgan (Michael Madsen and Linden Ashby). Warren finally makes an appearance, played by Jim Caviezel. James Earp, playing more of a role than the real one did in the O.K. Corral incident, is portrayed by David Andrews. Joanna Going appears in the role of Josie Marcus, with Mare Winningham as Wyatt's first "wife" Mattie Blaylock. Isabelle Rossellini, daughter of the fabulous Ingrid Bergman, gets the part of Big Nose Kate. JoBeth Williams is Jim's Bessie, with stepdaughter Sally played by Tea Leoni, leaving Catherine O'Hara and Alison Elliott to appear as Virgil and Morgan's wives. Bill Pullman and Tom Sizemore caught the roles of Ed and Bat Masterson. Other friends of the Lawman crowd include Todd Allen as Sherm McMaster, Adam Taylor as Texas Jack, and Rusty Hendrickson as Turkey Creek Jack. The role of Mayor John Clum went to Randall Mell with questionable Sheriff John Behan played by Marc Harmon (who went on to star in the *NCIS* TV series). Boots Southerland plays Marshal Fred White and John Lawlor portrays Judge Spicer.

Screenwriter Dan Gordon allows but two Clantons, Ike and Billy, with the parts given to Jeff Fahey and Adrian Golsey. Frank and Tom McLaury's roles go to Rex Linn and Adam Baldwin. Also featured: Lewis Smith as Curly Bill Brocious, John Dennis Johnson as Frank Stillwell, Kirk Fox as Pete Spence, Norman Howell as Johnny Ringo, Kris Kamm as Billy Breckenridge, and Scotty Augare as Indian Charlie.

Vulgar and violent, Quaid's Holliday re-established everything evil his mythic character has come to represent. Doc is uncouth, profane, and deadly, but he delivers his much-used killer lines with such aplomb as to almost mesmerize the audience. Employing a powerful, ruthless image of the deadly dentist, this picture about the life of Earp would have been deadly boring without the dramatic Holliday character. Although characterized by some as "misunderstood," Quaid's portrayal did not set well with many of Doc's proponents, and simply could not stand up to the superb performance turned in by Kilmer the previous year.

In 1994, Hugh O'Brian, Bruce Leitner, and Paul Brinegar appeared in a movie written by Daniel P. Ullman and Rob Word, *Wyatt Earp: Return to Tombstone*.[92] The independent film used new shots combined with many colorized clips from the old *Life and Times of Wyatt Earp* TV episodes. Hugh O'Brian still plays the marshal, who returns to his old haunts. No gunplay is featured, however, as he visits old friends, teaches some bad guys a few tricks still up his sleeve, and tells some new stories of his early days. Douglas Fowley ("Doc Fabrique") remains at Wyatt's right hand but only in flashback scenes, as do Virgil and Morgan played by John Anderson and Ray Boyle. Ike, Billy and Old Man Clanton also appear in old clips. The only fresh faces are characters unfamiliar to the saga: Bruce Boxleitner

Dennis Quaid as a rail thin and deadly Doc in *Wyatt Earp* (1994) (courtesy of Michael F. Blake).

as Sam, the Cochise County sheriff, Jim Brinegar as Jim "Dog" Kelly, Harry Carey, Jr., as Digger Phelps, Bo Hopkins as Rattlesnake Reynolds, Alex Hyde-White as Woodworth Clum, Marvin Kove as Ed Ross, and Don Meredith as Clay *et al.*

Interestingly, *Tombstone* and *Wyatt Earp* were not the first in which the Doc Holliday character stole the show. Preston Foster certainly cut a charming figure in *The Arizonian*, and there are proponents who favor Kirk Douglas' Holliday over Burt Lancaster's Earp in *Gunfight at the O.K. Corral*. No one is going to come right out and say Henry Fonda or James Garner could be outdone on the screen in their efforts as the lawman, but Arthur Kennedy was certainly a more jovial Doc in *Cheyenne Autumn*. Stacy Keach without a doubt took the accolades from Harris Yulin in *Doc*. It would be interesting to see what Dennis Hopper would have made of his *Wild Times* Doc if he had been expanded, but it's almost impossible to outshine Sam Elliott. Of course, that roan pony in *The Outlaw* did a great job. (But is it factually a roan? That film is black and white.)

Although the decision is up to you, it has been said that Kilmer's Doc Holliday was "a man for every man, and for every women who was glad of it."

In 1999 TNT came out with the made-for-television *Purgatory*, in which Holliday and numerous other bad guys of the West are earthbound in a mystic town.[93] Randy Quaid appears as Doc in this effort, where everybody is given a second chance at redemption if virtue and honor can triumph over their more human frailties. Doc comes off well in *Purgatory*. The last Doc Holliday film of the century still asks the question, good man or bad man?

These varied, shifting images of Doc Holliday during the Twentieth Century confirm the observation that historical accounts, as always, are seriously compromised when so little is known and so much surmised about a person. In this case, the creative imaginations of authors, screenwriters and viewers have utilized the few known facts of Doc Holliday's life to fashion them into a fabulous frontier legend. Undoubtedly, Doc was a killer, gambler, consumptive, and friend. Yet each generation, although generally choosing to cast him in a negative light, tolerates glimmers of good, with shifting climates of political and social opinion playing a major part in the shaping of his diverse image.

As the world teetered on the brink of a new millennium, so did Doc Holliday's reputation.

TEN

Doc Holliday in the New Millennium

The 21st century dawned, the first year declared "International Year for the Culture of Peace." The biggest business merger in history made news when AOL purchased Time Warner. Florida abolished death by the electric chair, as matters of social justice became familiar topics. *Cast Away* was the top box office draw with *The Sopranos* grabbing the award for best television drama.[1] Music was still going country with classical making an unsuccessful bid for baby boomers. The British Parliament was taking steps to forever undermine centuries of citizen-government relations. Seventeen United States Naval personnel were killed when Yemeni terrorists attacked the destroyer USS *Cole*, stating clearly that hope for peace was seriously exaggerated.

O.K., The Corral, The Earps and Doc Holliday, by novelist Paul West, was published the first year of the new millennium.[2] The novel turns early to Wyatt's first interview with *The San Francisco Examiner*, using his 1896 words to introduce Doc as a philosopher.[3] West proceeds to place a great deal of importance on Doc's "love affair" with his cousin, by then Sister Mary Melanie of the Savannah, Georgia, Sisters of Mercy convent.[4] Since the letters were destroyed and that time was but a flash in the overall life of Doc, it renders the book somewhat fanciful, as does his speaking for Doc in the first person. West's toying with the facts leaves much to the reader's evaluation.

An anonymous writer, not likely Wyatt, published *Wyatt Earp Tells of the Gunfight Near the O.K. Corral* in 2000.[5] Richard Churchill's book on Masterson's, Wyatt's and Doc's *Colorado Careers* was reprinted in 2001.[6] Bruce Olds published *Bucking the Tiger*, another novel, the same year.[7] Although several literary critics likened it to a "three-way crash" and "a genre burning collage," one declared Olds to be "the poet of Doc Holliday."[8] *John Ringo: The Final Hours* (2001) by Michael M. Hickey contains copies of many documents, including a map that had allegedly belonged to Wyatt.[9] Hickey's books are somewhat like a murder mystery, especially for the reader who likes both myth and documentation commandeered to reach the truth. Thorndyke Press, the leader in large print books, released Nelson C. Nye's 1960 *Gunfight at the O.K. Corral*. A second edition of Karen Holliday Tanner's *Doc Holliday: A Family Portrait*, with a foreword by Robert K. DeArment, was released in paperback that year.[10]

September 11, 2001, most Americans believed, would be (like December 7, 1941) a date to "live in infamy."[11] Soon, however, politicians and the media decreed the nation must forget the whole thing and move on. Less than a year later, only a few courageous country singers were willing to mention it publicly.

Interest in Doc Holliday and his contemporaries continued, and even picked up considerably in 2002. Thom Ross' *Gunfight at the O.K. Corral in Words and Pictures*, with a foreword by Paul A. Hutton, presents contemporary images that remain both historical and mythical.[12] *Doc Holliday* was published in French that year, with Paul West and Rémy Lambrechts proving the United Kingdom not the only European country interested in our gambling dentist.[13] *John H. Behan: Sacrificed Sheriff*, by prolific researcher–writer Bob Alexander, of necessity mentions Doc.[14] It does, however, have little good to say of either him or his friends. Matt Braun's *Tombstone*, also in 2002, is a Luke Starbuck novel, finding him in Tombstone bent on killing Wyatt.[15] For just a good read on the Texas trails that Doc haunted, try *Lawrence Clayton: A Clear Fork Chronicle*.[16]

Two thousand two, three, and four found all of Europe accepting a new monetary exchange, leaving the U.S. dollar and British pound to continue in their devaluation. In some kind of response to the 2001 horror, President George W. Bush signed the Homeland Security Act in November of 2002. A Pulitzer Prize–winning author announced in 2003 that he believed ignorance of our history among the country's youth was a threat to national security. Much less prestigious Americans had figured that out long before. In 2004 the Olympic games were back in Greece after a 108-year absence and vied nicely with the national election scene in the United States. Strife and uprisings called attention to Russia, Iran, Pakistan, Haiti, and the Sudan. In November, United States troops launched an attack on Falluja, stronghold of the Iraqi insurgency.

One children's book on the street fight appeared in 2003.[17][18] For a nice addition to your library, check out James Reasoner's *Draw: The Greatest Gunfights of the American West*.[19] L.T. Brooks' 2004 *The Last Gamble of*

Doc Holliday takes Doc "as a myth, a legend ... and makes him a man." Brooks' first effort is certainly a novel way to approach Doc's biography.[20] Gene Carlisle's *Why Doc Holliday Left Georgia* asks again the age-old question.[21] Bob Boze Bell made another worthwhile contribution to the Tombstone legend in 2005 with his *Holliday in Tombstone*.[22] Ed Finn's *Look West Series* published "The Legend of the O.K. Corral."[23] *Bravo of the Brazos: John Larn of Fort Griffin, Texas* offered more of general interest concerning Doc's years in that area.[24]

As the first decade of the twenty-first century slipped past the halfway mark, books on Doc Holliday and other prominent Tombstone figures continued to flourish. By the end of 2006, Doc's definitive biography was published and not a living soul could be disappointed.[25] Of Gary L. Roberts' *The Life and Legend of Doc Holliday*, *Publisher's Weekly* put it most succinctly: "You can't beat this story for drama.... An omnibus of everything ever known, spoken, or written about Doc Holliday." Simply put, this book is a must for every person with even the hint of an interest in one of Georgia's, and the Old West's, most famous men.

Hollywood and the O.K. Corral by leading film historian Michael Blake takes the prize for as a unique book on the subject.[26] Blake presents an interesting read with behind-the-scenes stories and photographs. *Analysis of the Gunfight at the O.K. Corral* (2006) finds Ben T. Traywick back on the trail.[27] Next came the audio book *Doc Holliday*.[28] *Borrowed Time*, the first of a Tombstone trilogy, was published in 2007, followed in 2008 by the continuing historic fiction *Holliday in Tombstone (Doc Holliday)*.[29] Susan Ballard's *Death Takes a Holliday* continues the fantasy with Doc leaving a young son behind in Tombstone.[30] Jack Kincade, Hollywood screenwriting veteran, brought Doc to the fore for the younger generation with his *Fighting for Air — The Unknown Adventures of Young Doc Holliday*.[31] *Gunfight at the O.K. Corral* (2008) by Gayle Martin is also a good read for ages eight and up.[32] Tim Barnes published *Doc Holliday's Road to Tombstone: The Life and Times of John Henry Holliday* the same year.[33] The original radio script *My Darling Clementine* by William Keighley added a new facet to Holliday memorabilia in 2009.[34] Ongoing interest in Doc's Texas Trail days came in *Famous Gunfighters of the Western Frontier: Wyatt Earp, Doc Holliday, Luke Short and Others*.[35] Allegedly told by Bat Masterson, much of this material has been covered elsewhere.

The second decade of the new century found several writers thinking about Doc and his environs. Kate was the focus of 2010's interest in Doc, with a book by the same name.[36] This Ballard novel fantasizes Kate's life with Doc and what "drove her" to Johnny Ringo, a matter often appearing in film. Ballard continued to discuss *Doc Holliday's Dilemma* later that year.[37] *They Call Me Doc: The Story Behind the Legend of John Henry Holliday* is D.J. Herda's take on the gambling dentist.[38] An audio book encompassing a mass of sinners, entitled *Gunfighters: Billy the Kid, Jesse James, The Earps & Doc Holliday*, appeared the same year.[39]

Gunfight at the O.K. Corral and Other Western Adventures (2011) got well into the familiar tale.[40] *The Arizona War and The Gunfight at the O.K. Corral* by SB Jeffrey and "History of Cochise County, Arizona: Gunfight at the O.K. Corral, Wyatt Earp, Doc Holliday, Earp Vendetta Ride" both have 2011 origins in Wikipedia.[41] *Hour of the Gun (1967): Deconstructing Wyatt Earp* summed up the year's commentaries.[42] *Western Legend* by John Alder focused on alleged conversations with Virgil. For the first time recorded, Virgil stated Doc was a manic depressive.[43] It is questionable the term was in use that early.

Doc, by prolific Mary Doria Russell started off 2012.[44] Jeff Guinn's *Last Gunfight: The Real O.K. Corral and How It Changed the American West* provides an excellent chronological study of factors leading up to and following the big event.[45] Despite the fact it was far from the last, the book got tremendous reviews. The cover of *Holliday* shows a .9mm gun and goes on to interpret Doc in modern-day terminology.[46] *Wyatt: Doc Holliday's Account of an Intimate Friendship* is another light take on the two friends.[47] Paul Lee Johnson shed more light on the controversial McLaury brothers[48] and Peter Brand continued his insight into the vendetta riders with *The Story of Texas Jack Vermillion* in 2012.[49]

Kindle, the replacement for our old friends, books, carries many of these stories written on the O.K. Corral and its participants.

Two thousand had gotten off to a slow start in the magazine and journal department, generally speaking. *True West* featured R.K. DeArment in January and Karen Holliday Tanner in August.[50] Old Fort Griffin is the focus of DeArment's article, and high time. A lot yet remains to be learned concerning Doc's years there. Unfortunately, the records are sketchy at best. Tanner addresses gunfighter mythology as it pertains to Doc, a topic always of interest. Charles River Editors produced *Wyatt Earp & Doc Holliday: The West's Greatest Gunslingers* for Kindle.

Doc Holliday at the O.K. Corral had, by the end of the twentieth century, been viewed from every possible angle, or so we thought. The Vendetta Ride, his second claim to fame in the spring of 1882, came under closer inspection in the twenty-first century. Despite its having been exaggerated in the film *Tombstone*, earlier writing and movies had little to say. Warren Earp's participation was determined fairly soon, but several researchers, around the turn of the century, questioned just who made that infamous ride.

Charley Smith had been re-discovered by Robert F. Palmquist in 1997.[51] Before 2000 was over, all sorts of furor appeared on Origen Charles Smith, which turned out to be a slew of fake letters and a mysterious newspaper article. Karen Holliday Tanner and Clifton Brewer addressed this in "Doc Holliday's Last Days."[52] Tanner's hypothesis was based on an article found by Brewer in an old trunk. This debate, together with conclusions by experts of the day, was discussed over the next few years. The clipping was seemingly related directly to one of the men who accompanied Doc on the vendetta ride and into Colorado. It had somehow found its way into the Sulphur *Oklahoma Headlight* in February 1899. Smith alleges to have traveled from Leadville to Glenwood Springs with Doc and Kate, where the two shared Doc's last days. That the newspaper article exists is obviously true; history proves the tale definitely was not. Gary L. Roberts, a Holliday authority, put the matter to rest for all intents and purposes in 2004.[53] His work received WOLA's Outstanding Article award that year. Charlie Smith was further discussed at some length in Roberts' 2006 book on Doc Holliday.

In 1998 Paul Cool had cleared up the correct spelling of Sherman McMaster's name.[54] Peter Brand offered considerably more on McMaster in his 1999 "The El Paso Salt War, Texas Rangers & Tombstone."[55] These two efforts, combined with data in Gary Roberts' *Doc Holliday*, offered a fairly complete insight into McMaster's life.[56] That he was in the pool hall when Morgan was murdered explains his standing with the Earps, but he did not suffer the grizzly death told in the film. He kept with the riders into Silver City and Albuquerque, New Mexico, and stayed with them in Gunnison, Colorado, where they split up.

Daniel G. Tipton was born in New York and, as a Federal Deputy appointed as Earp bodyguards, was with them the night Morgan was shot.[57] Peter Brand's 2000 "Daniel G. Tipton & the Earp Vendetta Posse" sheds more light on the man and his history.[58] The Australian researcher and writer contributes more interesting finds on Tipton, who rode with Doc and Wyatt after Morgan's murder[59]: "The man trusted to deliver the much needed money and information was a tough miner named Daniel Tipton." Roberts' 2006 book and Brand's further discoveries of "Big Tip" reveal him to be a real mystery man.[60] Tipton stayed with Doc after the post-gunfight split, going on to Denver with him.

"Turkey Creek Jack" Johnson is fairly well remembered from *Tombstone*, with veteran western actor Buck Taylor in the role. Little had been known of him prior to Wyatt Earp's testimony at the Lotta Crabtree estate hearings in 1926, which can be found in J.R. Stephens' *Wyatt Earp Speaks!*[61] While in Tombstone he was called "mysterious" and "unknown." Peter

Brand conducted personal interviews and research prior to writing his 2003 "Wyatt Earp, Jack Johnson & the Notorious Blount Brothers" for NOLA.[62] It is fairly certain that "Turkey Creek Jacks'" real name was John W. Blount and it was Stuart Lake who gave him the catchy moniker.

"Texas Jack" Vermillion, Brand proclaims, is the most difficult of all to find. He was first mentioned in Pat Jahn's *Frontier World of Doc Holliday*; she was unable to furnish her source.[63] Brand's "Wyatt Earp's Vendetta Posse" in the April 2007 *Wild West Magazine* went far into pulling the whole matter together.[64] Brand went to Virginia and spent some time where John Vermillion had allegedly returned and lived a long life as an exemplary church member and citizen.[65] No one in the family had any inkling of his infamous days as "Texas Jack" in Cochise County. Brand's later research confirmed he was not John Wilson Vermillion, but John Oberland Vermillion. This mystery man has been thoroughly researched in Brand's 2012 book. Brand gives much of the credit for his research in the States to his most capable assistant, Jean Smith of Stafford, Arizona.

True West in December 2001 was a Doc Holliday Collector's Edition and can still be purchased from some sources.[66] In addition to Vendetta data, cited above, the issue contains eight articles by some of the field's best research writers with expert Gary L. Roberts contributing four. Roberts begins the issue with a tale of how his fascination with Doc began.[67] His second article deals with Kate, querying, "Mrs. John Holliday?" and conjecturing it was a relationship more of mutual respect and loyalty than love.[68] Doc's Leadville, Colorado, years are the subject of Roberts' third article, addressing a fairly new topic in the legend.[69] It supposes Doc did not heed the warning issued by a *Tourists Guide to Leadville*, that people with weak lungs avoid the altitude. Leadville, however, was simply a magnet for gamblers, and that's what Doc was. Chuck Hornung joined Roberts in the disputed matter of "Did Doc & Wyatt Split Because of a Racial Slur?"[70] Doc's belief that Wyatt was too pro–Semitic is clearly identified in a letter from former New Mexico governor (and widely read writer) Miguel A. Otero, Jr. It does raise the question, however, that Doc, as a staunch Rebel and Southerner, might have once been on speaking terms with the Ku Klux Klan. Confederate veterans organized the Night Riders in 1865, and it was active throughout Doc's teen and last few years in Georgia. If we are expected to believe he shot and killed blacks at his family swimming hole and attempted to blow up a Freedman's Bureau, it is but one short step for the imagination. While neither of these stories is suggested as truth, they simply carry supposition to the next level.

Feature article writers were on a roll the following year. *Wild West* in June found Lee A. Silva questioning what happened to the (probably Wells

Fargo) shotgun with which Doc blasted Tom McLaury and then threw down in the street.[71] Silva presents a believable tale of Wyatt and Virgil's giving the weapon to a famous frontiersman in Quartsite, Arizona. His son remembers it as a new hammerless model that fired both barrels at once. The weapon is seemingly lost, but not its story. Casey Tefertiller and Jeff Morey take a long look at all the guns and the gunfight in an October *Wild West*.[72]

Jeff Morey's centerfold feature addresses Doc's character and performance in the days preceding and during the gunfight.[73] A part of the title proclaims "Doc Holliday vs. Everyone" and it weakens the point made by others that Doc wanted to provoke a fight with Ike Clanton. It cites his returning from Tucson with Morgan Earp the evening of October 22, certainly not on any kind of hurried mission. With maps and graphics by Gus Walker, Morey's article insightfully draws the first really clear picture of Holliday's role in the controversial events. An enhanced version appears in the Tombstone archives, online.[74]

Victoria Wilcox's article in this special edition, "Mischievous Minor: From Lad to Lunger," repeats much of the folklore.[75] Wilcox does explain the established mourning customs of the South, and the blatant way young John Henry's father ignored them in his early remarriage. Things were further disrupted when his uncle filed suit against newlywed Henry Holliday for control of his dead sister's estate. Anything of worth attained thereby for young John was, however, put in trust with his father, making it all something of a lesson in futility. Doc was able to sell his holdings in Georgia to finance his trip West.

"No, he didn't. Yes, he did" by Karen Holliday Tanner and Howard Bryan addresses the question of Mike Gordon's death in Las Vegas, New Mexico.[76] Tanner disputes the two-years-later *Optic* newspaper account as having no basis in fact, while Bryan maintains that it's the truth. Neither mentions that Wyatt Earp listed Mike Gordon as one of the "three men Doc Holliday killed" in his 1896 interview with the *San Francisco Examiner*. Gary Roberts gives further facts in his biography of Doc.[77] Roger Jay, another relatively new writer on the scene, completed the "Friends and Enemies" piece about an oft-mentioned figure in Doc Holliday's life, Johnny Tyler.[78] "Looking for Doc in Dallas" finds Erik Wright casting back to Texas for early information on the gambling dentist.[79] A map of 1876 Dallas indicating the spot of Doc's dental practice accompanies the article.

Two other writers in this special edition tackle the issue of Doc in Dodge City.[80] His ad from the *Dodge City Times* is shown, together with a newly acquired "pocket dentist" kit for creating gold fillings. The article claims ownership and penmanship engraving as belonging to none other than Doc. He is reported to have given it, shortly before his death, to one Maggie May McKenzie. Its present owner, unknown, acquired it from a small museum in Colorado. One unique feature of this issue is a piece regarding the numerous real and mistaken photographs of Doc.[81] Ben Carlton Mead adds "Painting Doc's Personality," by the artist who sketched him for the January-February 1960 *True West* that queried "The West's Greatest Gunman?"[82] "Is There a Doctor in the House?" was the prelude to an article in the following January issue of *True West*, "Real to Reel."[83] Carried over from the special edition, the article looks at Doc in film, showing how Hollywood has altered the many facets of his personality.

Four quite intriguing articles dealing with Doc, and one with an Earp brother, appeared between July and December 2003. R. G. Robertson uses the talent of Thom Ross to discuss "Painting the Mythical West."[84] Veteran writer John Boessenecker wrote interestingly in the August issue of *Wild West*, discussing Sheriff Bob Paul's connection with Doc and Wyatt, especially while Doc was jailed in Denver.[85] The article offers interesting insight into Paul's life and credibility before Arizona, suggesting he was simply out-maneuvered when he attempted to extradite Doc. His career was not damaged by the failure, and historians today get yet another slant to the story from his memoirs. Roger Jay proved his serious attention to detail in a December *WOLA Journal*, again bringing new material to the forefront. Doc Holliday is the focus of Jay's article on "The Lake County Independent Club, 1882" which contains much Leadville information heretofore unpublished.[86] Jay wound up the year with another article in *Wild West*, "Doc Holliday: Last Stand in Leadville."[87] The necessity for Doc's staying in Colorado, not the healthiest climate for his tuberculosis, is heartbreakingly true. It must have been galling that his weakened condition prevented his being the stand-up man he had once been. However, hearing that a man to whom he owed a pittance of five dollars was gunning for him, left him no choice: one that could clearly open the door to his extradition to Arizona. True to form, Doc missed his shot at six feet but, almost on top of Billy Allen, managed to hit him in the arm. Using all the wiles he had learned with the Denver newspapers and aided by a brace of good attorneys, he was acquitted on the grounds of self-defense. "Spitting Lead in Leadville: Holliday's Last Stand" appeared in a 2003 *Wild West*.[88] Roger Jay continued his pursuit of Doc in northern Colorado with some exciting new information in that winter's *WOLA Journal*.[89]

Robert B. McCubbin gives an insightful study into the fact and fiction regarding pictures of Doc Holliday in the March 2004 *True West*. "It Ain't Really Him! ... Or Is It?" discusses the four most popular photographs, stating that the problem with Doc is we have too many, rather than the standard too few of most famous westerners.[90] In October, Roger Jay tackled Tombstone in a *Wild West* article entitled, "The Gambler's War in Tombstone."[91]

The December 2006 *True West* celebrated the 125th anniversary of the O.K. Corral. Two specific questions about Doc were asked in "Dying Doc, Withered Wyatt?" and "Doc Holliday's Racist Killing?"[92] Pam Potter wrote about the O.K. Corral's international fascination.[93] *Wild West* responded with Gary Roberts' "Doc Holliday, the Earps' Strangest Ally."[94]

"Frontier Doc: The tuberculosis bullet that eventually took Doc Holliday's life" appeared in the April 2008 *True West*.[95] Jeff Morey's "The Streetfight: What We Know and Why We Know It" was published in the Tombstone History Archives in early 2009.[96] Robert K. DeArment addressed Doc Holliday in *WWHA Journal* issues that year with "Four Awful Badmen."[97] Roy B. Young's "The Assassination of Frank Stilwell" gave one more point of view on that matter.[98] That same year, Peter Brand published a booklet entitled The *Life and Times of Perry Malon*, which can also be found at www.tombstonevendetta.com.[99] Brand followed the subject in the June *Wild West* with "The Man Who Arrested Doc Holliday."[100] "Interview with Bat Masterson" by Robert DeArment was published in 2010.[101]

Paul A. Hutton solved nearly a century of mystery in a 2012 *True West* item in BBB's Blog.[102] Hutton makes an excellent case of Bert Lindley in the role of Wyatt Earp in William S. Hart's *Wild Bill Hickok*. Hutton believes this verifies a Doc Holliday appearance, as well.

Other than documentaries, moviemakers failed to address the Arizona legend early in the twenty-first century. Horse operas continued, just not with the verve the old-timers might have wanted. Remakes of *High Noon* and *The Virginian* kicked things off in 2000, together with the story of how the Texas Rangers were founded.[103] Viewers had not yet fully grasped the horror that remakes would constitute. Tom Selleck, one of America's favorite cowboys, appeared in Louis L'Amour's *Crossfire Trail* in 2001.[104] The most distressing news yet was westerns being reviewed as "fantasy." The year 2003 offered two really great westerns, *Monte Walsh* starring Tom Selleck and *Open Range*, co-starring Robert Duvall and Kevin Costner.[105] The Selleck film, a remake of a 1970 Lee Marvin movie, grabbed immediate success with the new casting. The following year's remake of *The Alamo* met with mixed emotions and opinions.[106] Casting and financial problems plagued production from the outset and the decision to show Davy Crockett dying as a prisoner of war, rather than going down fighting with his men, did not sit well with many. It could be said that right or wrong, it is still hard to buck John Wayne.

On the home front, Congress was allegedly concerned with ethics, but military activities in Iraq and Israel made the world scene decidedly violent. A baffling mixture of the IRA, obesity in children, fighting on multiple fronts, and concern over the U.S. fiscal condition grappled for the headlines. Two thousand six saw more threats of a deficit increase, while random and multiple shootings seemed to escalate in schools and public buildings. Congress refused to adopt a Constitutional amendment to make the desecration of the American flag a crime. Scientists discovered water on a Saturn moon: Texans wished they could do the same.

Marches for relaxed immigration laws were evidenced across the country and it is doubtful the reported 2.5 percent rise in national crime came as any surprise. News of terrorist activities around the globe was commonplace. On the brighter side, Google bought YouTube and on October 19, 2006, the Dow Jones closed at an all-time high.

Despite continued worldwide intrigue, a few worthwhile westerns appeared. The TV mini-series *Broken Trail* (2006) with Robert Duvall was sufficient to keep every horse opera fan content.[107] Despite being another remake, 2007's *3:10 to Yuma* seemed to be the exception in possibly surpassing the 1957 film.[108] *The Assassination of Jesse James by the Coward Robert Ford* ran a close second.[109] *Appaloosa* has become the favorite of the 2008 westerns.[110] Two thousand nine failed to deliver in the traditional western genre and ran head long into another John Wayne controversy with the remake of *True Grit* in 2010.[111] Although it was nominated for ten Academy Awards and declared a "re-creation," most long-time western fans still stood with the Duke. In 2011, traditional westerns disappeared into *Cowboys and Aliens*, strengthened by a strong cast including Harrison Ford and Daniel Craig.[112]

John Henry (Doc) Holliday appears in *The Legend of Hell's Gate*.[113] Released late in 2011, the story of the mysterious cliff formation rising up from Possum Kingdom Lake, Texas, is definitely a traditional western. Jamie Thomas King plays Doc. The visuals are pure Texas beauty. Despite Val Kilmer's appearance as the famous lawman, *Wyatt Earp's Revenge* (2012) is likely doomed to the B category.[114] Wilson Bethel is a scarcely noticed Doc Holliday.

Despite Hollywood's complete disregard for the boys in Tombstone, television contributed a great deal on the subject.

The Discovery Channel's *Unsolved History* featured *Shoot Out at the O.K. Corral*.[115] Distinguished historian and author Paul A. Hutton served as commentator for a new take on the old story. *Unsolved History* incorporates a forensic point of view, using both archaeological and existing photographs. It then utilizes carefully selected interviews from "eyewitnesses" to carefully reconstruct what happened in the days leading up to the event. Employing firearms, simulators, ballistic reports, police detectives, and a computer-generated map, the program seeks to determine if the shooting was "justified or homicide."

"A dozen six-shooters burst into a frenzy of gunfire" might be something of an exaggeration; there were only seven shooters. That the marshals "stood unscathed" at the end is definitely a departure from the truth: Virgil Earp was shot in the calf and his brother Morgan suffered an even more serious wound. If "order was restored," as the Discovery Channel would have us believe, the following six months were surely less so for Virgil Earp, crippled for life in December, and for Morgan, shot dead some five months later. Certainly a great deal was happening in and around Tombstone up to and after these events, including the "vendetta" killings. It would be many a long time before any modicum of the alleged "peace" was restored to Cochise County.

BBC marshaled Western historian Jeff Morey for its 2003 *The Wild West: The Gunfight at the OK Corral*.[116] Despite having the best money could buy, they essentially proved once again that England understands the American West on a level with Hollywood's comprehension of the Scottish Wars for Independence. The film does take the unique tack of studying the event from the Wells Spicer Court hearings and asks, "Was justice to be found in the rule of the law or the rule of the gun?" It focuses almost exclusively on Wyatt and Ike Clanton; Doc, played by George Asprey, is scarcely mentioned. The first version of the street fight pictures no shotgun, but following a discussion of the trial, the second take has it in full view, then being thrown to the ground. With the exception of narrator Michael Praed and the Wyatt Earp character (Liam Cunningham), most of the cast sounds as if it may have seen *Gone with the Wind* a few too many times. Only Doc truly had a Georgian accent, the Earps would have been scandalized. The faked Southern accent; together with the English trait of dropping the "h," prevents the documentary from being as strong as it might have.

Jeff Morey does contribute some solid truths to be carried into, optimistically, future O.K. Corral history. He admitted that often, in the early West, law and order did grow out of chaos. Morey additionally likens the vendetta ride to Old Testament retribution, admitting it was not only an act of vengeance, but also one of natural law. He makes the astute observation that, as always, whatever decision has been or will be made remains contingent on interpretation and evaluation.

The History Channel's "Doc Holliday: The Man Behind the Myth" (2004) may have created more myths than it resolved.[117] Despite the appearance of Holliday researcher-historian Jeff Morey, it managed to confuse some issues for which verification was available by that date. Rob Word, producer of "Wyatt Earp, Return to Tombstone" (1994), refers to Doc as a "flamboyant ... rock star of the era." Word calls on the old cliché that Doc was "never afraid to die because he was dying already." Despite this being a case often made, it does not explain the actions of a great many other more prolific and certainly careless gunfighters. Why, then, were James Butler (Wild Bill) Hickok, Billy the Kid, John Wesley Hardin and others, healthy so far as we know, seemingly just as unafraid of death? A first-time-ever statement is made, as if there were not enough snakes already plowed up, alleging that Doc told Ike the night before the street fight he had killed Old Man Clanton.

Kate's place in Doc's life is one of the documentary's most glaring mistakes. The story told by Earp of the paramour's heroics following his knifing of Ed Bailey in Texas is repeated. It expands the error by showing Kate as remaining by Doc's side in Leadville and until his death in Glenwood Springs.

The best new-to-television material is taken from Karen Holliday Tanner's book and family collection.[118] Although the episode begins with at least two photographs long known to *not* be John Henry, Tanner has provided the audience with several baby and childhood shots of the young Holliday, including his college graduation picture. Jeff Morey sticks to the best of Doc Holliday by declaring him a combination of elegance and decadence, "the cobblestones of the Victorian era." He is on the mark when insisting it is this strange combination in our gambling dentist that continues to fascinate.

Investigating History: Wyatt Earp at the O.K. Corral, one of Bill Kurtis' western investigations, was released on May 24, 2004.[119] It focuses primarily on Wyatt but Doc is given some spot of fame in this documentary that opens with the question, "Is this the finest hour of American law enforcement?" Narration says that Doc "wears trouble like a neon sign," and the enmity between Holliday and Ike Clanton is mentioned early. The well-recognized picture of Doc, taken in Prescott just prior to his arrival in Tombstone, is shown. A second alleged picture is now questioned. Allan Barra refers to Doc as the "wild card" of the law faction, while Bruce Dingus of the Arizona Historical Society adds the usual commentary that Doc knew he was going to die and it was "easy to say that he's reckless." Ben Traywick, Tombstone resident and voluminous writer on the topic, declares that all Doc wanted to do was go back to Georgia. Really? The statement is made that Doc Holliday had killed a man in Las Vegas, New Mexico, with nothing said of the Texas murder for which he is often accused, likely committed, and for which Wyatt gave him full credit. The dentist's friendship with one of the stage robbers is noted, and how it acerbated the ire of both the cowboys and the townspeople.

As the film, co-produced by Kurtis and Paul A. Hutton, takes a look at the "official version," it is pointed out that the scene of the street fight took place in a 15' × 20' lot and the ages-old question of "Who fired first?" is addressed. Although legal professor Stephen Lubet declares the law of physics is against what actually appears to have happened, he readily admits a charge of first-degree murder could simply never have stuck. Lubet states some facts as "certain," but follows that word with "we'll never know." Precisely what everyone has been saying since 1881.

It is strongly intimated that Doc would gladly have killed Frank Stillwell, who bragged of having gunned down his fun-loving buddy Morgan Earp. Wyatt, however, readily confessed to the railroad station shooting, and whether Doc contributed to the excessive number of cartridge and shotgun shells found in the body is something of a moot point. Doc is also included, by inference, in the statement that the U.S. marshalcy was solidly behind the Earps up until the vendetta, and that both Wyatt and Holliday stayed within the law until Morgan was murdered. Although the narrator claims the O.K. Corral to be a story of American justice outside

Visualization of ace-high, four kings poker hand (all Doc Holliday enactors): Val Kilmer (*Tombstone* 1993) is certainly the highest valued player. Left to right are: Jason Robards (*Hour of the Gun* (1967), Anthony Quinn (*Warlock* 1959), Kilmer, Kirk Douglas (*Gunfight at the O.K. Corral*, 1957), and Walter Huston in Howard Hughes' *The Outlaw* (1943) (Shirley Ayn Linder Collection).

the law and Wyatt Earp a cold-blooded killer, Hutton sums things up pretty well. Although we substitute "Doc" for "Wyatt," it probably goes without saying, "he would have been amazed at what we have made of him."

"Wyatt Earp," an episode of *The American Experience*, mentions Doc but sticks true to its topic.[120] Jeff Morey consulted on this production, which includes new viewpoints and experts.

The Twenty-first Century opened up an entirely new genre for presenting the gambling dentist.

SUNDOWN, A Musical About the Legend of Doc Holliday opened in Dallas, Texas, in 2002 to rave reviews. Broadway discovered Doc in 2004.[121] Claims that "Doc Holliday himself being worthy of opera" tend to choke up traditional western fans. The musical, however, won the 2003 ASCAP award and was declared one of the top ten best theatrical albums of 2004. It is available on CD for the more musically inclined Holliday aficionados.

Outride the Devil: A Morning with Doc Holliday is something completely different.[122] Kit Hussey does an excellent interpretation of how Doc might perceive himself had he lived a longer life. Proponents of Doc's wit will particularly enjoy this.

Mark Hopkins sculpted "Doc Holliday" in bronze early in the new century's second decade.[123] Hopkins evidently studied all the known pictures available of Doc, for the likeness is astonishing in most details.

Jon Chandler's haunting "Linwood," winner of the Western Writers of America Spur Award for best western song in 2009, is a melancholy

Doc Holliday ©Mark Hopkins Sculpture, available at 83SpringStreet.com

reminder of the man who has challenged so many to so much.[124] It whispers of how Doc gazes out the hotel window to the cemetery that would soon be his final resting place:

"Linwood"

He'd stand at his second floor window and gaze to the west
Above the wooden false fronts and newly mortared brick and stone buildings on the opposite side of the street
Across the valley to the Red Mountain
And the evergreens would remind him of his boyhood in Georgia
He'd always preferred the fresh scent of pine to the heavy fragrance of magnolia
At the end, his bed was against a wall opposite the window
And he would lay on what passed for a mattress and watch the snow-filled clouds pass over the great red slope
The interplay of light and shadow gave him comfort
And he thought himself fortunate to die in such a lovely place
He spoke of a girl he'd known before he was sent to Philadelphia to take up dentistry
His beautiful cousin
And wondered if she still ministered to the poor and sick
Or taught children that would never be her own
He fought back tears for his mother after so many years
And spoke his long-dead brother's name
He woke from dreams of Kate, and Wyatt, but his only regular visitor was the kid who worked at the hotel
The kid who brought him whisky, and laudanum
In his delirium, he was back in the Arizona heat
Trying to stop his finger from pulling the shotgun's trigger
As Tom McLaury screamed, "No!"
His heart beat a little quicker at the thought that he'd soon be able to apologize
He asked the kid about the boneyard here in Glenwood Springs. Did it have a name?
"Don't know," the kid replied, and left to find out
He returned later with a fresh bottle and said, "Linwood"
"Hmm," Doc mused. "It ends in Linwood"

I deal myself another hand, the morning sunlight fades
King of Diamonds, Ace of Hearts, dog-eared trey of spades
True companions all, they are, my life's only friends
The Queen withholds her judgment, the Jack seeks no amends
Rye whisky burns like hellfire, dulls the deeper pain
Mad dogs need to feel the flame, or their spirit starts to wane
I traveled down a twisted trail that ends in this cheap room
What went before is dust and rage, what lies ahead is gloom

Thoughts of Kansas swirl around
As I lay here in this mountain town
Soon they'll lay my body down in Linwood

Ten cent novel's out of reach, dropped down to the floor
It says that I killed 40 men and shot as many more
Somewhere some kid's reading these tall tales of gun and knife
I pray he never has the chance to take another's life
I traveled to these mountains in hopes of hanging on
But time now has no meaning, anticipation's gone
So I try to conjure places, let my memory travel time
Familiar, long gone faces, and a church bell's distant chime

Ban this devil from my soul
Maybe death will make me whole
They'll lay me in a six-foot hole in Linwood

My boots sit on the rough hewn floor
My pistol hangs behind the door
I guess they'll even up the score in Linwood

(Lyrics reprinted by permission of Jon Chandler.)

John H. (Doc) Holliday continues to inspire in the twenty-first century, just as he did in the two previous millennia. There is obviously no end to his legend. We have but paused here to do as the reporter noted in *The Man Who Shot Liberty Valance*[125]: "When the legend becomes fact, print the legend."

JOHN HENRY (DOC) HOLLIDAY
ONGOING LEGEND

Chapter Notes

Introduction

1. Bertram Wyatt-Brown, *Southern Honor: Ethics and Behavior in the Old South*. (New York: Oxford University Press, 1983).

Chapter One

1. Karen Holliday Tanner, *Doc Holliday: A Family Portrait* (Norman: University of Oklahoma Press, 1998); Gary L. Roberts, *Doc Holliday: The Life and Legend* (New York: John Wiley & Sons, Inc., 2006).
2. *Tombstone*, 1993; *Wyatt Earp*, 1994.
3. Susan McKey Thomas, letter to author dated April 6, 1996, and phone conversations with author, 1995–1996, attesting to facts in the family Bible and to John Henry's early years.
4. U.S. National Archives (Washington, DC), Henry B. Holliday, SC-1908, Special Orders No. 86, Mexican War Pension, February 9, 1887, W-3780; Georgia State Archives, Civil War Records; Roster of Twenty-seventh Georgia Volunteer Infantry; Payroll Records (June 14, 1862).
5. Thomas.
6. Albert S. Pendleton, Jr., and Susan McKey Thomas, "Doc Holliday's Georgia Background," *Journal of Arizona History* 14 (Autumn 1974): 185–204; William Alexander Griffith, *New Orleans Daily Picayune*, April 16, 1885; *Valdosta Daily Times*, April 18, 1885.
7. Susan McKey Thomas.
8. "The Sixteenth Annual Commencement of the Pennsylvania College of Dental Surgery," *The Dental Times*, April 4, 1872, 148–150; "Annual Commencement," *Pennsylvania Inquirer*, March 2, 1872; "Dentists," *The Philadelphia Inquirer*, March 11, 1875.
9. Roberts, 51–52.
10. William Barclay Masterson, "Famous Gunfighters of the Western Frontier: Doc Holliday," *Human Life*, May 1907, 5.
11. "Card," *Atlanta Constitution*, August 15, 1872. Clipping from Frontier Historical Society, Glenwood Springs, Colorado.
12. Spalding County, GA, Deed Book F, 1, 95.
13. Pendleton and Thomas, 201.
14. Roberts, 58.
15. James Mackay, *William Wallace: Brave Heart* (Edinburgh: Mainstream Publishing Company, 1995), 20, 91, 107, 109.
16. Martin Kaufman, "Step Right Up, Ladies and Gentlemen," *American History Illustrated*, August 1981, 39–45.
17. Rita L. Benischek, M.A., University of New Mexico, email to author, June 16, 2005.
18. Bob Boze Bell, *The Illustrated Life and Times of Doc Holliday* (Phoenix: Tri Star-Boze, 1995), 17–18.
19. "Dallas City Directory," *Dallas Daily Commercial*, February 13, 1874.
20. "Awards on Friday," *Dallas Weekly Herald*, October 11, 1873.
21. *Dallas Daily Commercial*, March 2, 1874.
22. "Recollections, M.F. Holliday," *Gunnison Daily-News Democrat*, June 18, 1882.
23. *State of Texas vs. J.H. Holliday*, Dallas County Court Minutes, 1874–78, Case No. 2236, May 12, 1874; 209, 256–57.
24. Tanner, 94–96.
25. *Dallas Herald*, January 2, 1875.
26. State of Texas v. J.H. Holliday, Dallas County Court Minutes, 1874–78, Case No. 2643, January 18, 1875.
27. *Ibid.*, Case No. 2236, April 13, 1875.
28. B. W. Aston and Donathan Taylor,

Along the Texas Forts Trail (Denton: University of North Texas, 1997).

29. Shackelford County, Texas, District Court Docket, 1; Pat Jahns *The Frontier World of Doc Holliday* (New York: Hastings House, 1957), 61; This court record has since disappeared from the docket.

30. Roberts, 76.

31. "Awful Arizona," *Denver Republican*, May 22, 1882. John H. Holliday interview.

32. Robert K. DeArment, *Bat Masterson: The Man and the Legend* (Norman: University of Oklahoma Press, 1975).

33. Roberts, 433n; Transcript of Recollections of Mary Katherine (Harony) Cummings as given to Anton Mazzanovich, 5–7. Private collection of Kevin J. Mulkins.

33. U.S. National Archives, Records of the War Department, Office of the Quartermaster (Washington, DC). Master General, Reservation File, 1889. Microfilm.

34. Roberts, 77–78.

35. B.W. Aston and Donathan Taylor, *Along the Texas Forts Trail* (Denton, TX: University of North Texas Press, 1997), 3–5.

36. Roberts, 434n.

37. Neither the Sweetwater Cantonment nor the Eagle Pass theories preclude the mining town stories. They do give credence to the tales that Doc and Kate may well have spent a large part of this time along the Texas Fort Trails. They could conceivably have begun at Forts Richardson and Griffin, located across the northern rim of this rectangular-shaped route, then followed the trail south through the Abilene and San Angelo vicinities. A quick turn east at Eldorado, near Eagle Pass, would have led them back to the arrival point, Ft. Mason, again on the Texas Fort Trail.

38. *Dallas Weekly Herald*, June 7, 1877.

39. Tanner, 106–107.

40. Notes of Stuart N. Lake in interviews with Wyatt Earp held in California (1924–1929) microfilm, Huntington Library, San Marino, Berkeley Collections. Hereafter referred to as Earp/Lake Papers.

41. *San Francisco Examiner*, August 2, 1896. Written under Wyatt Earp's name. It was actually Masterson who captured Rudabaugh several months later.

42. Doc and Kate disagreed on many issues, but both indicated a profound appetite for liquor. Whatever their differences or similarities, they were undoubtedly a twosome during much of the time for which Doc has achieved his greatest fame. Kate's memoir, written when she was nearly ninety, is fraught with contradictions.

43. Tanner, 115.

44. Casey Tefertiller, *Wyatt Earp: The Life Behind the Legend* (New York: John Wiley & Sons,1997).

45. Craig Minor, *Wichita: The Early Years* (Lincoln: Bison, 1982), 110.

46. *The (National) Police Gazette*, George Wilkes, founder. (New York: 1845–1982). August 10 1878.

47. "Dentistry," *Dodge City Times*, June 8, 1878, 3:2.

48. Earp/Lake Papers; *San Francisco Examiner*, August 1896.

49. Frontier Historical Society Collections, Glenwood Springs, CO. Miscellaneous files.

50. San Miguel County, New Mexico, Territory Criminal Record Book (1876–79), 391.

51. E. Richard Churchill, *Doc Holliday, Bat Masterson & Wyatt Earp, Their Colorado Careers* (Gunnison: B&B Printers, 1973), 41; Richard O'Connor, *Iron Wheels and Broken Men: The Railroad Barons and the Plunder of the West* (New York: G.P. Putnam's Sons, 1973), 203. It was in Trinidad that Bud Ryan allegedly took exception to Holliday's card playing skills and, according to O'Connor, was "disemboweled" for his ire. In fact, Ryan's throat was cut, and he survived to cause Doc further trouble in Leadville several years later.

52. *Otero County Optic*, Otero, NM, June 5, 1879, 6:4.

53. *Gazette*, Las Vegas, NM, July 26, 1879.

54. *Gazette*, July 26, 1879; *Santa Fe New Mexican*, August 2, 1879.

55. *Daily Optic*, Las Vegas, NM, July 20, 1881.

56. San Miguel County, New Mexico, Territory Criminal Record Book, 1876–79, 401–2.

57. Robert K. DeArment, *Knights of the Green Cloth: The Saga of the Frontier Gamblers* (Norman: University of Oklahoma Press, 1982).

58. Tefertiller, 280.

59. Earp/Lake Papers.

60. John P. McWilliams, "Trail's End," *New Mexico: A Glimpse into an Enchanted Land* (Scottsdale: Inkwell, 2012).

61. Cecil B. Hartley, *Life & Times of Col. Daniel Boone* (New York: Derby & Jackson, 1860).

62. Roger Jay, "'The Peoria Bummer': Wyatt Earp's Lost Year," *Wild West*, August 2003, 46–53.

63. Dr. Robert Himmerich y Valencia, University of New Mexico, ret. Native of Santa Ana, now Sandoval County, NM.

64. Tefertiller, 32, 36; Roberts, 114–115.

Notes. Chapter One

65. Earp/Lake Papers.
66. United States Government, 1880 Census Enumeration, Prescott, Yavapai County, Arizona Territory, Enumeration District 26, Household 52, 4.
67. Roberts, 117–121.
68. San Miguel County Deed Book, Las Vegas, NM, Book 12, Line 182.
69. Jahns, 136, 139–141.
70. Miguel Antonio Otero, *My Life on the Frontier, 1864–1882* (New York: The Press of the Pioneers, Inc., 1935), 216–18.
71. *The Great Register for Pima County*, September 27, 1880, "Number, 1483; Name, Holliday, J. H.: age, 24; local residence, Precinct No. 17."
72. Don Chaput, *The Earp Papers: In a Brothers' Image* (Encampment, WY: Affiliated Writers of America, 1993), 37.
73. Cochise County [AZ] mill sites Book 1, February 3, 1881, Cochise County Recorder's Office, Bisbee, AZ.
74. *Tombstone Daily Epitaph*, October 18, 1880; Earp/Lake Papers.
75. Earp/Lake Papers.
76. William Breckenridge, *Helldorado: Bringing the Law to the Mesquite* (Boston: Houghton Mifflin, 1927).
77. Roberts, 142.
78. John P. Clum, "Autobiography," *University of Arizona Times*, Box 1, Chapter 16 (Tucson: University of Arizona Collections), 13.
79. Walter Noble Burns Papers, 1908–1964 (bulk 1922–1932), Col. AZ-194, 3.3 lin ft., Arizona Archives Online, http://www.azarchivesonline.org.
80. Carolyn Lake, ed., *Under Cover for Wells Fargo: The Unvarnished Recollections of Fred Dodge* (Norman: University of Oklahoma Press, 1997), 24.
81. Roberts, 76; www.tombstonehistory.tripod.com/cbindex.html.
82. Roy B. Young, *Cochise County Cowboy War* (Apache, OK: Young and Sons Enterprises, 1999).
83. "Pete Spence, Escaping the Wrath of the Earps," *Legends of America*, www.legendsofamerica.com, 2003–2009.
84. Breckenridge, *Helldorado*, 212–213; Walter Noble Burns, *Tombstone: An Iliad of the Southwest* (New York: Doubleday, 1927), 172; Stuart N. Lake, *Wyatt Earp: Frontier Marshal* (Boston: Houghton Mifflin Co., 1931), 215; John Richard Stephens, ed. *Wyatt Earp Speaks!* (Cambria: Fern Canyon Press, 1998), 49; Lorenzo Walters, *Tombstone's Yesterday* (Tucson: Acme, 1928), 93.
85. Roberts, 94, 462n.
86. Earp/Lake Papers.
87. Casey Tefertiller and Jeff Morey, "O.K. Corral: A Gunfight Shrouded in Mystery," *Wild West*, October 2009, 38–44, 70, 72.
88. Gary Roberts, email to author dated May 17, 2012.
89. Morey and Tefertiller are discussed in detail later.
90. Alford E. Turner, ed., *The O.K. Corral Inquest* (College Station, TX: Creative Publishing, 1980) 97.
91. See Chapter Ten.
92. Earp/Lake Papers.
93. Lake, *Wyatt Earp*, 291.
94. Roberts, 233, 243–244, 249, 252–253, 260–262, 267, 270–272, 280, 284–285, 328; Peter Brand, "Dan Tipton and the Earp Vendetta Posse," *True West*, 48:8, December 2001, 54.
95. Mark Dworkin for Peter Brand, "Daniel G. Tipton 1844–1898," *WOLA Journal* (Western Outlaw-Lawmen History Association), Fall 2006.
96. "Murderers' Methods. Capture in Denver of 'Doc' Holliday," *Denver Tribune*, May 16, 1882, 1:5–6.
97. Peter Brand, *The Life and Times of Perry Mallon*, booklet, independent publication, 2006, 25–35. www.tombstonevendetta.com.
98. "'Doc' Holliday. Man-Killer, or an Abused Man, Which?" *Denver Daily Times*, May 16, 1882, 2–3, 4.
99. "Caught in Denver," *The Denver Republican*, May 16, 1882, 1:8.
100. "Doc Holladay in a New Role," *The Denver Daily Times*, May 18, 1882, 3:4.
101. "The Holladay Case," *The Denver Daily Times*, May 20, 1882, 2:4.
102. "The Arizona Feud," *Denver Tribune*, May 20, 1882, 1:8.
103. "Awful Arizona," *Denver Republican*, May 22, 1882, 1:5.
104. "Started Many Graveyards," *Daily Denver Times*, June 15, 1886; *Valdosta Times*, June 19, 1886.
105. "Holliday Out on Bail," *Trinidad Daily News*, June 3, 1882, II:2.
106. *Leadville City Directory*, 1883, 153.
107. Tanner, 203.
108. Gary Roberts, "The Leadville Years," *True West* (Cave Creek, AZ: Rick Baish, Bob Boze Bell, and Bob McCubbin, 1954–present, December 2001, 66–71.
109. *The People of the State of Colorado v. John Holliday*, Lake County Superior Court, Case No. 258.
110. Roger Jay, "The Lake County Independent Club, 1882," *WOLA Journal* (Winter 2003) 4, 24–29.
111. *Ibid*.

112. *Ibid.*
113. Roger Jay, "Doc Holliday: Last Stand in Leadville," *Wild West* (Leesburg: Primedia Enthusiasts Publication Group), December 2004, 38–74.
114. Josephine Sarah Marcus Earp, Mabel Earp Cason, and Vinnolia Earp Ackerman, "She Married Wyatt Earp: The Recollections of Josephine Earp," unpublished manuscript, circa 1938, C. Lee Simmons Collection, Sonoita, Arizona (as reported in Roberts' *Doc Holliday*, 365–366, 493n).
115. Virginia Crowne, "Reminiscing: An Account of Early Days in Glenwood Springs, CO," 1948. Frontier Historical Museum (copy of a newspaper clipping with no source or date).
116. The October 17, 2004, edition of the *Glenwood Springs Post*, 5A, contains a picture and article of a "new and correct" tombstone erected in Doc Holliday's memory at the Linwood Cemetery.
117. Lena Urquhart, *The First Ninety Years: 1886–1976: A History of the First Presbyterian Church, Glenwood Springs, Co.* (Glenwood Springs, CO: Glenwood Springs Historical Society, n.d.), B-66.
118. W.W. Crook, M.D., letter dated May 23, 1943, copy in Glenwood Springs Historical Museum, Glenwood Springs, CO.
119. "Holliday's Trail of Blood," *Denver Republican*, December 25, 1887, 1:14.

Chapter Two

1. *Las Vegas Optic*, July 1889.
2. Cited in a number of Colorado newspapers including *The Denver Republican, Denver Daily Times, Denver Tribune, Trinidad Daily News, Valdosta Times,* and *Trinidad Daily News*.
3. Gary L. Roberts, *Doc Holliday: The Life and Legend* (New York: John Wiley & Sons, Inc., 2006), 387–388.
4. *Ibid.*, 384.
5. *San Francisco Examiner*, August 2, 1896.
6. *Ibid.*
7. Gary L. Roberts, 322–323.
8. Jack Burrows, *John Ringo: The Gunfighter Who Never Was* (Tucson: University of Arizona Press, 1987).
9. Alfred Henry Lewis, *Wolfville* (New York: F.A. Stokes, 1897).
10. Alfred Henry Lewis, *Wolfville Days* (New York: F.A. Stokes, 1902); Alfred Henry Lewis, *Wolfville Nights* (New York: F.A. Stokes, 1902),
11. Alfred Henry Lewis, *The Sunset Trail* (Unknown publisher, 1906.)
12. Roberts, 380–381, 495n.
13. Masterson, William Barclay, "Famous Gunfighters of the Western Frontier: Doc Holliday," *Human Life,* May 1907, 5, 79.
14. *Ibid.*, 81.
15. Glenwood Springs, CO, Frontier Museum.
16. Robert G. McCubbin, "It Aint' Really Him!... Or Is It?" *True West*, March 2004, 25–26.
17. Walter Noble Burns, *Tombstone: An Iliad of the Southwest* (New York: Doubleday, 1927); William B. Breckenridge, *Helldorado: Bringing the Law to the Mesquite* (Boston: Houghton-Mifflin Co., 1927); Lorenzo Walters, *Tombstone's Yesterday* (Tucson, AZ: Acme Printing, 1928).
18. Burns, 32, 46–47.
19. *Ibid.* 163–170; *San Francisco Examiner*.
20. Walter Noble Burns, *The Saga of Billy the Kid* (New York: Grossett & Dunlap, 1925); Walter Noble Burns, *The Robin Hood of Eldorado* (Berkeley: Coward-McCann, Inc., 1932).
21. Breckenridge, 89, 123–25, 145–47.
22. *Tombstone*, 1993.
23. William B. Breckenridge, Richard Maxwell Brown, ed. *Helldorado: Bringing the Law to the Mesquite* (Lincoln: University of Nebraska Press, 1992).
24. Walters, 52–69.
25. Sherman McMaster's last name was misspelled as McMasters until research in the late 1990s and early 21st century. Peter Brand and Paul Cool offered documentation for the correct spelling.
26. Many of these issues have been addressed in Gary L. Roberts' *Doc Holliday*, 2006.
27. Walters.
28. *Tucson Star*, April 6, 1926.
29. Catherine Ann Curry, Ph.D., January 18, 1999. *Western Cattle Markets and News*, San Francisco, December 15, 1930.
30. http:www.everything2.com. dragoon, May 17, 2002.
31. Cool, Paul. "The World of Sherman McMaster(s)." *WOLA Journal*, Autumn, 1998, 10–22.
32. Stuart N. Lake, *Wyatt Earp: Frontier Marshal* (Boston: Houghton-Mifflin Co., 1931).
33. Earp/Lake Papers.
34. Lake.
35. *The Capture of the Biddle Brothers*, 1902.
36. *The Great Train Robbery*, 1903.
37. *Birth of a Nation*, 1915.

38. *Police Gazette.*
39. Owen Wister, *The Virginian: A Horseman of the Plains* (New York: Macmillan Company, 1904); Frederic S. Remington (October 4, 1861–Dec. 26, 1909); Charles M. Russell (March 19, 1864–October 24 October, 1926).
40. Joseph Brooks, dir., *Ben Hur,* New York City: Broadway Theater (November 29, 1899).
41. "Eye Witness to History.com." February 28, 2006, cites William S. Hart, *My Life East and West,* 1968; Lonn Taylor and Ingrid Maar, *The American Cowboy,* 1983.
42. Ronald L. Davis, *John Ford: Hollywood's Old Master* (Norman: University of Oklahoma Press, 1995).
43. Michael Munn, *John Wayne: The Man Behind the Myth* (New York: New American Library, 2003).
44. *In Old Arizona.*
45. *The Virginian.*
46. *The Big Trail.*
47. *Wild Bill Hickok.* Paul A. Hutton, Appearance of Bert Lindley in *Wild Bill Hickok.* BBB's Blog, *True West,* Jan. 26, 2012. blog.truewestmagazine.com.

Chapter Three

1. W.R. Burnett, *Saint Johnson* (New York: A.L. Burt Co.).
2. *Little Caesar,* 1931; *Scarface,* 1932; *High Sierra,* 1941.
3. Graham Cassidy, *Tombstone Pistoleers* (New York: Phoenix Press, 1936).
4. Jack O'Connor, *Boom Town* (New York: A.A. Knopf, 1938).
5. Frank A. Dunn, D.D.S. "Celebrating a Holliday," *Oral Hygiene,* September 1933, 1339–1343.
6. "Dodge's First Dentist Was a Pistoleer," The *Dodge City Globe,* September 18, 1933.
7. "The Films of Edward L. Cahn," *Classic Film and Television,* http://mikegrost.com/film.htm.
8. *Law and Order,* 1932.
9. Jon Tuska, *The Filming of the West* (UK: Robert Hale, 1978).
10. Harry Carey, Jr., Personal Interview with author. July 29, 1998, Cody, WY.
11. *Frontier Marshal,* 1934.
12. *The Arizonian,* 1935.
13. *The Informer,* 1935; *Stagecoach,* 1939.
14. *Tombstone,* 1993.
15. *Law for Tombstone,* 1937.
16. *Don Juan,* 1927.
17. *Wild West Days,* 1937.
18. *In Early Arizona,* 1938.
19. *The Marshal of Mesa City,* 1939.
20. *Gone with the Wind,* 1939; *Wuthering Heights,* 1939; *Gunga Din,* 1939.
21. *Frontier Marshal,* 1939.
22. *Sands of Iwo Jima,* 1950.
23. www.ovguide.com.

Chapter Four

1. *The Grapes of Wrath,* 1940; *The Great Dictator,* 1941; *Fantasia,* 1940.
2. *For Whom the Bell Tolls,* 1943.
3. Letter from Mary K. Cummings reproduced in Bob Boze Bell's *The Illustrated Life and Times of Doc Holliday* (Phoenix: Tri Star-Boze Publications, Inc., 1995), 106–110.
4. *Tombstone,* 1993.
5. E.B. Mann, *The Blue-Eyed Kid* (New York: Triangle Books, 1944).
6. Lee E. Wells, *Guns of Happy Valley* (New York: Curtis Books, 1947).
7. *Law and Order/Man from Cheyenne,* 1940.
8. *Tombstone, the Town Too Tough to Die,* 1942.
9. Michael S. Taylor, "McLowery" descendant, in correspondence and personal interview, identified the proper spelling as originally McClaughry, later McLaury. The name underwent several popular spellings, the most prevalent being McLowery.
10. *The Kansan,* 1943.
11. www.InternetActive.com.
12. Richard Aquila, ed. *Wanted Dead or Alive: The American West in Popular Culture* (Urbana: University of Illinois Press, 1996), 118.
13. *The Outlaw,* 1943.
14. *My Darling Clementine,* 1946); *Stagecoach,* 1939.
15. Davis, *John Ford,* 181.
16. Richard Griffith, *New Movies Review* (Frontier Historical Museum, January 22, 1947), 6–8.

Chapter Five

1. John Myers Myers, *Tombstone's Early Years* (New York: E.P. Dutton & Co., Inc., 1950).
2. John Clum, ed. *Tombstone Epitaph* (Tombstone, AZ: 1880–1882).
3. Harry M. Woods, ed. *Tombstone Nugget* (Tombstone, AZ: Tombstone Epitaph, 1880–1882).

4. Tom J. Hopkins, *Trouble in Tombstone* (Garden City: Doubleday & Co., Inc., 1951).
5. Clarence B. Kelland, *Tombstone* (New York: Harper & Brothers Publishers, 1952).
6. Will Henry (Henry Wilson Allen), *Who Rides with Wyatt* (New York: Random House, 1954).
7. W.R. Burnett, *Bitter Ground* (New York: Random House, 1954).
8. John Myers Myers, *Doc Holliday* (Boston: Little, Brown & Company, Inc., 1955).
9. John Myers Myers, "Doc Holliday: The West's Greatest Gunman," *SAGA: True Adventures for Men*, March 1955, 12–15; 87–93.
10. Carl Coke Rister, *Fort Griffin of the Texas Frontier* (Norman: University of Oklahoma Press, 1956).
11. Richard O'Connor, *Bat Masterson* (Garden City: Doubleday & Co., Inc., 1957).
12. Jahns, *The Frontier World of Doc Holliday*, 223.
13. Douglas D. Martin, *Tombstone's Epitaph* (Norman: University of Oklahoma Press, 1958).
14. Jeff Morey, "Blaze Away! Doc Holliday's Role in the West's Most Famous Gunfight," *True West*, November/December, 2001, 34.
15. Leslie Scott, *Tombstone Showdown* (New York: Pyramid Books, 1958).
16. www.Biblio.com, Comic World via Abe Books (Canada, 1959).
17. Oakley Hall, *Warlock* (New York: The Viking Press, Inc., 1958).
18. Wallace Stegner, *Angle of Repose* (Penguin Classics, December 2000).
19. Robert Stone, "Warlock," *New York Book Reviews*, 2005.
20. Lea F. McCarty, *The Gunfighters* (Oakland: Scenic Art, Inc., 1959).
21. Jack Foster, ed. "Doc Holliday Gained Fame with His Fast Draw," *Rocky Mountain News* (Denver, CO), July 26, 1953.
22. Wayne Gard, "One Dallas Dentist Rightly Forgotten," *Dallas News* (Dallas, TX), Sept. 28, 1954.
23. *Law and Order*, 1953.
24. *Powder River*, 1953.
25. *Dawn at Socorr*, 1954.
26. *New Frontier*, 1939; *Big Jake*, 1971.
27. *Masterson of Kansas*, 1954.
28. *Wichita*, 1955.
29. *Gunfight at the O.K. Corral*, 1957.
30. *Tombstone: The Town Too Tough to Die*, 1942.
31. *Warlock*, 1959.
32. *Warlock*, 1989.
33. Gary Yoggy, *Riding the Video Range: The Rise and Fall of the Western on Television* (Jefferson, NC: McFarland, 1995).
34. "Duel at the O.K. Corral," *Cavalcade of America*, 1954.
35. "Doc Holliday," *Stories of the Century*, 1954.
36. "Gunfight at the OK Corral," *You Are There*, 1953.
37. Doc Holliday," CBS Radio Western, July 19, 1952.
38. *Gunsmoke* CBS, Arness Production, 1955–1975.
39. *The Life and Legend of Wyatt Earp*, 1955–1961.
40. *Life and Legend*, Doug Fowley as Doc Holliday, 52 episode credits, 1956–1957; 1959–1961.
41. *Life and Legend*, Myron Healey as Doc Holliday, 13 episode credits, 1958–1959.
42. "Little Brother," *Life and Legend*, 1958.
43. "Tombstone," *Life and Legend*, 1959.
44. *Life and Legend*, Final 5 episodes (Aug. 29, 1961–Sept. 26, 1961).
45. "First Possee," *Buffalo Bill, Jr.*, 1955.
46. *Maverick*, September 22, 1957–July 8, 1962, 124 episodes.
47. The Quick and the Dead," *Maverick*, 1957.
48. "Seed of Deception," *Maverick*, 1958.
49. *Tombstone Territory*, October 16, 1957–September 17, 1958.
50. "Doc Holliday in Durango," *Tombstone Territory*, 1958.
51. "Johnny Ringo's Last Ride," *Tombstone Territory*, 1958.
52. *Lawman*, October 5, 1958–October 9, 1962, 156 episodes; "The Wayfarer," *Lawman*, 1959.
53. *Colt .45*, a/k/a *Thundercloud*, 1959–1960; "The Devil's Godson," *Colt .45*, 1959.
54. *Sugarfoot*, Sept. 17, 1957–July 3, 1961; "The Trial of the Canary Kid" *Sugarfoot*, 1959.
55. *Zane Grey Theater*, October 5, 1945–May 18, 1961; "Man of Fear," *Zane Grey Theater*, 1958.
56. *Tales of Wells Fargo*, March 18, 1957–September 8, 1962; "Doc Holliday," *Tales of Wells Fargo*, 1959.
57. *Cheyenne*, 108 episodes, 1955–1962; "Birth of a Nation," *Cheyenne*, ABC, 1959, not aired.

Chapter Six

1. Frank Waters, The *Earp Brothers of Tombstone: The Story of Mrs. Virgil Earp* (New York: C.N. Potter, 1960).
2. Robert E. Ladd, *Vengeance at the O.K.*

Corral (Tucson: Arizona Historical Society, 1963).

3. Glen G. Boyer, *Illustrated Life of Doc Holliday* (Glenwood Springs, CO, Reminder Publishing Co., 1966).

4. Glenn G. Boyer, *Suppressed Murder of Wyatt Earp* (San Antonio: Naylor Co, 1967).

5. Joseph G. Rosa, *The Gunfighter: Man or Myth?* (Norman: University of Oklahoma, 1969).

6. Lake, *Wyatt Earp*.

7. Harris M. Lentz III, *Western and Frontier Film and Television Credits* (Jefferson, NC: McFarland, 1996).

8. Charles L. Sonnischen, *From Hopalong to Hud: Thoughts on Western Fiction* (Lubbock: Texas Tech University Press, 1978).

9. *Cheyenne Autumn*, 1964.

10. Richard Slotkin, *Gunfighter Nation* (Norman: University of Oklahoma Press, 1998), 629.

11. *Stagecoach*, 1966.

12. *Hour of the Gun*, 1967.

13. *Maverick*, September 22, 1957–July 8, 1962.

14. "Triple Indemnity," *Maverick*, 1961.

15. "A Technical Error," *Maverick*, 1961.

16. "Marshal Maverick," *Maverick*, 1962.

17. "The Maverick Report," 1962.

18. "One of Our Trains Is Missing," *Maverick*, 1962.

19. "Rovin' Gambler," *The Tall Man*, 1961.

20. "Calamity Over the Comstock," *Bonanza*, 1963.

21. *Death Valley Days*, 1952–1975, 452 episodes.

22. "After the O.K. Corral," *Death Valley Days*, 1964.

23. The epdisodes were titled, "The Quiet and the Fury" and "Fighting Sky Pilot."

24. "Doc Holliday's Gold Bars," *Death Valley Days*, 1966.

25. *Wagon Train*, "The Silver Lady," 1965.

26. *Dr. No* (1962); *From Russia with Love* (1963); *Goldfinger* (1964); *Thunderball* (1965); *You Only Live Twice* (1967); *On Her Majesty's Secret Service* (1969).

27. *Bonnie and Clyde* (1967); *Wild in the Streets* (1968); *Easy Rider* (1969).

28. *The Graduate* (1967).

29. "A Holliday for the Doctor," *Doctor Who*, 1966; "Don't Shoot the Pianist," *Doctor Who*, 1966; " Johnny Ringo," *Doctor Who*; "The O.K. Corral" *Doctor Who*, 1966.

30. "Spectre of the Gun," *Star Trek*, 1966.

31. Shootout at the O'Day Corral," *Pistols 'n' Petticoats*, 1967.

32. "Doctor from Dodge," *The High Chaparral*, 1967.

Chapter Seven

1. Ben T. Traywick, *Tombstone: 1877–1900* 4th. ed. (Tombstone: Self-published, 1970).

2. Dale Key Schoenberger, *The Gunfighters* (Caldwell, ID: Caxton Printers, Ltd., 1971), 139–180.

3. George Turner, *Book of Gunfighters* (Amarillo: Baxter Lane Co., 1972), 32–33.

4. Albert S. Pendleton and Susan McKey Thomas, *In Search of the Hollidays* (Valdosta, GA: Little River Press, 1973).

5. Glenwood Springs Historical Society Collection.

6. Ben T. Traywick, *The Residents of Tombstone's Boothill* (Tombstone: Self-published, 1971).

7. Ben T. Traywick, *Tombstone's Immortals* (Tombstone: Self-published, 1973).

8. *Tombstone* (1993).

9. O'Connor, *Iron Wheels and Broken Men*, 202–203.

10. Churchill, *Doc Holliday, Bat Masterson & Wyatt Earp, Their Colorado Careers*.

11. W. Eugene Hollon, *Frontier Violence: Another Look* (New York: Oxford University Press, 1974).

12. Frederick Jackson Turner, *The Significance of the Frontier in American History: Chicago World's Columbian Exposition, 1893*. (Albuquerque: University of New Mexico Press, 1993).

13. Glenn G. Boyer, *I Married Wyatt Earp: The Recollections of Josephine Sarah Marcus Earp* (Tucson: University of Arizona Press, 1976).

14. Ben T. Traywick, *The Earp Years: 1880–1882* (Tombstone: Tombstone Epitaph, 1974); Traywick, *The Wild Bunch: The Most Unusual and Exciting Western Show Found Anywhere on Earth* (Tombstone: Self-published, 1975).

15. Howard Robert Lamar, *The Reader's Encyclopedia of the American West* (New York: Thomas Y. Crowell Co., 1977).

16. Larry D. Ball, *The United States Marshals of New Mexico and Arizona Territories, 1846–1912* (Albuquerque: University of New Mexico Press, 1978), 107–133.

17. Jeffrey J. Morey in email, July 10, 2011.

18. Gary L. Roberts "Gunfight at O.K. Corral: The Wells Spicer Decision, 1881," *Montana, The Magazine of Western History* XX (January 1970), 62–74.

19. Wayne Montgomery, "A Little Ride with Doc," *Real Frontier* (April 1971), 41.

20. Martha Anne Holliday (Sister M. Melanie, Sisters of Mercy, 1849–1939).

21. Story related by phone from Mrs.

Susan McKey Thomas, family member, July 19, 1996.
22. Glenn G. Boyer, "John Henry Holliday, DDS," *Journal of Arizona History* (Autumn, 1973), 14.
23. Zoltan Malocsay, "OK Corral: 100 Years of Lies, " *Westerner* (July-Aug., 1973), 34.
24. Stanley R. Korf, "Doc Holliday: The Legend and the Dentist," *Jada* (Atlanta: Vol. 88, Jan. 1974), 16-30.
25. Sam Ripple, "Doc Holliday's Girl," *Westerner* (Nov./Dec. 1971), 48; Wayne Montgomery, "The Deadly Doctor Holliday" (April 1973), 14.
26. Wayne Montgomery, "Tom 'Pole Cat'" Adams Recalls Doc Holliday," *NOLA Magazine* (National Outlaw-Lawmen Association) Summer 1975, 14.
27. Carl W. Briehan, "Desperate Men, Desperate Guns," *True West* (Annual, Winter 1977-78), 16.
28. Jane Polley, "Good Guys & Co.: The Men with the Six-Pointed Star," *Readers' Digest Assn., Inc.* (New York: American Folklore and Legend, 1978), 320-322.
29. Glenn G. Boyer, "Postscripts to Historical Fiction About Wyatt Earp in Tombstone," *Arizona and the West* (Vol. 18, Autumn 1976) 217-236).
30. Gary L. Roberts. "The Real Tombstone Travesty: The Earp Controversy from Bechdolt to Boyer" *WOLA Journal* (V, VIII, 1999). Also available at http://home.earthlink.net/knuthcol.
31. Gary L. Roberts, *Doc Holliday*.
32. A.W.Bork and Glenn G. Boyer, "The O.K. Corral Fight at Tombstone: A Footnote by Kate Elder," *Arizona and the West* (Tucson: Arizona Historical Society, 1977), 65-84.
33. *Doc*, 1971.
34. "Showdown at O.K. Corral," *Appointment with Destiny*, 1971; "Which Way to the O.K. Corral?" *Appointment with Destiny*, 1972.
35. *Alias Smith and Jones*, Jan. 1971-1973.
36. "Which Way to the O.K. Corral?" *Alias Smith and Jones*, 1972.
37. "The Day That Shook Kid Curry," *Alias Smith and Jones*, 1972.
38. *Sesame Street*, Season 7, Episode 19, 60 min, 25 Dec. 1975.
39. Robert F. Palmquist, "Good-Bye Old Friend," *Real West* (May 1979), 24-53.

Chapter Eight

1. Aaron Spelling, ex. prod. *Dynasty* (Hollywood: ABC, 47 min. Jan. 12, 1981–May 11, 1989); Michael Mann, ex. prod. *Miami Vice* (Hollywood: NBC, USA Network, 48 min. 28 Sept. 1984–25 Jan. 1990); Sidney Sheldon, screenwriter, *Hart to Hart* (Hollywood: ABC, 60 min. 25 Aug. 1979–22 May 1984).
2. Alford E. Turner, *The Earps Talk* (College Station: Creative Publishing Co., 1980).
3. Wyatt Boyer [sic] and Glenn G. Earp [sic]. *Wyatt Earp* (Tombstone, AZ: Y.V. Bissette, 1981).
4. W.R. Garwood, *Ringo's Tombstone* (Ann Arbor, MI: Bath Street Press, 1981).
5. Alford E. Turner, ed. *The O.K. Corral Inquest* (Minneapolis: Creative Publishing, 1981).
6. Masterson, Bat, annotated and illustrated by Jack DeMattos) *The 75th Anniversary of Famous Gunfighters of the Western Frontier* "Doc Holliday, Chapter 4 (Monroe, WA: Weatherford Press, January 1982) 75-84.
7. DeMattos, Jack, "Doc Holliday," *Real West* (Spring, 1985) 30.
8. Ben T. Traywick, *A Town Called Tombstone* (Tombstone, AZ: Red Marie's, 1982).
9. Paul A. Hutton, *American West* "Celluloid Lawman: Wyatt Earp goes to Hollywood" (XXI: 3, May/June 1984) 58-65.
10. Ben T. Traywick, *Tombstone's Deadliest Gun: John Henry Holliday* (Tombstone: Red Marie's, 1984).
11. Ben T. Traywick, Traywick, *Tombstone's Outlaw Album: The Gunfight at O.K. Corral and Incidents Following* (Tombstone: Red Marie's, 1984); Ben T. Traywick, *Wyatt Earp: The Lion of Tombstone* (Tombstone: Red Marie's, 1984).
12. Ben T. Traywick, *Tombstone Outlaw Album*.
13. Peter Hertzog, *Outlaws of New Mexico* (Santa Fe: Sunstone Press, 1984).
14. Ben T. Traywick, *The National Tombstone Epitaph; Marshal of Tombstone Virgil Walter Earp and John Peters Ringo: Mythical Gunfighter* (Tombstone: Red Marie's, 1985).
15. DeMattos, "Doc Holliday."
16. John Alder, *Western Legend* (Casper, WY: Whiskey Creek Press, 1985).
17. Jon Tuska, *The American West in Film: Critical Approaches to the Western* (Santa Barbara: Greenwood Press, 1985).
18. Carl W. Breihan and Wayne Montgomery, *Forty Years on the Wild Frontier* (Greenwich: Devin-Adair, Publishers, 1985).
19. Paul I. Wellman, *A Dynasty of Western Outlaws* (Lincoln: University of Nebraska, 1985).
20. Carl Coke Rister, *Fort Griffin on the Texas Frontier* (Norman: University of Oklahoma Press, 1986).

21. Loren D. Estleman, *Bloody Season* (New York: Bantam Books, Inc. 1987).
22. David Everitt, *Legends: The Story of Wyatt Earp* (New York: Paper Jacks, 1988).
23. Edward Schieffelin, and Ben T. Traywick. *History of the Discovery of Tombstone, Arizona, as Told by the Discoverer, Edward Lawrence Schieffelin*. (Tombstone, AZ: Red Marie's, 1988).
24. Joseph G. Rosa and Waldo E. Coop, *Rowdy Joe Lowe: Gambler with a Gun* (Norman: University of Oklahoma Press, 1989); Preston Lewis, *The Lady and Doc Holliday* (Austin: Diamond Books, 1989).
25. Jeff J. Morey, *Equivocation at the O.K. Corral* (Tucson: Arizona Historical Society Archives, 1989).
26. Paula Mitchell Marks, *And Die in the West: The Story of the O.K. Corral Gunfight* (Norman: University of Oklahoma Press, 1989).
27. *Wild Times*, prod. Wes Sheldon, dir. Richard Compton, TV mini-series, 195 min. (Santa Fe, NM: Rattlesnake Productions, Inc., Jan. 24, 1980).
28. *The New York Times*. Movies. "Wild Times," Feb. 24, 2009.
29. *Damon Runyon's Pueblo*, prod. Al Kochka, dir. John Henry Johnson, 40 min. (Pueblo, CO: Tamarack Productions, 1981).
30. *I Married Wyatt Earp*, 1983.
31. *Stagecoach*, 1986.
32. *The Young Maverick*, prod. Ric de Alzevedo, dir. Hy Averback, et al., 60 min. (California: CBS/Warner Brothers Television, 1979–80, 8 episodes.); *The Chisholms*, prod. Paul Freeman, dir. Edward M. Abroms and Mel Stuart, 50 min. (Colorado: CBS/Alan Landsburg Productions, 1979–1980, 13 episodes); *Bret Maverick*, prod. Gordon Lawson, dir. Ivan Dixon, et al., 60 min. (California: NBC/Cherokee Productions, 1981–1982, 18 episodes).
33. *Dallas*, prod. James H. Brown, dir. Dwight Adair, et al., 60 min. (Hollywood: CBS/Warner Brothers 1978–1991, 357 episodes); *Yellow Rose*, prod. Paul Freeman, dir. Lee H. Katzin, et al., 60 min. (Hollywood: NCB, 1983–1984, 22 episodes).
34. *Sesame Street*, prod. Melissa Dino, et al., dir. Ted May, et al., 60 min. (Hollywood: Season 21, Episode 5, 17 Nov, 1989).
35. *Pale Rider*, 1985.
36. *Young Guns*, 1988.
37. *Indiana Jones and Raiders of the Lost Ark*, 1989; *Die Hard*, 1988; *Rambo: First Blood*, 1982; *Rambo First Blood Part II*, 1985; *Rambo III*, 1988; *Lethal Weapon*, 1987; *Lethal Weapon 2*, 1989.

Chapter Nine

1. http://www.tombstonehistoryarchives.com.
2. Richard Maxwell Brown, *No Duty to Retreat* (Norman: University of Oklahoma, 1991).
3. Ben T. Traywick, *The Chronicles of Tombstone to a Lady Called Red Marie* (Tombstone: Red Marie's, 1990).
4. Richard F. Selcer, *Hell's Half Acre: Life and Legend of a Red Light District*. Chisholm Trail Series No. 9 (Dallas: Texas Christian University Press, 1991), 364.
5. Richard E. Erwin, *The Truth About Wyatt Earp* (Carpinteria: O.K. Press, 1993).
6. Charles M. Robinson, *The Frontier World of Fort Griffin: The Life and Death of a Western Town* (Norman: Arthur H. Clark, 1992).
7. Slotkin, *Gunfighter Nation*.
8. Larry D. Ball, *Desert Lawmen: The High Sheriffs of New Mexico and Arizona 1846–1912* (Albuquerque: University of New Mexico Press, 1992).
9. Ben T. Traywick, *Legendary Characters of Southwest Arizona* (Tombstone: Red Marie's, 1992).
10. *Unforgiven*, 1992.
11. *Tombstone*, 1993; *Wyatt Earp*, 1994.
12. Ben T. Traywick, *Hell's Belles of Tombstone* (Tombstone: Red Marie's, 1993); Glenn G. Boyer & Ben T. Traywick. *Wyatt Earp's Tombstone Vendetta* (Honolulu: Talei Publishers, Inc., 1993).
13. J.R. Roberts, *The Gunsmith Giant 01: Trouble in Tombstone* (Berkeley: Jove, Special Giant Edition Book, 1993).
14. Jack Fiske, *My Friend Doc Holliday*. (Tombstone, AZ: J. Fiske, 1994).
15. Don Cusic, *Cowboys and the Wild West* (New York: Facts on File, 1994).
16. Chaput, *The Earp Papers*.
17. Sylvia Lynch, *Aristocracy's Outlaw* (New Tazwell: Iris Press, 1994).
18. Emma Walling, *John "Doc" Holliday Colorado Trials and Triumphs* (Snowmass, CO: Kollene Sublett, 1994).
19. Ben T. Traywick, *The Chronicles of Tombstone, Historical Documents and Photographs of Tombstone, Tombstone Clippings* (Tombstone: Red Marie's, 1994).
20. Traywick, *The Chronicle of Tombstone*, 2d. ed., 1994.
21. Glenn G. Boyer, *Wyatt Earp's Tombstone Vendetta* (New York: G.K. Hall Large Print Book Series, 1994).
22. Paul Beck, *The Gunfight at O.K. Corral and Incidents Following* (Tombstone: Red Marie's, 1994).

23. Arizona, *A Guide to Public Records in the Arizona State Archives* (Phoenix, AZ.: Archives Division, Dept. of Library, Archives & Public Records, State of Arizona, 1994).

24. Bell, *The Illustrated Life and Times of Doc Holliday*.

25. Gene Autry, *The Loser's View of the O.K. Corral/Dalton Gang's Mystery Rider/Tombstone's Boot Hill* (Cowles History Group, October 1995) Wild West: Vol. 8, No. 3.

26. Jane Candia Coleman, *Doc Holliday's Woman* (New York: Warner Books, Inc., 1995).

27. Carl R. Green and William R. Sanford, *Outlaws and Lawmen of the Wild West* (Berkeley Heights, NJ: Enslow Publishers, 1995).

28. H. Sheffer, *Gunfight at the O.K. Corral* (Detroit: Norseman Publishing, 1995).

29. Lynn R. Bailey, ed. *A Tenderfoot in Tombstone: The Private Journal of George Whitwell Parsons: The Turbulent Years, 1800-82, Vol. 65 of Great West and Indian* Series (Tucson: Westernlore Press, 1996).

30. Ralph Compton, *The Killing Season, The Autumn of the Gun* (New York: Penguin Books, 1996, 1997).

31. Preston Lewis, *Mix-Up at the O.K. Corral* (New York: Book Creations, Inc., 1996).

32. Leon Claire Metz, *The Shooters* (Knoxville, TN: Berkeley Trade, 1996).

33. Ben T. Traywick, *John Henry: The "Doc" Holliday Story* (Tombstone: Red Marie's Bookstore, 1996); www.americanwest.com/pages/docholid.htm.

34. Traywick, *The Clantons of Tombstone* (Tombstone: Red Marie's, 1996).

35. Ben T. Traywick, Wallace Clayton, Dana Shull, et al. [sic]. *OK Corral Gunfight Symposium*. 2 audiocassette tapes, 1996.

36. Tefertiller, *op cit*.

37. Tefertiller (Carson and Ackerman), "She Married Wyatt Earp" 278-279, 378n.

38. Tefertiller, 18.

39. Matt Braun, *Doc Holliday* (New York: St. Martin's Paperbacks, 1997).

40. Neil B. Carmony, ed. *Apache Days and Tombstone Nights: John Clum's Autobiography, 1877-1887* (Silver City, NM: High Lonesome Books, 1997).

41. Buck Rainey, *Western Gunslingers in Fact and on Film: Hollywood's Famous Lawmen and Outlaws* (Jefferson, NC: McFarland,1997).

42. Ty Cashion, *A Texas Frontier: The Clear Fork Country and Fort Griffin, 1849-1887* (Norman: University of Oklahoma Press, 1997).

43. Glenn G. Boyer. *Suppressed Murder of Wyatt Earp; Trailing an American Myth & Those Marryin' Earp Men* (Wyatt Earp Facts, Vol. 3) (Missoula: Historical Research Associates, Inc., 1997).

44. Glenn G. Boyer. *Who Was Sheriff Johnny Behan? (Wyatt Earp: Family Friends & Foes, Vol. 2); Who Killed John Ringo: Wyatt Earp, Family Friends & Foes, Vol. 5* (Missoula: Historical Research Associates, Inc., 1997).

45. Steven Gibson and Ken Ravell, *Outlaws and Lawmen of the Wild West* (Mesa, AZ: Terrell Publishing Co., 1997).

46. Tanner, *Doc Holliday*.

47. Randy Lee Eickhoff, *The Fourth Horseman* (New York: A Tom Doherty Associates Book, 1998).

48. Allen Barra, *Inventing Wyatt Earp: His Life and Many Legends* (New York: Carroll & Graf Publishers, 1998).

49. Phillip W. Steele, John D. Levan, *Outlaws and Gunfighters of the Old West*, audiocassette (Gretna, LA: Pelican Press, 1998).

50. John Richard Stephens, ed. *Wyatt Earp Speaks!* (Cambria Pines by the Sea, CA: Fern Canyon Press, 1998).

51. Josephine Sarah Marcus, *Wyatt's Woman: She Married Wyatt Earp, The Life and Times of Josephine Sarah Marcus* (Tucson: E. Chafin Press, 1998).

52. Ben T. Traywick, *Wyatt Earp's 13 Dead Men*. (Tombstone: Red Marie's, 1998).

53. Buck Rainey, *Western Gunslingers in Fact and on Film* (Jefferson, NC: McFarland, 1998).

54. Kathleen Chamberlain, Compiler. *Wild Westerners, A Bibliography*. Richard W. Etulain, Series Editor. Center for the American West, Department of History (Albuquerque, University of New Mexico, 1998).

55. Young, *Cochise County Cowboy War*.

56. Ben T. Traywick, ed. *Tombstone Paper Trails* (Tombstone: Red Marie's, 1999).

57. Alfred H. Lewis, ed. *Gunfighters of the Western Frontier: A Memoir of the Old West* (by William Barclay 'Bat" Masterson (Old West Library, 1999).

58. Richard Etulain and Glenda Riley, ed. *With Badges and Bullets: Lawmen and Outlaws in the Old West* (Bolden: Fulcrum Publishers, 1999).

59. Michael M. Hickey, *Street Fight in Tombstone Near the O.K. Corral* (Honolulu: Talei Publishers, Inc., 1991).

60. J.R. Kirkpatrick, "Doc Holliday's Missing Grave," *True West* (October 1990), 46.

61. David J. Hall, "John Henry 'Doc' Holliday and His Street Howitzer," *NOLA Magazine* (Jan.–March 1993), 12-15.

62. Chuck Parsons, "Answer Man" column. *True West* (Jan. 1993), 13; (Feb. 1993), 12; (June 1993), 12.
63. Chuck Parsons, "Answer Man" column, *True West* (Jan. 1994), 12; Robert Barr Smith. "The West's Deadliest Dentist, *Wild West* (April 1994), 64.
64. Glenn G. Boyer, "Wyatt Earp: Part XII: Tombstone's Helen of Troy, *True West* (July 1994), 12-17.
65. Jeffrey J. Morey, "The Curious Vendetta of Glenn G. Boyer," *NOLA Magazine* (October-Dec. 1994), 22-28; Tombstone History Archives. http://disc.yourwebapps.com/Indices/39627.html.
66. Leo W. Banks, "Wyatt Earp: Fearless Lawman, Loyal Friend and Deadly Enemy" *Arizona Highways* (Phoenix: Arizona Dept. of Transportation, 1970) Vol. 70, No. 7, 4-13.
67. Terry "Ike" Clanton, "Wyatt Earp Murdered My Cousin" (Hilton Head, SC: TriComm Productions, 1994).
68. Paul A. Hutton, "Showdown at the Hollywood Corral," *Montana, The Magazine of Western History* (Summer 1995), 2-31.
69. Randy Lee Eickhoff, "A Young Doc Holliday," *True West* (March 1995), 12-16.
70. Dana Shull "The Losers View of the O.K. Corral," *Wild West* (October 1995), 50-72.
71. Randy Lee Eickhoff, Western column, "Doc Data Disputed, Letter & Response by Author," *True West* (June 1995), 4; Chuck Parsons Answer Man column, "Doc Holliday—Fact and Fancy," *True West* (October 1995), 58.
72. "Did Loan Play Role at O.K. Corral?" *The Arizona Republic* Life (18 March 1996). University of Arizona collection of Jacobs family records.
73. Chuck Parsons,"Doc Holliday's Life," "Answer Man" column, *True West* (October. 1996), 58.
74. Ben Traywick, "Doc Holliday," *True West* (April 1997), 31; Victoria Wilcox, "Doc Holliday's White Columns in Georgia," *True West* (April 1997), 24; Sylvia Wittels, MD. "Doc's Disease," *True West* (April 1997), 20.
75. Rick Cartledge, "Doc Holliday and the Whipit Gun," *True West* (April 1997), 14.
76. Randy D. Smith, "Wyatt Earp, Doc Holliday: The Stuff of Legends," *Old West* (Summer 1997), 41.
77. P.A. Mallory, "The Dodge City War," *Wild West* (June 1997), 32; Ben Traywick, "The Real Doc Holliday," *Wild West* (October 1997), 36; Chuck Parsons, "Another Shot at Doc," *True West* (Nov. 1997), 58.
78. Robert F. Palmquist. "Mining, Keno and the Law, The Tombstone Careers of Bob Winders, Charley Smith and Fred Dodge, 1879-1888," *The Journal of Arizona History* (Summer, 1997).
79. Paul Cool, "The World of Sherman McMaster(s)," *WOLA Journal*, Autumn 1998, 10-22.
80. Gary L. Roberts, "Trailing an American Mythmaker: Glenn G. Boyer," *The WOLA Journal*, 1998 6:3) 5-25.
81. Tamie Ross "Memories Ride Trail Back to Frontier City's Beginning," *Sunday Oklahoman*, Travel and Entertainment (May 17, 1998).
82. Chuck Hornung, "Wyatt Earp and Doc Holliday in Las Vegas, New Mexico," *True West* (May 1999) 12); Hornung, "Wyatt Earp's New Mexico Adventures," *Old West* (Summer 1999) 12; Karen Holliday Tanner, "Vision of a Legend," *NOLA Magazine* (23: 2, 1999) 30.
83. Gary L. Roberts, "The Real Tombstone Travesty," *WOLA Journal* (Fall, 1999).
84. Peter Brand, "The El Paso Salt War, Texas Rangers & Tombstone." *WOLA Journal* (Winter 1999) 2-19.
85. Pila Martinez, "UA May Sever Ties to Wyatt Earp Book," *Arizona Daily Star*, Dec. 9, 1999, Sec B, 3.
86. *Real West*, prod. David L. Wolper, dir. Yan Debonne, A&E Channel. Remastered by The History Channel in 2008. Ultimate Collections, *The Real West* in four discs. Disc four is Cowboys & Outlaws. Available individually or in the set.
87. Howard Bryan, *Wildest of the Wild West: True Tales of a Town on the Santa Fe Trail* (Santa Fe: Clear Light Publishers, 1988).
88. *Daily Optic*, 20 July 1881.
89. *Gunfighters of the West: The Earp Brothers*, prod. Phillip Boag, dir. Kevin McCarey, 50 min. (Mescal, AZ: TLC/The Learning Channel, WinStar, 11 May 1998).
90. *Tombstone*; *Wyatt Earp*, op cit.
91. *Law and Order*, 1932, op cit.
92. *Wyatt Earp: Return to* Tombstone, dir. Paul Landres, 100 min. (Old Tombstone: Associated Images, July 1, 1994).
93. *Purgatory*, prod. Daniel Schneider, dir. Uli Edell. 94 min. (Hollywood: TNT, Jan. 10, 1999).

Chapter Ten

1. *Cast Away*, 2000; *The Sopranos*, prod. Brad Gray, dir. Tim Van Patten, 60 min. (New Jersey: HBO, 1999-2000, 86 episodes).
2. Paul West, *O.K.: The Corral, the Earps, and Doc Holliday* (New York: Scribner, 2000).

3. *San Francisco Examiner.*
4. Roberts, 340.
5. Wyatt Earp and John Richard Stephens, *Wyatt Earp Tells of the Gunfight Near the O.K. Corral* (Cambria, CA: Fern Canyon Press, 2000).
6. E. Richard Churchill, *Doc Holliday, Bat Masterson, and Wyatt Earp: Their Colorado Careers* (Colorado: Western Reflections Publishing Co., 2001).
7. Bruce Olds, *Bucking the Tiger* (UK: Picador, 2001).
8. Nathan Ward, *Library Journal,* 2001.
9. Michael Hickey, *John Ringo: His Final Hours* (Hawaii: Talei Publishers, 2001).
10. Karen Holliday Tanner, *Doc Holliday: A Family Portrait* (Norman: University of Oklahoma, 2001).
11. Franklin D. Roosevelt, January 7, 1941.
12. Thom Ross, *Gunfight at the O.K. Corral in Words and Pictures* (Golden: Fulcrum Publishing, 2001).
13. Paul West and Rémy Lambrechts, *Doc Holliday* (France: Gallimard Press, 2001)
14. Bob Alexander, *John H. Behan: Sacrificed Sheriff* (Silver City, NM: High Lonesome Books, 2002).
15. Matt Braun, *Tombstone* (New York: Saint Martin's Paperbacks, 2002).
16. Lou H. Rodenberger and David Coffey, *31 by Lawrence Clayton: A Clear Fork Chronicle* (College Station, TX: State House Press, 2002).
17. Scott Waldman, *Gunfight at the O.K. Corral: Wyatt Earp Takes on the Clanton Gang* (New York: Rosen Publishing Group, 2003).
18. Rosen is an educational press with materials aimed primarily at teen readers.
19. James Reasoner, *Draw: The Greatest Gunfights of the American West* (Berkley: Berkley Trade, 2003).
20. L. T. Brooks, *The Last Gamble of Doc Holliday* (North Carolina: Pentland Press, 2004).
21. Gene Carlisle, *Why Doc Holliday Left Georgia* (Ohio: Carlisle Publishing, Inc., 2004).
22. Bob Bell Boze, Gus Walker, and Robert G. McCubbin, *Classic Gunfights: Blaze Away! The 25 Gunfights Behind the O.K. Corral Vol. 2 Vol. 2.* Phoenix: Tri Star-Boze, 2005.
23. Ed Finn, *The Legend of the O.K. Corral* (Tucson: Rio Nuevo Publishing, 2005).
24. Robert K. DeArment, *Bravo of the Brazos: John Larn of Fort Griffin, Texas* (Norman: University of Oklahoma Press, 2005).
25. Roberts, *op cit.*
26. Michael F. Blake, *Hollywood and the O.K. Corral* (Jefferson, NC: McFarland, 2006).
27. Ben T. Traywick, *Analysis of the Gunfight at the O.K. Corral* (Tombstone: Red Marie's, 2006).
28. *Doc Holliday,* audio book, narrated by William Conrad (New York: Radio Spirits, June 21, 2007).
29. S.M. Ballard and Lee Emory, *Borrowed Time; A Holliday in Tombstone (Doc Holliday)* (Arizona: Treble Heart Books/Sundowners, March 2007, March 2008). Ballard, S. M. Borrowed Time. Sierra Vista, AZ: Sundowners, 2007.
30. S. M. Ballard, *Death Takes a Holliday* (Arizona: Treble Heart books/Sundowners, 2009).
31. Jack Kincade, *Fighting for Air: The Unknown Adventures of Young Doc Holliday* (Create Space, 2008).
32. Gayle Martin, *Gunfight at the O.K. Corral* (Chandler, AZ: Five Star Publications, 2008).
33. Tim Barnes, *Doc Holliday's Road to Tombstone: The Life and Times of John Henry Holliday* (Xlibris, 2008).
34. *My Darling Clementine,* audio book written by William Keighley (Amazon Digital: Shamrock Eden Publishing, 2009).
35. *Famous Gunfighters of the Western Frontier: Wyatt Earp, Doc Holliday, Luke Short and Others* (New York: Dover Publications, 2009).
36. S. M. Ballard, *Kate* (Tombstone: Goose Flats Publishing, 2010).
37. S. M. Ballard, *Doc Holliday's Dilemma* (Tombstone: Amazon Digital Services, 2010).
38. D.J. Herda, *They Call Me Doc: The Story Behind the Legend of John Henry Holliday* (Connecticut: Lyons Press, 2010.
39. Jimmy Gray, Donnie Blanz, Joe Loesch and Bennie Shipley, *Gunfighters: Billy the Kid, Jesse James, The Earps & Doc Holliday* (Readio Theater, Ltd., 2010).
40. George Scullin, Steve Frazee and Paul Leslie Peil, *Gunfight at the O.K. Corral and Other Western Adventures* (Montana: Literary Licensing, 2011).
41. SB Jeffrey, *The Arizona War and The Gunfight at The O.K. Corral* (Webster's Digital Services); "History of Cochise County, Arizona: Gunfight at the O.K. Corral, Wyatt Earp, Doc Holliday, Earp Vendetta Ride," Wikipedia, 2011.
42. John DiLeo, *Hour of the Gun (1967): Deconstructing Wyatt Earp* (New Jersey: Hansen Publishing Group, 2011).
43. John Alder, *Western Legend* (Texas: Whiskey Creek Press, 1985; Amazon Digital Services, 2011).
44. Mary Doria Russell, *Doc* (New York: Ballentine Books, 2012).
45. Jeff Guinn, *The Last Gunfight: The*

Real Story of the Shootout at the O.K. Corral — And How It Changed the American West (New York: Simon and Schuster, 2012).

46. Nate Bowden, *Doc* (Portland: Oni Press, 2012).

47. Dale Chase, *Wyatt: Doc Holliday's Account of an Intimate Friendship* (New York: Bold Strokes Books, 2012).

48. Paul Lee Johnson, *The McLaurys in Tombstone, Arizona: An O.K. Corral Obituary* (Denton: University of North Texas, 2012).

49. Peter Brand, *Wyatt Earp's Posse Rider: The Story of Texas Jack Vermillion* (New South Wales, AUS: Peter Brand, 2012) 17–27.

50. R. K. DeArment, "The Sporting Crowd at Old Fort Griffin, *True West*, January 2000) 16; Karen Holliday Tanner, "Gunfighter Mythology: Doc Holliday," *True West*, August 2000, 32.

51. Palmquist. "Mining, Keno..." *op cit.* Cool, "The World of Sherman..." *op cit.*

52. Karen Holliday Tanner and Clifton Brewer. "Doc Holliday's Last Days," *True West* (Spring 2003) 29–48.

53. Gary L. Roberts, "The Charlie Smith Papers: Real or Fake," *WOLA Journal* (Spring 2004) 29–48.

54. Cool, *op cit.*

55. Peter Brand, *op cit.*

56. Roberts, *Doc Holliday*, 239–240, 243–246, 253, 267, 284.

57. Roberts, *Doc Holliday*, 244.

58. Peter Brand, "Daniel G. Tipton & The Earp Vendetta Posse. *NOLA Magazine* (October–December 2000), 17–27.

59. Peter Brand, "Friends and Enemies: Dan Tipton and the Earp Vendetta Posse," *True West* (December 2001) 54.

60. Roberts, *Doc*. 233, 243–44, 249, 252–53, 260, 262, 267, 270, 272, 280, 284–285, 328.

61. Stephens.

62. Peter Brand, "Wyatt Earp, Jack Johnson and the Notorious Blount Brothers," *NOLA Magazine* (Oct.–Dec. 2003), 36–47.

63. Jahns, 223–24, 232, 234, 235.

64. Peter Brand, "Wyatt Earp's Vendetta Posse." *Wild West* (April 2007), 36–47.

65. Peter Brand, "Duty Bound" The Story of John Wilson Vermillion & The Mystery of Tombstone's Texas Jack," *WWHA Journal* (August 2010), 5–19.

66. "Doc Holliday Collector's Edition," *True West* (December 2001).

67. Gary L. Roberts. "The Lure of the Legend," *True West* (December 2001), 14.

68. Roberts, "Mrs. John Holliday?" *True West* (December 2001) 26–28.

69. Roberts, "The Leadville Years."

70. Chuck Hornung and Gary L. Roberts, "The Split: Did Doc & Wyatt Split Because of a Racial Slur?" *True West* (December 2001), 58–61.

71. Lee A. Silva, "The Shotgun Used by Doc Holliday in the Gunfight at the O.K. Corral Has Never Surfaced ... Or Did It?" *Wild West — Guns of the West Department*, June 2001), 14–75.

72. Casey Tefertiller and Jeff Morey, "O.K. Corral: A Gunfight Shrouded in Mystery," *Wild West* (October 2001).

73. Jeffrey J. Morey, "Blaze Away! Doc Holliday Vs. Everyone: Three Men Hurled into Eternity: Bullet Spitting Son O' Thunder," *True West* (December 2001), 34–40.

74. www.tombstonehistoryarchives.com.

75. Victoria Wilcox, "Mischievous Minor: From Lad to Lunger," *True West* (December 2001), 18–22.

76. Karen Holliday Tanner and Howard Bryan, "TEN PACES: No, he didn't. Yes, he did," *True West* (December 2001), 31.

77. Roberts, 109–112, 398.

78. Roger Jay, "Doc's Nemesis: Johnny Tyler," *True West* (December 2001), 54.

79. Erik Wright, "Looking for Doc in Dallas," *True West* (December 2001), 42–43.

80. Roger Hedgecoth and Vickie Wilcox, "Living in the Wild Wild West," *True West* (December 2001), 45.

81. Ben Carlton Mead, "Spittin' Images of Doc," *True West* (December 2001) 47; "Painting Doc's Personality," 50.

82. Ben Carlton Mead, "Spittin' Images of Doc," *True West* (December 2001) 47; "Painting Doc's Personality," 50.

83. Shirley Ayn Linder, "Real to Reel," *True West* (January 2002), 66–71.

84. R. G. Robertson, "Painting the Mythical West," *True West* (July 2003), 84.

85. John Boessenecher, "Lawman Bob Paul's Doc and Wyatt Connection," *Wild West* (August 2003), 39–45.

86. Roger Jay, "The Lake..."

87. Roger Jay, "...Last Stand..."

88. Roger Jay, "Spitting Lead in Leadville: Holliday's Last Stand," *Wild West* (December 2003).

89. Roger Jay, "The Lake..."

90. Robert G. McCubbin, "It Ain't Really Him! (Chapter One.)

91. Roger Jay, "The Gamblers' War in Tombstone," *Wild West* (October 2004), 38.

92. Mark Boardman, "Dying Doc, Withered Wyatt?" *True West* (October 2006), 44–45; Allen Barra, "Doc Holliday's Racist Killing?" *True West* (October 2006), 49–52.

93. Pamela J. Potter, "The International O.K. Corral," *True West* (October 2006), 46–48.

94. Gary Roberts, "Doc Holliday, the Earps' Strangest Ally," *Wild West* (October, 2006), 42–47.

95. "Frontier Doc: The Tuberculosis Bullet That Eventually Took Doc Holliday's Life," *True West* (April 2008.)

96. Jeff J. Morey, "The Streetfight: What We Know and Why We Know It," www.tombstonehistoryarchives.com. , 2009.

97. Robert K. DeArment, "Four Awful Badmen," *WWHA Journal* (October, 2008) 34–38, 48.

98. Roy B. Young, "The Assassination of Frank Stillwell," *WWHA Journal* (August 2008), 16–33.

99. Peter Brand, *The Life and Times of Perry Mallon* (Indep.) Publication, www.tombstonevendetta.com, 2006), 25–35.

100. Peter Brand, "The Man Who Arrested Doc Holliday," *Wild West* (June 2009), 48–53.

101. Robert K. DeArment, "Interview with Bat Masterson," *WWHA Journal* (February 2010).

102. Paul A. Hutton, "Appearance of Bert Lindley in *Wild Bill Hickok*," BBB's Blog, *True West* (January 26, 2012) blog.truewestmagazine.com.

103. *High Noon* (TV remake), 2000; *The Virginian* (TV remake), 2000; *Texas Rangers*, prod. and dir. Steve Miner, 90 min. (Alberta: Griesman Productions, 2001).

104. *Crossfire Trail*, prod. and dir. Simon Wincer, 92 min. (Alberta: TWS Productions, 2001).

105. *Monte Walsh*, prod. Hal Landers, dir. William A. Fraker, 106 min. (Hollywood: Paladin Pictures, 1970); *Monte Walsh*, prod. John Albanis, dir. Simon Wincer, 117 min. (Alberta: Brandman Productions/TCN, 2003); *Open Range*, prod. and dir. Kevin Costner, 139 min. (Alberta: Touchstone Pictures, 2003).

106. *The Alamo*, prod. Ron Howard, dir. John Lee Hancock, 137 min. (Texas: Touchstone Pictures, 2004).

107. *Broken Trail*, prod. Michael Frislev and Robert Duvall, dir. Walter Hill, 184 min. (Alberta: Butcher's Run Films, 2006).

108. *3:10 to Yuma*, prod. Kathy Conrad, dir. James Mangold, 122 min. (New Mexico: Relativity Media, 2007).

109. *The Assassination of Jesse James by Robert Ford the Coward*, prod. Ridley Scott, dir. Andrew Dominik, 160 min. (Calgary: Warner Bros. and Plan B Entertainment, 2007).

110. *Appaloosa*, prod. and dir. Ed Harris, 115 min. (Texas: Warner Brothers, 2008).

111. *True Grit*, prod. and dir. by Joel and Ethan Cohen, 111 min. (Austin, TX: Paramount Pictures, 2010).

112. *Cowboys and Aliens*, prod. Brian Grazer and Ron Howard, dir. Jon Favreau, 119 min. (New Mexico: Universal Pictures, 2011).

113. *The Legend of Hell's Gate*, prod. Jay Michaelson, dir. Tanner Beard, 108 min. (ND/Texas: 4GO West Productions, 2011).

114. *Wyatt Earp's Revenge*, prod. Barry Barnholtz, dir. Michael Feifer, 92 min. (California: Feifer Worldwide/Hybrid Productions, Inc., March 6, 2012).

115. "Shoot Out at the O.K. Corral," *Unsolved History*, Dan Levitt, creator (Discovery Channel/Termite Art Productions), Episode 10, 22 Jan. 2003.

116. David Stewart, prod. and dir. *The Wild West: The Gunfight at the OK Corral* (Tucson, London: BBC/Discovery Channel Productions, 2003). BBC.co.uk/history.

117. *Doc Holliday: The Man Behind the Myth*, prod. and dir. Tim Evans (Biography Channel, Graystone Communications, Inc., A&E Home Video, 2004).

118. Tanner, *Doc Holliday*; Karen Tanner Holliday Collection.

119. *Investigating History: Wyatt Earp at the O.K. Corral*, prod. Paul Hutton and Bill Curtis, dir. Ken Curtis (Mescal & Tucson, AZ: The History Channel/Kurtis Productions, 24 May 2004).

120. *Wyatt Earp*," *The American Experience*, prod. and dir. Rod Rapley (Arizona: PBS, 2010).

121. *Sundown: A Musical About the Legend of Doc Holliday*, created and written by Steve Link (Dallas, 2003; New York: 2004).

122. *Outride the Devil: A Morning with Doc Holliday*, 2007.

123. "Doc Holliday," Mark Hopkins, 19" × 12" × 12" (© Mark Hopkins Sculpture, available at 83SpringStreet.com).

124. "Linwood," written and sung by Jon Chandler (from his CD *The Grand Dame of the Rockies*, 2004).

125. *The Man Who Shot Liberty Valance*, 1962.

Filmography

Films

The Arizonian, assoc. prod. Clief Reid, dir. Charles Vidor, 75 min. (Hollywood: RKO Pictures, June 18, 1935.)

Cheyenne Autumn, prod. and dir. John Ford, 154 min. (Hollywood: Warner Bros., Oct. 3, 1964.)

"Cowboys & Outlaws," *Real West* (disc four), prod. David L. Wolper, dir. Yan Debonne, A&E Channel. Remastered by The History Channel in 2008. Ultimate Collections, *The Real West* in four discs. Available individually or in the set.

Damon Runyon's Pueblo, prod. Al Kochka, dir. John Henry Johnson, 40 min. (Pueblo, CO: Tamarack Productions, 1981.)

Dawn at Socorro, prod. William Alland, dir. George Sherman, 80 min. (Hollywood: Universal International, Sept. 1, 1954.)

Doc, prod. and dir. Frank Perry, 96 min. (Hollywood: United Artists, Aug. 1, 1971.)

"Doc Holliday," *Stories of the Century*, dir. William Whitney, 25 min. (Hollywood: Republic Pictures, 1954–56.) Series 1 (Episode 10, March 25, 1954.)

Doc Holliday: The Man Behind the Myth, prod. and dir. Tim Evans (Biography Channel, Graystone Communications, Inc., A&E Home Video, 2004.)

"Duel at the O.K. Corral," *Cavalcade of America*, prod. Jack Cherkot, dir. Wilheim Thiele, 60 min. (1952–1957), *Duel at the O.K.* (Season 2, Episode 20, March 9, 1954.)

Frontier Marshal, prod. Sol M. Wurtzel, dir. Lewis Seiler, 66 min. (Hollywood: Fox Pictures, Jan. 19, 1934.)

Gunfight at the O.K. Corral, prod. Hal Wallis, dir. John Sturgis, 122 min. (Hollywood: Paramount Pictures, May 30, 1957.)

"Gunfight at the OK Corral," *You Are There*, prod. James D. Fonda, dir. Charles Russell, John Frankenheimer, 22–24 min. (1953–1971.) (Series 4, Episode: 8, Nov. 6, 1955.)

"The Gunfight at the OK Corral," *The Wild West*. prod and dir., David Stewart (Tucson, London: BBC/Discovery Channel Productions, 2003.), BBC.co.uk/history.

Gunfighters of the West: The Earp Brothers, prod. Phillip Boag, dir. Kevin McCarey, 50 min. (Mescal, AZ: TLC/ The Learning Channel, WinStar, May 11, 1998.)

Hour of the Gun, prod. and dir. John Sturges, 100 min. (Hollywood: Mirisch Corporation, Nov. 1, 1967.)

I Married Wyatt Earp, prod. Richard D. Briggs, dir. Michael O'Herlihy, 100 min. (Comworld Productions, Jan. 10, 1983.)

In Early Arizona, prod. Larry Darmour, dir. Joseph Levering, 53 min. (Hollywood: Columbia Pictures, Nov. 2, 1938.)

Law and Order, prod. Carl Laemmie, Jr., dir., Edward L. Cahn, 75 min. (Hollywood: Universal Pictures, March 1, 1932.)

Law and Order, prod. John W. Woods, dir. Nathan Duran, 80 min. (Hollywood: Universal Pictures, May 13, 1953.)

Law for Tombstone, dir., W. B. Eason and Buck Jones, 59 min. (Hollywood: Universal Pictures, A Buck Jones Production, Oct. 10, 1937.)

The Legend of Hell's Gate, prod. Jay Michaelson, dir. Tanner Beard, 108 min. (ND/Texas: 4GO West Productions, 2011.)

Masterson of Kansas, prod. Sam Katzman, dir. William Castle, 73 min. (Hollywood: Republic Pictures, Dec. 1, 1954.)

My Darling Clementine, prod. Samuel C. Engel, dir. John Ford, 97 min. (Hollywood: 20th Century–Fox, Dec. 3, 1946.)

The Outlaw, prod. and dir. Howard Hughes, 116 min. (Hollywood: Paramount Pictures, Feb. 5, 1943–Dec. 1947.)

Powder River, prod. André Hakim, dir. Louis King, 78 min. (Hollywood: 20th Century–Fox, June 8, 1953.)

Purgatory, prod. Daniel Schneider, dir. Uli Edell. 94 min. (Hollywood: TNT, Jan. 10, 1999.)

"Showdown at O.K. Corral," *Appointment with Destiny*, prod. David L. Wolper, dir. Nicholas Webster, 60 min. (Tombstone/Tucson, AZ: CBS/David L. Wolper Productions, Nov. 19, 1971; "Which Way to the O.K. Corral?" (Season 2, Episode 20, Feb. 10, 1972.)

"Shoot Out at the O.K. Corral," *Unsolved History*, Dan Levitt, creator (Discovery Channel/Termite Art Productions), Episode 10, Jan. 22, 2003.

Stagecoach, prod. Walter Wanger, dir. John Ford, 96 min. (Hollywood: United Artists, March 2, 1939.)

Stagecoach, prod. Martin Rackin, dir. Gordon Douglas, 115 min. (10th Century–Fox Productions, June 15, 1966.)

Stagecoach, prod. Hal W. Polaire, dir. Ted Post, 115 min. (Old Tucson: Hermitage Entertainment, Inc., 1986).

Tombstone, prod. James Jacks, dir. George P. Cosmatos, 130 min. (Cinergi Pictures Entertainment, 1993.)

Tombstone, the Town Too Tough to Die, prod. Harry Sherman, dir. William C. McGann, 79 min. (Hollywood: Paramount Pictures, June 13, 1942.)

Warlock, prod. and dir. Edward Dmytryk, 122 min. (Hollywood: 20th Century–Fox, April 1, 1959.)

Wild Bill Hickok, prod. William S. Hart, dir. Clifford Smith, 70 min. (Victorville: Famous Players-Lasky Corporation, Nov. 18, 1923.)

Wild Times, prod. Wes Sheldon, dir. Richard Compton, MTV mini-series, 195 min. (Santa Fe, NM: Rattlesnake Productions, Inc., Jan. 24, 1980.)

Wild West Days, prod. Ben Koenig, dir. Ford Beebe and Cliff Smith, 268 min. (Hollywood: Universal Pictures, July 5, 1937.)

Wyatt Earp, prod.-dir. Lawrence Kasdan, 191 min. (Warner Bros., 1994.)

"Wyatt Earp at the O.K. Corral," *Investigating History*, prod. Paul Hutton and Bill Kurtis, dir. Bill Kurtis (Mescal & Tucson, AZ: The History Channel/Kurtis Productions, May 24, 2004).

Wyatt Earp: Return to Tombstone, prod. Phil May et al., dir. Paul Landres, 100 min. (Old Tombstone: Associated Images, July 1, 1994.)

"Wyatt Earp," *The American Experience*, prod. and dir. Rod Rapley (AZ: PBS, 2010.)

Wyatt Earp's Revenge, prod. Barry Barnholtz, dir. Michael Feifer, 92 min. (California: Feifer Worldwide/Hybrid Production, Inc., March 6, 2012.)

Television Series of the Fifties and Sixties

Bonanza, prod. Fred Hamilton, created by David Dortort, 60 min. (California: NBC, 430 episodes, 1959–1973). "Calamity Over the Comstock," dir. Charles R. Rondeau, 60 min. (Season 8, episode 8, Nov. 3, 1963.)

Buffalo Bill, Jr., prod. Gene Autry, dir. Frank Navarro, 30 min. (Hollywood: Flying A Productions, 1955–56.) "First Possee," (Series 1, Episode 10, April 1, 1955.)

Colt .45, a/k/a *Thundercloud*, prod. Harry Tatleman, dir. Edward L. Marin, 74 min. (Hollywood: Warner Bros., 1959–1960, 67 episodes). "The Devil's Godson," prod. William T. Orr, dir. Herbert L. Strock, 30 min. (Series 3, Episode 3, Oct. 18, 1959.)

Cheyenne, prod. Roy Huggins, Leslie H. Martinson, dir. 60 min. (ABC, Hollywood: Warner Bros. Burbank Studios, 108 episodes, 1955–1962.) "Birth of a Nation," *Cheyenne*, ABC, 1959, not aired.

Death Valley Days, prod. Darrell McGowan et al., dir. Edward Ludlum, Frank McDonald, 30 min (Arizona: McGowan Productions/Filmaster Productions/CBA, 452 episodes, 1952–1972.)

"After the O.K. Corral," and "The Quiet and the Fury," *Death Valley Days*. (Season 12, Episodes 23 and 24, April 18 and April 25, 1964); "Doc Holliday's Gold Bars." (Season 15, episode 14, Dec. 30, 1966.)

Doctor Who, dir. Rex Tucker, 45 min. (UK: Production Code Z, BBC, 1963–1969; 2005–2007.)

"A Holliday for the Doctor," (April 30,

1966); "Don't Shoot the Pianist," (May 7, 1966); "Johnny Ringo," (May 14, 1966); "The OK Corral," (May 21, 1966.)
Law and Order/Man from Cheyenne, prod. Joseph Kane, dir. Ray Taylor, 57 min. (Hollywood: Universal, Oct. 18, 1940.)
Lawman, prod. Jules Sherma, dir. Lee Sholem, 30 min. (Hollywood: Warner Bros.; 30 min., Oct. 5, 1958–Oct. 9, 1962) 156 episodes. "The Wayfarer," 30 min. (Season 1, Episode 36, June 7, 1959.)
The Life and Legend of Wyatt Earp, prod. Frank McDonald et al., dir. Roy Rowland. (Hollywood: Desilu Productions, 1955–59; ABC 1959–1961, Sept. 6, 1955– Sept. 26, 1961). Doug Fowley as Doc Holliday, 52 episode credits, 1956–1957; 1959–1961, Final 5 episodes (Aug. 29, 1961–Sept. 26, 1961). Myron Healey as Doc Holliday, 13 episode credits, 1958– 1959. "Wyatt Meets Doc Holliday," 30 min. (Season 2, Episode 33, April 23, 1957); "Wells Fargo v Doc Holliday," 30 min. (Season 3, Episode 15, Oct. 15, 1957); "Doc Holliday Rewrites History," 30 min. (Season 3, Episode 34, May 6, 1958); "Little Brother," 30 min. (Season 4, Episode 15, Dec. 23, 1958); "The Reformation of Doc Holliday," 30 min. (Season 4, Episode 16, Dec. 30, 1958); "Tombstone," 30 min. (Season 5, Episode 23, Sept. 15, 1959); "The Trail to Tombstone," 30 min. (Season 5, Episode 2, Sept. 9, 1959); "The Court vs. Doc Holliday," 30 min. (Season 5, Episode 35, April 26, 1960); "Doc Holliday Faces Death," 30 min. (Season 6, Episode 21, Feb. 28, 1961); "The Gunfight at the O.K. Corral," 30 min. (Season 6, Episode 36, April 6, 1961); "The Outlaws Cry Murder," 30 min. (Season 6, Episode 37, June 27, 1961.)
Maverick, prod. Roy Huggins, dir. Robert Altman, 60 min. (Hollywood: Warner Bros., Sept. 22, 1957–July 8, 1962), 124 episodes. "The Quick and the Dead," dir. Douglas Heyes, 60 min. (Series 1, Episode 12, Dec. 8, 1957); "Seed of Deception," dir. Richard L. Bare, 60 min. (Season 1, Episode 27, April 13, 1958); "Triple Indemnity," dir. Leslie H. Martinson, 60 min. (Season 4, Episode 5, March 19, 1961); "A Technical Error," dir. Leslie H. Martinson, 60 min. (Season 5, Episode 5, Nov. 16, 1961); "The Maverick Report," dir. Irving J. Moore, 60 min. (Season 5, Episode 9, March 4, 1962); "Marshal Maverick," dir. Sidney Salkow, 60 min.

(Season 5, Episode 10, March 11, 1962); "One of Our Trains Is Missing," dir. Lee Sholem, 60 min. (Season 5, Episode 13, April 11, 1962.)
Pistols 'n' Petticoats, prod. Joe Connelly, dir. Leslie Goodwins, 30 min. (Hollywood: CBS, 26 episodes, 1966–1967.) "Shootout at the O'Day Corral." (Series 1, Episode 12, Dec. 3, 1967.)
Star Trek, prod. Gene L. Coon, dir. Vincent McEveety, 51 min. (Hollywood: NBC, 27 episodes, Sept. 8, 1966–Sept. 2, 1967.) "Spectre of the Gun." (Season 3, episode 6, Oct. 25, 1966.)
Sugarfoot, prod. William T. Orr, dir. Montgomery Pitman, 60 min. (Hollywood: Warner Bros., Sept. 17, 1957–July 3, 1961.) "The Trial of the Canary Kid." (Series 3, Episode 1, Sept. 15, 1959.)
Tales of Wells Fargo, prod. Nat Holt, dir. Earl Bellamy, 30–60 min. (Hollywood: Revue Productions/Overland Productions, March 18, 1957–Sept. 8, 1962.) "Doc Holliday," 60 min. (Season 3, Episode 53, May 4, 1959.)
The High Chaparral, prod. William F. Claxton, dir. William F. Claxton and James Schmerer, 60 min. (Hollywood: NBC, Sept. 10, 1967–March 12, 1971.) "Doctor from Dodge" (Series 1, Episode 9, Oct. 19, 1967.); "The Marshal of Mesa City," prod. Bert Gilroy, dir. David Howard, 62 min. (Hollywood: Republic Pictures, Nov. 3, 1939.)
The Tall Man, prod. Edward Montagne et al., dir. Tay Garnett et al., 30 min. (Hollywood: NBC, 2 seasons, 1960–1962.) "Rovin' Gambler," dir. William Whitney. (Season 1, Episode 27, March 18, 1961.)
Tombstone Territory, prod. Frank Pittman et al., dir. Richard L. Bare et al., dir. 30 min. (Hollywood: Ziv TV, Oct. 16, 1957– Sept. 17, 1958.) "Doc Holliday in Durango," 30 min. (Series 1, Episode 29, April 20, 1958.) "Johnny Ringo's Last Ride," 30 min. (Series 1, Episode 19, Feb. 19, 1958.)
Wagon Train, prod. Howard Christie, et al., dir. Andrew V. McLaglen, 60 min. (Hollywood: ABC, 284 episodes, 1957–1965.) "The Silver Lady," 60 min. (Series 8, episode 25, April 25, 1965.)
Zane Grey Theater, prod. Helen Ainsworth, dir. James Sheldon, 60 min. (Hollywood: CBS, Oct. 5, 1945–May 18, 1961.); "Man of Fear," 60 min. (Season 2, Episode 22, March 14, 1958.)

Bibliography

This bibliography is divided into seven parts: Books, Articles, Government Documents, Collections, Select Newspapers, Personal Correspondence and Interviews, and Recordings.

Books

Alexander, Bob. *John H. Behan: Sacrificed Sheriff*. Silver City, NM: High Lonesome Books, 2002.

Aquila, Richard, ed. *Wanted Dead or Alive: The American West in Popular Culture*. Urbana: University of Illinois Press, 1996.

Aston, B. W., and Donathan Taylor. *Along the Texas Forts Trail*. Denton, TX: University of North Texas Press, 1997.

Autry, Gene et al. *The Loser's View of the O.K. Corral/Dalton Gang's Mystery Rider/Tombstone's Boot Hill*. Leesburg, VA: Cowles History Group, 1995.

Bailey, Lynn R., ed. *A Tenderfoot in Tombstone: The Private Journal of George Whitwell Parsons: The Turbulent Years, 1800–82*. Vol. 63 of Great West and Indian Series. Tucson, AZ: Westernlore Press, 1996.

Ball, Larry D. *Desert Lawmen: The High Sheriffs of Arizona and New Mexico, 1846–1912*. Albuquerque: University of New Mexico Press, 1992.

_____. *The United States Marshals of the Arizona and New Mexico Territories, 1846–1912*. Albuquerque: University of New Mexico Press, 1978.

Ballard, S. M. *Death Takes a Holliday*. Sierra Vista, AZ. Treble Heart Books/Sundowners, 2009.

_____. *A Holliday in Tombstone (Doc Holliday)*. Sierra Vista, AZ: Treble Heart Books/Sundowners, 2008.

_____. *Kate*. Tombstone, AZ: Goose Flats Publishing, 2010.

_____, and Lee Emory. *Borrowed Time*. Sierra Vista, AZ: Treble Heart Books/Sundowners, 2007.

Barnes, Tim. *Doc Holliday's Road to Tombstone: The Life and Times of John Henry Holliday*. Xlibris, 2008.

Barra, Allen. *Inventing Wyatt Earp: His Life and Many Legends*. New York: Carroll & Graf Publishers, 1998.

Beck, Paul. *The Gunfight at O.K. Corral and Incidents Following*. Tombstone, AZ: Red Marie's, 1994.

Bell, Bob Boze. *Classic Gunfights*, Vol. 2. Cave Creek, AZ: Bob Boze Bell Productions, 2005.

_____. *The Illustrated Life and Times of Doc Holliday*. Phoenix, AZ: Tri Star-Boze Publications, 1995.

Blake, Michael F. *Hollywood and the O.K. Corral*. Jefferson, NC: McFarland, 2006.

Bowden, Nate. *Doc*. Portland, OR: Oni Press, 2012.

Boyer, Glenn G. *I Married Wyatt Earp: The Recollections of Josephine Sarah Marcus Earp*. Tucson: University of Arizona Press, 1976.

_____. *Illustrated Life of Doc Holliday*.

Glenwood Springs, CO: Reminder Publishing, 1966.
_____. *The Suppressed Murder of Wyatt Earp*. San Antonio, TX: Naylor, 1967.
_____. *Suppressed Murder of Wyatt Earp: Trailing an American Myth & Those Marryin' Earp Men (Wyatt Earp Facts.)* Vol. 3, Missoula, MT: Historical Research Associates, 1997.
_____. *Who Killed John Ringo? (Wyatt Earp: Family Friends & Foes.)* Vol. 5, Missoula, MT: Historical Research Associates, 1997.
_____. *Who Was Sheriff Johnny Behan? (Wyatt Earp: Family Friends & Foes.)* Vol. 2, Missoula, MT: Historical Research Associates, 1997.
_____. *Wyatt Earp's Tombstone Vendetta*. New York: G.K. Hall Large Print Book Series, 1994.
_____, and Ben T. Traywick. *Wyatt Earp's Tombstone Vendetta*. Honolulu, HI: Talei Publishers, 1993.
Brand, Peter. *The Life and Times of Perry Mallon*. (Booklet) Published independently, 2006.
_____. *Wyatt Earp Vendetta Posse's Ride: The Story of Texas Jack Vermillion*. New South Wales, AUS: Peter Brand, 2012.
Braun, Matt. *Doc Holliday*. Gunfighter Series. New York: St. Martin's Press, 1997.
_____. *Tombstone*. New York: Saint Martin's Paperbacks, 2002.
Breckenridge, William B. *Helldorado: Bringing the Law to the Mesquite*. Boston, MA: Houghton-Mifflin, 1927.
_____, and Richard Maxwell Brown, ed. *Helldorado: Bringing the Law to the Mesquite*. Lincoln: University of Nebraska, 1992.
Briehan, Carl W., and Wayne Montgomery. *Forty Years on the Wild Frontier*. Greenwich, CT: Devin-Adair, 1985.
Brooks, L. T. *The Last Gamble of Doc Holliday*. Raleigh, NC: Pentland Press, 2004.
Brown, Richard Maxwell. *No Duty to Retreat*. Norman: University of Oklahoma Press, 1991.
Bryan, Howard. *Wildest of the Wild West: True Tales of a Town on the Santa Fe Trail*. Santa Fe, NM: Clear Light Publishers, 1988.
Burnett, William Riley. *Bitter Ground*. New York: Random House, 1954.
_____. *Saint Johnson*. New York: A.L. Burt Company, 1930.
Burns, Walter Noble. *The Robin Hood of Eldorado*. Berkeley, CA: Coward-McCann, 1932.
_____. *The Saga of Billy the Kid*. New York: Grossett & Dunlap, 1925.
_____. *Tombstone: An Iliad of the Southwest*. New York: Doubleday, 1927.
Burrows, Jack. *John Ringo: The Gunfighter Who Never Was*. Tucson: University of Arizona Press, 1987.
Carlisle, Gene. *Why Doc Holliday Left Georgia*. Carlisle, PA: Carlisle Publishing, 2004.
Carmony, Neil B, ed. *Apache Days and Tombstone Nights*. Silver City, NM: High Lonesome Books, 1997.
_____. *John Clum's Autobiography*. Silver City, NM: High Lonesome Books, 1997.
Cashion, Ty. *A Texas Frontier: the Clear Fork Country and Fort Griffin, 1849–1887*. Norman: University of Oklahoma Press, 1997.
Cassidy, Graham. *Tombstone Pistoleers*. New York: Phoenix Press, 1936.
Chamberlain, Kathleen. *Wild Westerners: A Bibliography*. Albuquerque: University of New Mexico Press, 1998.
Chaput, Don. *The Earp Papers: In a Brother's Image*. Encampment, WY: Affiliated Writers of America, 1994.
Chase, Dale. *Wyatt: Doc Holliday's Account of an Intimate Friendship*. New York: Bold Strokes Books, 2012.
Churchill, E. Richard. *Doc Holliday, Bat Masterson and Wyatt Earp: Their Colorado Careers*. Denver, CO: Timberline Books, 1974. Reprint. Lake City, CO: Western Reflections Publishing, 2001.
Clum, John, ed. *Tombstone Epitaph*. Tombstone, AZ: Tombstone Epitaph, 1880–1882.
Coleman, Jane Candia. *Doc Holliday's Woman*. New York: Warner Books, 1995.
Compton, Ralph. *Autumn of the Gun*. New York: Penguin Books, 1997.
_____. *The Killing Season*. New York: Penguin Books, 1996.
Cusic, Don. *Cowboys and the Wild West*. New York: Facts on File, 1994.
Davis, Ronald L. *John Ford: Hollywood's Old Master*. Norman: University of Oklahoma, 1995.

DeArment, Robert K. *Bat Masterson: The Man and the Legend.* Norman: University of Oklahoma Press, 1995.
___. *Bravo of the Brazos: John Larn of Fort Griffin, Texas.* Norman: University of Oklahoma Press, 2005.
___. *Deadly Dozen: Forgotten Gunfighters of the Old West.* Norman: University of Oklahoma Press, 2009.
___. *Knights of the Green Cloth: The Saga of the Frontier Gamblers.* Norman: University of Oklahoma Press, 1982.
DiLeo, John. *Hour of the Gun (1967): Deconstructing Wyatt Earp.* East Brunswick, NJ: Hansen Publishing Group, 2011.
Earp, Wyatt, and Glenn G. Boyer. *Wyatt Earp.* Sierra Vista, AZ: Y.V. Bissette, 1981.
Eickhoff, Randy Lee. *The Fourth Horseman.* New York: A Tom Doherty Associates book, 1998.
Erwin, Richard E. *The Truth About Wyatt Earp.* Carpenteria, CA: O.K. Press, 1993.
Estleman, Loren D. *Bloody Season.* New York: Bantam Books, 1987.
Etulain, Richard W., Series Editor. *Wild Westerners.* Center for the American West, Department of History. Albuquerque: University of New Mexico, 1998.
Etulain, Richard W., and Glenda Riley. *With Badges and Bullets: Lawmen and Outlaws in the Old West.* Golden, CO: Fulcrum Pub., 1999.
Everitt, David. *Legends: The Story of Wyatt Earp.* New York: Paper Jacks, 1988.
Finn, Ed. *O.K. Corral.* Look West Series. Tucson, AZ: Rio Nuevo Publishing, 2005.
Fiske, Jack. *My Friend Doc Holliday.* Self-published, 1994.
Garwood, W.R. *Ringo's Tombstone.* Ann Arbor, MI: Bath Street Press, 1981.
Gibson, Steven, and Ken Ravell. *Outlaws and Lawmen of the Wild West.* Mesa, AZ: Terrell Publishing, 1997.
Green, Carl R., and William R. Sanford. *Outlaws and Lawmen of the Wild West.* Berkeley Heights, CA: Enslow Publishers, 1995.
Guinn, Jeff. *The Last Gunfight: The Real Story of the Shootout at the O.K. Corral and How It Changed the American West.* New York: Simon and Schuster, 2012.

Hall, Oakley M. *Warlock.* New York: Viking Press, 1958.
Hartley, Cecil J. *Life and Times of Col. Daniel Boone.* New York: Derby and Jackson, 1860.
Herda, D.J. *They Call Me Doc: The Story Behind the Legend of John Henry Holliday.* Springfield, TN: Lyons Press, 2010.
Henry, Will. *Who Rides with Wyatt?* New York: Random House, 1954.
Hertzog, Peter. *Outlaws of New Mexico.* Santa Fe, NM: Sunstone Press, 1984.
Hickey, Michael M. *John Ringo: His Final Hours.* Honolulu, HI: Talei Publishers, 2001.
___. *Street Fight in Tombstone Near the O.K. Corral.* Honolulu, HI: Talei Publishers, 1991.
Hollon, W. Eugene. *Frontier Violence: Another Look.* New York: Oxford University Press, 1974.
Hopkins, Tom J. *Trouble in Tombstone.* Garden City, NY: Doubleday, 1951.
Jahns, Pat. *The Frontier World of Doc Holliday.* New York: Hastings House, 1957.
Johnson, Paul Lee. *The McLaury's in Tombstone, Arizona: An O.K. Corral Obituary.* Denton, Texas: University of North Texas, 2012.
Kelland, Clarence B. *Tombstone.* New York: Harper, 1952.
Kincade, Jack. *Fighting for Air: The Unknown Adventures of Young Doc Holliday.* Create Space Self-publishing, amazon.com, 2008.
Ladd, Robert E. *Vengeance at the O.K. Corral.* Tucson: Arizona Historical Society, 1963.
Lake, Carolyn, ed. *Under Cover for Wells Fargo: The Unvarnished Recollections of Fred Dodge.* Norman: University of Oklahoma Press, 1997.
Lake, Stuart N. *Wyatt Earp: Frontier Marshal.* Boston, MA: Houghton-Mifflin, 1931.
Lamar, Howard Robert. *The Reader's Encyclopedia of the American West.* New York: Thomas Y. Crowell, 1977.
Lentz, Harris M., III. *Western and Frontier Film and Television Credits.* Jefferson, NC: McFarland, 1996.
Lewis, Alfred H. *Gunfighters of the Western Frontier: A Memoir of the Old West* (by William Barclay "Bat" Masterson. Old West Library, 1999.

_____. *The Sunset Trail.* Unknown publisher, 1906.
_____. *Wolfville.* New York: F.A. Stokes, 1897.
_____. *Wolfville Days.* New York: F.A. Stokes, 1902.
_____. *Wolfville Nights.* New York: F.A. Stokes, 1902.
Lewis, Preston. *The Lady and Doc Holliday.* Austin, TX: Diamond Books, 1989.
_____. *Mix-Up at the O.K. Corral.* New York: Book Creations, 1996.
Lynch, Sylvia. *Aristocracy's Outlaw.* New Tazewell, TN: Iris Press, 1994.
Mackay, James. *William Wallace: Brave Heart.* Edinburgh, Scotland: Mainstream Publishing, 1995.
Mann, E. B. *The Blue-Eyed Kid.* New York: Triangle Books, 1944.
Marcus, Josephine Sarah. *Wyatt's Woman: She Married Wyatt Earp: The Life and Times of Josephine Sarah Marcus.* Tucson, AZ: E. Chafin Press, 1998.
Marks, Paula Mitchell. *And Die in the West: The Story of the O.K. Corral Gunfight.* Norman: University of Oklahoma Press, 1989.
Martin, Douglas D. *Tombstone's Epitaph.* Norman: University of Oklahoma Press, 1958.
Martin, Gayle. *Gunfight at the O.K. Corral.* Chandler, AZ: Five Star Publications, 2008.
Masterson, Bat, and Jack DeMattos. *The 75th Anniversary of Famous Gunfighters of the Western Frontier.* Monroe, WA: Weatherford Press, 1982.
McCarty, Lea F. *The Gunfighters.* Oakland, CA: Scenic Art, 1959.
McWilliams, John P. *New Mexico: A Glimpse Into an Enchanted Land.* Scottsdale, NM: Inkwell Productions, 2012.
Metz, Leon Claire. *The Shooters.* Knoxville, TN: Berkeley Trade, 1996.
Minor, Craig. *Wichita: The Early Years.* Lincoln, NB: Bison, 1982.
Munn, Michael. *John Wayne: The Man Behind the Myth.* New York: New American Library, 2003.
Myers, John Myers. *Doc Holliday.* Boston, MA. Little, Brown, 1955.
_____. *Tombstone's Early Years.* New York: E.P. Dutton, 1950.

O'Connor, Jack. *Boom Town.* New York: A.A. Knopf, 1938.
O'Connor, Richard. *Bat Masterson.* Garden City, NY: Doubleday, 1957.
_____. *Iron Wheels and Broken Men: The Railroad Barons and the Plunder of the West.* New York: Putnam, 1973.
Olds, Bruce. *Bucking the Tiger.* New York: Picador Press, 2001.
Otero, Miguel Antonio. *My Life on the Frontier, 1864–1882.* New York: The Press of the Pioneers, 1935.
Pendleton, Albert S. Jr., and Susan McKey Thomas. *In Search of the Hollidays.* Valdosta, GA: Little River Press, 1973.
Rainey, Buck. *Hollywood's Famous Lawmen and Outlaws.* Jefferson, NC: McFarland, 1997.
_____. *Western Gunslingers in Fact and on Film.* Jefferson, NC: McFarland, 1997.
Reasoner, James. *Draw: The Greatest Gunfights of the American West.* Berkeley, CA: Berkeley Trade, 2003.
Rister, Carl Coke. *Fort Griffin on the Texas Frontier.* Norman: University of Oklahoma Press, 1956.
Roberts, Gary L. *Doc Holliday: The Life and Legend.* New York: John Wiley & Sons, 2006.
Roberts, J.R. *Trouble in Tombstone.* Berkeley, CA: Jove, Books, 1993.
Robinson, Charles M. *The Frontier World of Fort Griffin: The Life and Death of a Western Town.* Norman, OK: Norman H. Clark, 1992.
Rodenberger, Lou H., and David Coffey. *A Clear Fork Chronicle, 31 by Lawrence Clayton.* College Station, TX: State House Press, 2002.
Rosa, Joseph G. *The Gunfighter: Man or Myth?* Norman: University of Oklahoma Press, 1969.
_____, and Waldo E. Coop. *Rowdy Joe Young, Gambler with a Gun.* Norman: University of Oklahoma Press, 1989.
Ross, Thom. *Gunfight at the O.K. Corral in Words and Pictures.* Golden, CO: Fulcrum Publishing, 2001.
Russell, Mary Doria. *Doc.* New York: Ballentine Books, 2010.
Schieffelin, Edward, and Ben T. Traywick. *History of the Discovery of Tombstone, Arizona, as Told by the Discoverer, Edward Lawrence Schieffelin.* Tombstone, AZ: Red Marie's, 1988.

Schoenberger, Dale Key. *The Gunfighters.* Caldwell, ID: Caxton Printers, 1971.

Scott, Leslie. *Tombstone Showdown.* New York: Pyramid Books, 1958.

Scullin, George, Steve Frazee, and Paul Leslie Peil. *Gunfight at the O.K. Corral and Other Western Adventures.* Baker, MT: Literary Licensing, 2011.

Selcer, Richard F. *Hell's Half Acre: Life and Legend of a Red-Light District.* Dallas, TX: Christian University Press, 1991.

Sheffer, H. *Gunfight at the O.K. Corral.* Detroit, MI: Norseman Publishing, 1995.

Slotkin, Richard. *Gunfighter Nation: The Myth of the Frontier in Twentieth Century America.* New York: Antheneum Press, 1992.

Sonnischen, Charles L. *From Hopalong to Hud: Thoughts on Western Fiction.* Lubbock: Texas Tech University Press, 1978.

Steele, Phillip W. *Outlaws and Gunfighters of the Old West.* Gretna, LA: Pelican Pub., 1998.

Stegner, Wallace. *Angle of Repose.* New York: Penguin Classics, 2000.

Stephens, John Richard, ed. *Wyatt Earp Speaks!* Cambria, CA: Fern Canyon Press, 1998.

Stone, Robert. "Warlock." *New York Book Reviews:* 2005.

Tanner, Karen Holliday. *Doc Holliday: A Family Portrait.* Norman: University of Oklahoma Press, 1998. Reprint 2001.

Tefertiller, Casey. *Wyatt Earp: The Life Behind the Legend.* New York: John Wiley & Sons, 1997.

Thompson, George G. *Bat Masterson: The Dodge City Years.* Topeka: The Kansas State Printing Plant, 1943.

Traywick, Ben K. *Analysis of the Gunfight at the O.K. Corral.* Tombstone, AZ: Red Marie's: 2006.

_____. *The Chronicles of a Legend, to a Woman Named Red Marie.* Tombstone, AZ: Red Marie's, 1990.

_____. *The Chronicles of Tombstone, Historical Documents and Photographs of Tombstone, Tombstone Clippings.* Tombstone, AZ: Red Marie's, 1994.

_____. *The Clantons of Tombstone.* Tombstone, AZ: Red Marie's, 1996.

_____. *The Earp Years: 1880–1882.* Tombstone, AZ: Tombstone Epitaph, 1974.

_____. *Hell's Bells of Tombstone.* Tombstone, AZ: Red Marie's, 1992.

_____. *John Henry the "Doc" Holliday Story.* Tombstone, AZ: Red Marie's, 1996.

_____. *Legendary Characters of Southwest Arizona.* Tombstone, AZ: Coastwide T.L.C., 1993.

_____. *The National Tombstone Epitaph: Marshal of Tombstone Virgil Walter Earp and John Peters Ringo: Mythical Gunfighter.* Tombstone, AZ: Red Marie's, 1985.

_____. *The Residents of Tombstone's Boot Hill.* Tombstone, AZ: Self-published, 1971.

_____. *Tombstone's Deadliest Gun: John Henry Holliday.* Tombstone, AZ: Red Marie's, 1984.

_____. *Tombstone: 1877–1900.* Tombstone, AZ: Self-published, 1970.

_____. *Tombstone's Immortals.* Tombstone, AZ: Self-published, 1970.

_____. *Tombstone's Outlaw Album: The Gunfight at OK Corral and Incidents Following.* Tombstone, AZ: Red Marie's, 1984.

_____. *Tombstone's Wild Bunch.* Tombstone, AZ: Self-published, 1972.

_____. *A Town Called Tombstone.* Tombstone, AZ: Red Marie's, 1982.

_____. *The Wild Bunch: The Most Unusual and Exciting Western Show Found Anywhere on Earth.* Tombstone, AZ: Self-published, 1975.

_____. *Wyatt Earp: The Lion of Tombstone.* Tombstone, AZ: Red Marie's, 1984.

_____. *Wyatt Earp's 13 Dead Men.* Tombstone, AZ: Red Marie's, 1998.

_____, ed. *Tombstone Paper Trails.* Tombstone, AZ: Red Marie's, 1998.

Turner, Alford E. *The Earps Talk.* College Station, TX: Creative Publishing, 1980.

_____. *The O.K. Corral Inquest.* College Station, TX: Early West Publishers, 1981.

Turner, Frederick Jackson. *The Significance of the Frontier in American History.* Chicago, IL: Chicago World's Columbian Exposition, 1893. Albuquerque: University of New Mexico Press, 1993.

Turner, George. *Book of Gunfighters.* Amarillo, TX: Baxter Lane Col, 1972.

Tuska, Jon. *The American West in Film.* Santa Barbara, CA: Greenwood Press, 1985.

____. *The Filming of the West.* UK: Robert Hale, 1978.
Urquhart, Lena. *The First Ninety Years: 1886–1976: A History of the First Presbyterian Church, Glenwood Springs, Co.* Glenwood Springs Historical Society, Glenwood Springs, CO, B-66.
Waldman, Scott. *Gunfight at the O.K. Corral: Wyatt Earp Takes on the Clanton Gang.* New York: Rosen Publishing Group, 2003.
Walling, Emma. *John "Doc" Holliday Colorado Trials and Triumphs.* Snowmass, CO: Killene Sublett, 1994.
Walters, Lorenzo. *Tombstone's Yesterday.* Tucson, AZ: Acme Printing, 1928.
Waters, Frank. *The Earp Brothers of Tombstone: The Story of Mrs. Virgil Earp.* New York: C.N. Potter, 1960.
Wellman, Paul I. *A Dynasty of Western Outlaws.* Lincoln: University of Nebraska Press, 1985.
Wells, Lee E. *The Guns of Happy Valley.* New York: Curtis Books, 1937.
West, Paul. *O.K.: The Corral, the Earps, and Doc Holliday.* New York: Scribner, 2000.
____, and Rémy Lambrechs. *Doc Holliday.* Paris, France: Gallimard Press, 2001.
Wister, Owen. *The Virginian: A Horseman of the Plains.* New York: McMillan, 1904.
Woods, Harry M., ed. *Tombstone Nugget.* Tombstone, AZ: Tombstone Nugget, 1880–1882.
Wyatt-Brown, Bertram. *Southern Honor: Ethics and Behavior in the Old South.* NY: Oxford University Press, 1983.
Yoggy, Gary. *Riding the Video Range: The Rise and Fall of the Western on Television.* Jefferson, NC: McFarland, 1995.
Young, Roy B. *Chochise County Cowboy War.* Apache, OK: Young and Sons, Enterprises, 1999.

Articles

Banks, Leo W. "Wyatt Earp: Fearless Lawman, Loyal Friend and Deadly Enemy." *Arizona Highways*, Phoenix, AZ: Dept. of Transportation, 70-7, 1970) 4–13.
Barra, Allen. "Doc Holliday's Racist Killing?" *True West*, October 2006, 49–52.
Boardman, Mark. "Dying Doc, Withered Wyatt?" *True West*, October 2006, 44–45.
Boessenecher, John. "Lawman Bob Paul's Doc and Wyatt Connection." *Wild West*, August 2003, 39–45.
Bork, A. W., and Glenn G. Boyer. "The O.K. Corral Fight at Tombstone: A Footnote by Kate Elder." *Arizona and the West*, 1977, 65–84.
Boyer, Glenn. "John Henry Holliday, DDS." *Journal of Arizona History*, Autumn 1973, 14.
____. "Postscripts to Historical Fiction About Wyatt Earp in Tombstone." *Arizona and the West*, Autumn 1976, 217–236.
____. "Wyatt Earp: Part XII: Tombstone's Helen of Troy." *True West*, July 1994, 12–17.
Brand, Peter. "Dan Tipton and the Earp Vendetta Posse." *True West*, December 2001, 54.
____. "Daniel G. Tipton 1844–1898." Mark Dworkin for Peter Brand. *WOLA Journal*, Fall 2006.
____. "Duty Bound. The Story of John Wilson Vermillion and The Mystery of Tombstone's 'Texas Jack,'" *WWHA Journal*, August 2010, 5–19.
____. "The Man Who Arrested Doc Holliday," *Wild West*, June 2009, 48–53.
____. "Wyatt Earp, Jack Johnson & The Notorious Blount Brothers." *WWHA Journal*, Oct.–Dec. 2003, 36–47.
Briehan, Carl W. "Desperate Men, Desperate Guns." *True West*, Winter 1977-78, 16.
Cartledge, Rick. "Doc Holliday and the Whippit Gun." *True West*, April 1997, 14.
Cool, Paul. "The World of Sherman McMaster(s)." *WOLA Journal*, Autumn, 1998, 10–22.
DeArment, R.K. "Four Awful Badmen," *WWHA Journal*, October 2008, 34–38, 48.
____. "Interview with Bat Masterson, *WWHA Journal*, February 2010.
____. "The Sporting Crowd at Old Fort Griffin." *True West*, January 2000, 16.
DeMattos, Jack. "Doc Holliday." *Real West: Gunfighters of the Real West* special issue, Spring 1985, 30.
Eickhoff, Randy Lee. "Doc Data Disputed,

Letter & Response by Author." *True West*, June 1995, 4.

_____. "Frontier Doc: The tuberculosis bullet that eventually took Doc Holliday's life." *True West*, April 2008.

_____. "A Young Doc Holliday." *True West*, March 1995, 12–16.

Griffin, Richard. *New Movies Review*, 22 Jan 1947, 6–8.

Hall, David J. "John Henry "Doc" Holliday and His Street Howitzer." *NOLA Magazine*, Jan/Mar 1993, 12–15.

Hedgecoth, Roger, and Vickie Wilcox, "Living in the Wild Wild West." *True West*, December 2001, 45.

Hornung, Charles C., and Gary L. Roberts. "The Split: Did Doc & Wyatt Split Because of a Racial Slur?" *True West*, December 2001, 58–61.

Hornung, Chuck. "Wyatt Earp and Doc Holliday in Las Vegas, New Mexico." *True West*, May 1999, 12.

_____. "Wyatt Earp's New Mexico Adventures." *Old West*, Summer 1999, 12.

Hutton, Paul A. "Appearance of Bert Lindley in *Wild Bill Hickok*," BBB's Blog. *True West*, 25 Jan 2012.

_____. "Celluloid Lawman: Wyatt Earp Goes to Hollywood." *American West*, May/June 1984, 58–65.

_____. "Showdown at the Hollywood Corral." *Montana, The Magazine of Western History*, Summer 1995, 2–31.

Jay, Roger. "Doc Holliday: Last Stand in Leadville." *Wild West*, December 2004, 38–74.

_____. "Doc's Nemesis: Johnny Tyler." *True West*, December 2001, 54.

_____. "The Gambler's War in Tombstone." *Wild West*, October 2004, 38.

_____. "The Lake County Independent Club, 1882." *WOLA Journal*, XI 2003, 24–29.

_____. "The Peoria Bummer: Wyatt Earp's Lost Year." *Wild West*, August 2003, 46–53.

_____. "Spittin' Lead in Leadville: Holliday's Last Stand." *Wild West*, December 2003.

Kaufman, Martin. "Step Right up, Ladies and Gentlemen." *American History Illustrated*, August 1981, 39–45.

Kirkpatrick, J.R. "Doc Holliday's Missing Grave." *True West*, October 1990, 46.

Korf, Stanley R. "Doc Holliday: The Legend and the Dentist." *Jada*, January 1974, 16–30.

Linder, Shirley Ayn. "Real to Reel." *True West*, January 2002, 66–71.

Mallory, P.A. "The Dodge City War." *Wild West*, June 1997, 32.

Malocsay, Zoltan. "OK Corral: 100 Years of Lies." *Westerner*, July-Aug, 1973, 34.

Masterson, William Barclay. "Famous Gunfighters of the Western Frontier: Doc Holliday." *Human Life*, May 1907, 5.

McCubbin, Robert G. "It Ain't Really Him! ... Or Is It?" *True West*, March 2004, 25–26.

Mead, Ben Carlton. "Painting Doc's Personality." *True West*, December 2001, 50.

_____. "Spittin' Images of Doc." *True West*, December 2001, 47.

Montgomery, Wayne. "The Deadly Doctor Holliday." *Westerner*, April 1973, 14.

_____. "A Little Ride with Doc." *Real Frontier*, April 1971, 41.

_____. "Tom 'Pole Cat' Adams Recalls Doc Holliday." *NOLA Magazine*, Summer 1975, 14.

Morey, Jeffrey J. "Blaze Away! Doc Holliday's Role in the West's Most Famous Gunfight." *True West*, December 2001, 34–40.

_____. "The Curious Vendetta of Glenn G. Boyer." *NOLA Magazine*, Oct.–Dec. 1994, 22–28.

Parsons, Chuck. "Answer Man." *True West*, January 1993, 13; February 1993, 12; June 1993, 12.

_____. "Answer Man." *True West*, January 1994, 12.

_____. "Answer Man. Doc Holliday: Fact and Fancy." *True West*, October 1995, 58.

_____. "Answer Man. Doc Holliday's Life." *True West*, October 1996, 58.

_____. "Another Shot at Doc." *True West*, November 1997, 58.

Pendleton, Albert S., Jr., and Susan McKey Thomas. "Doc Holliday's Georgia Background." *Journal of Arizona History* 14 (1974) 185–204.

Potter, Pamela J. "The International O.K. Corral." *True West*, October 2006, 42–47.

Ripple, Sam. "Doc Holliday's Girl." *Westerner*, Nov./Dec. 1971, 48.

Polley, Jane. "Good Guys & Co." The Men

with the Six-Pointed Star." *Readers' Digest Assn. Inc.* American Folklore and Legend, 1978, 320–322.

Roberts, Gary, "The Charlie Smith Papers: Real or Fake." *WOLA Journal*, Spring 2004, 29–48.

_____. "Doc Holliday, the Earps' Strangest Ally." *Wild West*, October 2006, 42–47.

_____. "Gunfight at O.K. Corral: The Wells Spicer Decision, 1881." *Montana, The Magazine of Western History*, January 1970, 62–74.

_____. "The Leadville Years." *True West*, December 2001, 66–71.

_____. "The Lure of the Legend." *True West*, December 2001, 14, 16.

_____. "Mrs. John Holliday." *True West*, December 2001, 26–28.

_____. "The Real Tombstone Travesty: The Earp Controversy from Bechdolt to Boyer." *WOLA Journal*, V 1999.

_____. "Trailing an American Mythmaker: Glenn G. Boyer." *WOLA Journal*, 6:3, 5–25.

Robertson, R.G. "Painting the Mythical West." *True West*, July 2003, 84.

Shull, Dana. "The Losers View of the O.K. Corral." *Wild West*, Oct 1995, 50–72.

Silva, Lee A. "The Shotgun Used by Doc Holliday in the Gunfight at the O.K. Corral Has Never Surfaced ... or Did It?" *Wild West*, June 2001, 14–75.

Smith, Randy D. "Wyatt Earp, Doc Holliday: The Stuff of Legends." *Old West*, Summer 1997, 41.

Smith, Robert Barr. "The West's Deadliest Dentist." *Wild West*, April 1994, 64.

Tanner, Karen Holliday. "Gunfighter Mythology: Doc Holliday." *True West*, January 2000, 32.

_____. "Vision of a Legend." *NOLA Magazine*, 23:2, 1999, 30.

Tanner, Karen Holliday, and Clifton Brewer. "Doc Holliday's Last Days." *True West*, December 2001, 31.

_____, and Howard Bryan. "TEN PACES: No, he didn't. Yes, he did." *True West*, December 2001, 31.

Tefertiller, Casey, and Jeff Morey. "O.K. Corral: A Gunfight Shrouded in Mystery." *Wild West*, October 2009, 38–44.

Traywick, Ben T. "Doc Holliday," *True West*, April 1997, 31.

_____. "The Real Doc Holliday." *Wild West*, Oct 1997, 36.

Wilcox, Victoria. "Doc Holliday's White Columns in Georgia." *True West*, April 1997, 24.

_____. "Mischievous Minor: From Lad to Lunger." *True West*, December 2001, 18–22.

Wilkes, George, founder. *The (National) Police Gazette*. 10 Aug 1878.

Wittels, Sylvia, MD. "Doc's Disease." *True West*, April 1997, 20.

Wright, Erik. "Looking for Doc in Dallas." *True West*, December 2001, 42–43.

Young, Roy B. "The Assassination of Frank Stillwell," *WWHA Journal*, August 2008, 116–33.

Government Documents

Arizona Department of Library, Archives & Public Records. *A Guide to Public Records in the Arizona State Archives* (2d ed., 1994).

Arizona State Archives (Tucson, AZ), Letter from Wyatt Earp to Walter Noble Burns, Walter Noble Burns Papers, Box 3, Folder 2.

Cochise County, *Arizona Millsites, Book 1*, February 3, 1881, Cochise County Recorder's Office, Bisbee, AZ.

Colorado District Court Record (Denver, CO), GD No. 1851 (November 25, 1882).

Georgia State Archives (Atlanta, GA), *Civil War Records; Roster of Twenty-seventh Georgia Volunteer Infamy, Payroll Records* (June 14, 1862).

The Great Register for Pima County (Arizona). September 27, 1880.

Lake County, Colorado. *Superior Court Case No. 258*.

The People of the State of Colorado v. John Holliday. Lake County Superior Court, Case No. 258 (Roger Jay, 2003).

San Miguel County, New Mexico, *Deed Book*. Las Vegas, NM. Book 12, Line 182.

San Miguel County, New Mexico. *Territory Criminal Record Book, 1875–1879*.

Shackelford County, Texas. District Court Docket (1872).

Spalding County, Georgia. *Deed Book F*.

Texas State Archives (Austin, TX), *Dallas County Court Minutes, 1874–1888. Case No. 2236* (May 12, 1874); *Indictment No. 2643* (January 18, 1875); *Case No. 2643* (April 13, 1875).

United States National Archives (Washington, DC), 1880 Census Enumeration, Prescott, Yavapai County, Arizona Territory, Enumeration District 26, Household 52.

_____, Henry B. Holliday, SC-1908. *Special Orders No. 86, Mexican War Pension*, February 9, 1887, W-3780.

_____, Records of the War Department, Office of the Quartermaster, Master General, Reservation file, 1889. Microfilm.

Collections

Boyer Collection, Sharlot Hall Museum Library/Archives (Prescott, AZ).
C. Lee Simmons Collection, Sonoita, Arizona. "She Married Wyatt Earp: The Recollections of Josephine Earp," unpublished manuscript, circa 1928 (Roberts 365–366, 493n).
Catherine Ann Curry, Ph.D. collection. From P.M. O'Connell, "Arizona Fifty Years Ago."
Frontier Historical Museum, Glenwood Springs, Colorado.
Historical Society, Glenwood Springs, Colorado B-66.
Karen Holliday Tanner Collection.
Letter Box 10, Huntington Library, San Marino, California.
Letter Box 11, Huntington Library, San Marino, California.
Stuart N.Lake Collection. Berkeley Library, University of California at Berkeley, Berkeley, California.
Transcript of Recollections of Mary Katherine (Harony) Cummings as given to Anton Mazzanovich. Private Collection of Kevin J. Mulkins (Roberts, 433n).
University of Arizona Collections (Tucson, AZ). John P. Clum "Autobiography." Box 1, Chapter 16, Page 13.

Select Newspapers

Arizona Daily Star
The Atlanta Constitution
The Daily Commercial Record (Dallas)
Dallas Weekly Herald
The Dental Times
The Denver Daily News
The Denver Republican
The Denver Tribune
Dodge City Times
The Glenwood Springs Post
The Gunnison Daily-News Democrat
Las Vegas Optic
Leadville City Directory
The Daily Picayune (New Orleans)
The New York Times
Pennsylvania Inquirer
The Philadelphia Enquirer
The Pueblo (Colorado) *Ute-Chief*, November 10, 1887
San Francisco Examiner
Santa Fe New Mexican
Sunday Oklahoman
The Tombstone Epitaph
The Tombstone Nugget
The Trinidad Daily News
The University of Arizona Times
The Valdosta Daily Times
Western Cattle Markets and News

Personal Correspondence and Interviews

Susan McKey Thomas, Valdosta, Georgia. Letter dated April 6, 1996.
Harry Carey, Jr. Cody, Wyoming, Interview, July 28, 1998.
Rita L. Benischek, University of New Mexico. Email, June 16, 2005.
Jeff Morey, email, July 10, 2011.
Peter Brand, email, September 13, 2012.

Recordings

Chandler, Jon, et al. *The Grand Dame of the Rockies*. Album. Arroyo Records, 2008.
Gunsmoke. *Doc Holliday*, narrated by William Conrad. Audible Audio Edition. Radio Spirits, 2007.
Gray, Jimmy. *Gunfighters: Billy the Kid, Jesse James, The Earps & Doc Holliday*, narrated by Donnie Blanz, Joe Loesch, Bennie Shipley, and Jonathan Wise. Audible Audio Edition. Readio Theater, 2010.
Link, Peter, et al. *Sundown: An Original Cast Recording*. Georgetown, CN: Original Cast Records, 2004.

Index

Abilene, KS 18
Abilene, TX 14
Albuquerque, NM 30
Alias Smith and Jones (1972) 114–115
Allen, William J. (Billy) 34
And Die in the West 119
Anderson, Gilbert M. *see* Aronson, Max
Appointment with Destiny 114
The Arizonian (1935) 57–58, 62
Aronson, Max (a.k.a. Gilbert M. Anderson, "Broncho Billy") 48
The Aspen Daily Times 36
The Atlanta Constitution 10
Atwater, Barry 91

Babbitt's House, Denver 14, 32
Bailey, Ed 17–18, 40
Ballard, S.B. 142
Barnes, Johnny 27
Bartell, Harry 91–92
Bassett, Charlie 19
Beddoe, Dan 106–107
Behan, John H. (Johnny) 27, 29, 45, 75, 81, 131
Benson Stage robbery 26–28, 39, 45, 69
Bethel, Wilson 149
Birth of a Nation 49
Blaylock, Celia Ann (Mattie) 22
Blount, John W. ("Turkey Creek" Jack Johnson) 145
The Blue Eyed Kid 67
Bonanza (1959–1973) 103
Boom Town 53
Boyer, Glen G. 98, 110–111, 112, 113, 125, 129, 131
Brand, Peter 143, 148
Brandon, Henry 61–62
Breck, Peter 102–103
Breckenridge, William M. 27, 40, 43, 44–45

Brocious, "Curly Bill" (William Graham) 27, 30, 46
Brown, Johnny Mack 60, 67
Brown, Richard Maxwell 124
Buchanan, Edgar 68, 86
Burnett, William Riley 52
Burns, Walter Noble 7, 43–44, 46, 52, 57, 68

Calhoun, Rory 84
Carey, Harry 53–56, 63
Carey, Harry, Jr. 56
Cavalcade of America (1952–1957) 90
Chandler, Jon 153–154
Cheyenne Autumn 99–100, 139
Claiborne, Billy 29, 47
Clanton, Billy 27, 28, 67; death 29
Clanton, Ike 27, 29, 39, 45, 47, 50, 78, 131
Clark, Harvey 59
Clum, John 27, 77, 128
Colt .45 (1959–1960) 95
Colton (a.k.a. Kolton), Kid 41, 109
Confederate Cabinet: escape 8
Cool, Paul 132, 144
Cosmatos, George P. 134
Crabtree, Lotta, Estate 39, 40
Craig, James 67–69
Crane, Jim 27
Cronkrite, Walter 90–91
Cruz, Florentino 30
Cummings, Mary Katherine 14; *see also* Harony, Mary Katherine (Kate)
Curry, Catherine Ann 46

Dallas City Directory 12
The Dallas News 106–107
Dallas Weekly Herald 13, 15
Dark, Christopher 103
Dawn at Socorro (1954) 84
DeArment, Robert K. 143, 183, 187, 193

184 INDEX

Death Valley Days (1951–1975) 103–104
DeMunn, Jeffrey 120
The Dental Times 10
Denver & Rio Grande Railroad: feud with Santa Fe Railroad 20
Denver Daily Times 31, 31–33
The Denver Republican 31–33, 36, 83
Denver Tribune 30, 31
Doc (1971) 113–114, 115
Doc Holliday: A Family Portrait 129; *see also* Tanner, Karen Holliday
Doc Holliday: The Man Behind the Myth (2004) 150
"Dock": first reference to Doc by that name 14
Doctor Who (BBC 1963–1969; 2005–2007) 105–106
Dodge, Fred: recollections published 98–99; Wells Fargo agent 27
Dodge City, KS: Doc saves Wyatt's life 19; Doc's arrival 18
Dodge City Globe 53
Dodge City Times 147
Dorr, Lester 61
Douglas, Kirk 86–89, 100
Dupont Cavalcade Theater (1955–1961) 90
Dwan, Allan 60–62

Eagle Pass, TX 15
Earp, Allie 24
Earp, Bessie 22
Earp, James 22
Earp, Josephine Sarah Marcus 47, 58, 61–62, 110, 129, 131
Earp, Morgan 18, 27, 29, 67, 99, 102, 111, 128, 144
Earp, Sallie 22
Earp, Virgil 18, 22, 24–25, 29, 47, 66–67, 111, 128, 144
Earp, Warren 30, 45–46, 81, 143
Earp, Wyatt Berry Stapp: biography 128; interviews with Stuart N. Lake 46–48; life with Doc begins 16–37
Eason, W.B. 59
Edison, Thomas Alva 48
Edwards, Alan 56
Elder, Kate *see* Harony, Mary Katherine (Kate)
Elliott, Richard E. 38
Elliott, Sam 119, 135, 139, 154–155
Elliott, Wild Bill 60

Faro 21–22
First Presbyterian Church, Griffin, GA 7
Fisher, Kate *see* Harony, Mary Katherine (Kate)
Fletcher, Bill 115
Flood, John H., Jr. 55–56

Fly's Studio, Tombstone, AZ 42
Ford, Dr. Arthur C. 10
Ford, John 72–76, 99–100, 139
Fort Griffin, Shackelford Co., TX 13–14; Wyatt and Doc meet 16
Fort Sill, Indian Territory (Oklahoma) 14
Foster, Preston 57–59
Fowley, Douglas 92–93, 106–107
Frink, Dr. Lucian Frederick 10
Frontier History Museum (Glenwood Springs, CO) 36
Frontier Marshal: 1934 film 56–57; 1939 film 62–65
The Frontier World of Doc Holliday 80–81
"The Frontier World of Doc Holliday" (never aired proposed television pilot) 96

Gettysburg, PA, battle of 8
Gilman, Sam 106
Glenwood Springs, CO 36–37
Glenwood Springs Historical Society 19, 35–36, 83
Gone to Texas (*G.T.T.*) 12
Gordon, Mike 18, 20–21, 38, 40–41
Gosper, John J. 38
Great Register for Pima County (AZ) 25
Griffin, GA 7
Griffith, D.W. 49
Griffith, James 86, 93
Griffith, W.A. 9
Gunfight at the O.K. Corral (1957) 86–89, 100
"The Gunfight at the O.K. Corral" (*You Are There* episode) 91
Gunfighters of the West (1998) 133; *see also Legends of the Wild West*
Guns of Happy Valley 67
Gunsmoke (1952 radio show): "Doc Holliday" episode 91

Hall, Oakley 81
Halladay *see* Holliday, John Henry (Doc)
Harony, Mary Katherine (Kate): "Big Nose Kate" 14; Doc meets in St. Louis 10; Elder, Kate 2; Fisher, Kate 87, 116; letter to niece 66; "saves" Doc 17; trip to Tombstone 22–24; *see also* Cummings, Mary Katherine
Hart, William S. 49, 49–51
Head, Bill (Luther) 26
Healey, Myron 92–93
Helldorado: Bringing the Law to the Mesquite 27, 40, 43, 44–45
High Chaparral (1967–1971) 107
Holliday, Alice Jane McKey 7; *see also* McKey
Holliday, George 16

Index

Holliday, Henry Burroughs 146; father of Doc 7; remarriage 9
Holliday, John Henry (Doc): alledged shooting of Kid Colton 109; arrival in Las Vegs, NM 20; childrens' books 141–142; death 39; dental practice in Dodge City 19; diagnosis of tuberculosis 11; fire fighter in Leadville 34; grave 37; last meeting with Wyatt 35; Leadville years 33–35; O.K. Corral gunfight 28–29; pictures of 151; possible Scots ancestry 11; shotgun story 10, 45, 78; to Tombstone 22–24; trip to Texas 12
Holliday, Martha Jane (Mattie) 8; Sisters of Mercy convent 140
Homier, Skip 103–104
Hooker, Capt. Henry 40
Hopkins, Mark 153
Hopper, Dennis 119–120
Hour of the Gun (1963) 100–102
Houston and Texas Central Railroad 12
Hughes, Howard 69–72
Human Life magazine 41–42
Hussey, Kit 153
Huston, Walter 69–72
Hutton, Paul A. 50–51, 117, 131–132, 141, 148–149, 152–153

I Married Wyatt Earp (1983) 120–121
In Early Arizona (1938) 60–61
In Search of the Holidays 109
Ince, Thomas H. 49
Investigating History, "Wyatt Earp at the O.K. Corral" (2004) 151

Jacobs, Anthony 105–106
Jahns, Pat 80–81
James, Tim 114
Jarre, Kevin 199
Jay, Roger 30, 34–35, 146–148
Jeffrey, S.B. 143
Johnson, Chubby 83
Johnson, Turkey Creek Jack 46, 81; *see also* Blount, John W.
Jones, Buck 59; *see also Law for Tombstone*

Kansas City Journal 41
Kasdan, Lawrence 135–137
Keach, Stacy 70, 113–114, 115
Kelly, Jack 107
Kendrick, Arthur 35
Kennedy, Arthur 99–100
Kilmer, Val 134–136, 139, 149
King, Bill (Luther) 26, 27
King, James Thomas 149
Kolton (Colton), Kid 41, 44, 109
Kurtis, Bill 151
Lake, Stuart Nathaniel 46–48

Lamar, Howard R. 111
Landau, Martin 96
Lansing, Robert 103
Las Vegas, NM 18, 20–22, 24–25, 38, 40–41, 44, 133, 140, 151; Doc and Kate arrive 20
Las Vegas Gazette 21
Las Vegas (NM) Optic 20, 37, 38, 133, 146
Law and Order: 1932 film 53–56; 1940 film 83; 1956 film 83
Law and Order a.k.a. *Man from Cheyenne* (1940) 67–69
Law for Tombstone (1937) 59
Lawman (1958–1962) 95
Leadville, CO, Directory 33, 34
The Legend of Hell's Gate (2011) 149
Legend versus myth 6
Legends of the Wild West (1998) 133–134; *see also Gunfighters of the West*
Lentz, Harry M., III 99
Leonard, William 20, 26–28, 28
Leslie, Frank (Buckskin) 27, 40
Levering, Joseph 60–61
Lewis, Alfred Henry (Dan Quin) 40–41
The Life and Legend of Wyatt Earp (1955–1961) 92–93
Lindley, Bert 51, 148
"Linwood" 154

Mallen, Perry 30–31, 147
Man from Cheyenne a.k.a. *Law and Order* (1940) 67–69
Mannie Hyman's Monarch Saloon 33
Marcus, Josephine Sarah *see* Earp, Josephine Sara
Marks, Paula Mitchell 118–119, 119
Marshal of Mesa City (1939) 61–62
Martin, Dewey 96
Masterson, Ed 19
Masterson, Jim 18
Masterson, William Barclay (Bat): stories of Doc 10, 18, 26, 41; at Sweetwater Cantonment 14–15
Masterson of Kansas (1954) 86
Mature, Victor 72–76
Maverick (1957–1962) 93–94
McCubbin, Robert G. 42, 147, 159n
McDaniel, Hattie 57–59
McKey, Alice Jane 7; death 9
McKey, Tom 14
McLaury, Tom 18, 28–29, 40
McLowery *see* McLaury, Tom
McMaster, Sherman: often erroneously McMasters 144; vendetta ride and after 45
Mitchell, Cameron 84–85
Mitchum, Robert 134
Mohr, Gerald 93–95

Morey, Jeff 20, 133, 169, 173, 190, 193, 196–197, 199, 200
Music in Westerns 58–61
My Darling Clementine (1946) 72–76, 125; *see also* Ford, John
Myers, John Myers 77–80
Myth versus legend 6

Nelson, Willie 121–122
New York Herald Tribune 40
New York Sun 33
Newspapers: *The Aspen Daily Times* 36; *Atlanta Constitution* 10; *The Dallas News* 106–107; *Dallas Weekly Herald* 13, 15; *The Dental Times* 10; *Denver Daily Times* 31, 31–33; *The Denver Republican* 31–33, 36, 83; *Denver Tribune* 30, 31; *Dodge City Globe* 53; *Dodge City Times* 147; *Kansas City Journal* 41; *Las Vegas Gazette* 21; *Las Vegas Optic* 20, 37, 133, 146; *New York Herald Tribune* 40; *New York Sun* 33; *Otero Optic* 20; *Rocky Mountain News* 83; *St. Louis Republican* 18; *San Francisco Examiner* 40, 47; *Santa Fe New Mexican* 21; *The Tombstone Epitaph* 27, 77, 81; *The Tombstone Nugget* 27, 77; *Tucson Star* 46; *Ute Chief* 35; *Valdosta (Georgia) Times* 32–33
No Duty to Retreat 124

O'Brien, George 56–57, 61–62
O'Donnell, Anthony 46
Oral Hygiene 53
O'Rourk, John, (Johnny-Behind-the-Deuce) 40
Otero, Miguel Antonio, Jr. 25
Otero Optic 20
The Outlaw (1943) 69–72
Outride the Devil: A Morning with Doc Holliday 153

Palmquist, Bob 132, 144
Parsons, George Whitwell 127
Paul, Bob 26, 30, 147
Pearce, Shanghai 124
Pendelton, Albert, Jr. 109, 111–112
Pennsylvania College of Dental Surgery 10
Philpot, Bud 26
Pima County, AZ, census 25
Pistols 'n' Petticoats (1966–1967) 106–107
Pitkin, Frederick 32
Police Gazette 19
Porter, Edwin Stanton 48
Powder River (1953) 84–85
Prescott, AZ 38
Pueblo, CO 33
Purgatory (1999 MTV) 139

Quaid, Dennis 136–137, 138
Quaid, Randy 139
Quinn, Anthony 82, 89

Railroads: Denver & Rio Grande 48; Houston and Texas Central 12; Santa Fe 16, 20, 23; Union Pacific 14
Reader's Encyclopedia of the American West 111
Reagan, Ronald 83
Real West, "The Ten Most Wanted Outlaws" (2008) 132–133
Riding the Video Range 90
Ringo, Johnny 27, 45–46, 53; death 40
Robards, Jason 100–102
Roberts, Gary L. 10, 33–34, 111, 132, 133, 144–145, 148
Rocky Mountain News 83
Romero, Cesar 60–65
Rosa, Joseph G. 99, 118
Rudolph, Rev. 35

Saint Johnson 52–54, 60, 67, 80; *see also* Burnett, William Riley
St. Louis Republican 18
San Francisco Examiner 40, 47
Sandy Bob Stage 26–27
Santa Fe New Mexican 21
Santa Fe Railroad: feud with Denver & Rio Grande 20
Scots-Irish 7
sculpture of Doc 153
Seegar, Dr. John 12
Selman, John 16
Sesame Street (1989) 115, 122
Shaunessy, Johnny 16
Sherman, Gen. William T. 5, 8
Silva, Henry 104
Silver City, NM 30
Slotkin, Richard 124–125
Smith, Pvt. Jacob 15–16
Smith, Origen Charles (Charley) 144
Sonnischen, Carl 99
Spalding, Kim 90
"Specter of the Gun" (*Star Trek*) 106
Spence, Pete 27
Spicer, Wells 29
Stafford, Dan 103–104
Stagecoach: 1939 film 65; 1966 film 100; 1986 film 121
Star Trek (1966–1967) 106
Stilwell, "Dock" 45
Stilwell, Frank C. 27–28; death 31
Stories of the Century (1954) 90
Sturges, John 86–89, 100
Sugarfoot (1957–1961) 96
Sundown 153
Sweetwater Cantonement 14

Tales of Wells Fargo (1957–1962) 96
The Tall Man (1960–1962) 103
Talley, Jim 19
Tanner, Karen Holliday 33, 129, 133, 141, 143, 146, 151
Tefertiller, Casey 128
Television: *Alias Smith and Jones* 114–115; *The American Experience* 153; *Appointment with Destiny* 114; *Bonanza* 103; *Buffalo Bill, Jr.* 93; *Cavalcade of America* 90; *Cheyenne* proposed Doc Holliday pilot 96; *Damon Runyon's Pueblo* 120; *Death Valley Days* 103–104; *Doctor Who* (BBC TV series) 105–106; "Gunfight at the OK Corral" (*You Are There*) 90–92; *Gunfighters of the West* 133; *High Chaparral* 107; *Investigating History:* "Wyatt Earp at the O.K. Corral" 151; *Lawman* 95; *Legends of the West* 133–134; *Life and Legend of Wyatt Earp* 92–93; *The Man Behind The Myth* 150; *Maverick* 93–94; *Pistols 'n' Petticoats* 106–107; *Real West* 132–133; *Sesame Street* 115, 122; *Star Trek* "Spectre of the Gun" 106; *Stories of the Century* 90; *Sugarfoot* 96; *Tales of Wells Fargo* 96; *The Tall Man* 103; *The Ten Most Wanted Outlaws* 132–133; *Tombstone Territory* 93–95; *Unsolved History* 149–150; *Wagon Train* 104–105; *Wild Times* 119–120; *The Wild West: The Gunfight at the OK Corral* 150; "Wyatt Earp at the O.K. Corral" (*Investigating History*) 151; *You Are There:* "Gunfight at the OK Corral" 90–92; *Zane Grey Theater* 96
Texas: indicts Doc for murder 13
Texas Fort Trails 13, 80, 141, 142
The Texas House (Leadville, CO) 43–44
Thomas, Susan McKey 7, 109, 110, 112
Thompson, Bill 14–15
Thompson, Bob 14–15
Tilghman, Bill 19
Tipton, Daniel G. 30, 144
Tombstone (1993) 7, 134–136
Tombstone, AZ 22–33
Tombstone: An Iliad of the Southwest 7, 43–44, 46, 52, 57, 68
The Tombstone Epitaph 27, 77, 81
Tombstone History Archives 124, 148
The Tombstone Nugget 27, 77
Tombstone Pistoleers 53
Tombstone Territory (1956–58) 93–95
Tombstone: The Town Too Tough to Die (1942) 68–69
Tombstone's Yesterday 43, 45–46
"Trail's End," NM 23
Traywick, Ben T. 108, 108–109, 111, 117, 124–127, 130–132, 142, 151
Trinidad, CO 41–42, 52, 109

Tritle, Frederick A. 32
Tuberculosis, patent medicines and cure-alls 11–12
Tucson Star 46
Tuska, Jon 56, 117
Tyler, Johnny: confrontation with Doc 26; trouble in Leadville 34, 136, 146

Union Pacific Railroad 14
Unsolved History, "Shoot Out at the O.K. Corral" 149–150
Ute Chief 35

Valdosta, GA 8
The Valdosta Institute 8
Valdosta (Georgia) Times 32–33
Vanmetter, Ely 19
"Vendetta ride" 29, 42, 44–46, 65, 110, 143–144, 150
Vermillion, "Texas Jack" (John Oberland): vendetta research 143, 145; vendetta rider 45–46
Vicksburg, MS, fall of 8
Vidor, Charles 57–59

Wagon Train (1957–1965) 104–105
Wallace, Gov. Lew 20
Wallace, William 11
Walsh, Raoul 50
Walters, Lorenzo D. 43, 45–46
Warlock (1959 book) 81–82
Warlock (1959 film) 82, 89–90
West, Adam 95–96
Western Frontier Museum (Glenwood Springs, CO) 35
White (Wright), Charlie 25, 38
Wichita (1955) 86
Wichita, KS 18
Wild Bill Hickok 50–51, 148
Wild Times (1980) 119–120
Wild West Days (1937) 60
The Wild West: The Gunfight at the OK Corral (BBC 2003) 150
Windsor Hotel (Denver, CO) 35, 128
Wolfville stories 40–41
Wright (White), Charlie 25, 38
Wyatt Earp (1994) 7, 136–137
Wyatt Earp, Frontier Marshal: first edition 47–48; George O'Brian film 56
Wyatt Earp: Return to Tombstone (1994) 137–139
Wyatt Earp's Revenge (2012) 149

Yavapai County, AZ, 1880 census 24
Yoggy, Gary 90
You Are There (1953–1957) 90–92

Zane Grey Theater (1954–1961) 96

www.ingramcontent.com/pod-product-compliance
Ingram Content Group UK Ltd.
Pitfield, Milton Keynes, MK11 3LW, UK
UKHW042011140426
5217IPUK00015B/1112